Emerging Faith

Other Titles in the SEANET Series

Vol. 1: *Sharing Jesus in the Buddhist World*

Vol. 2: *Sharing Jesus Holistically in the Buddhist World*

Vol. 3: *Sharing Jesus Effectively in the Buddhist World*

Vol. 4: *Communicating Christ in the Buddhist World*

Vol. 5: *Communicating Christ Through Story and Song: Orality in Buddhist Contexts*

Vol. 6: *Communicating Christ in Asian Cities: Urban Issues in Buddhist Contexts*

Vol. 7: *Family and Faith in Asia: The Missional Impact of Social Networks*

Vol. 8: *Suffering: Christian Reflections on Buddhist Dukkha*

Vol. 9: *Complexities of Money and Missions in Asia*

Vol. 10: *Developing Indigenous Leaders: Lessons in Mission from Buddhist Asia*

Vol. 11: *Becoming the People of God: Creating Christ-Centered Communities in Buddhist Asia*

Vol. 12: *Seeking the Unseen: Spiritual Realities in the Buddhist World*

Vol. 13: *Restored to Freedom from Fear, Guilt and Shame: Lessons from the Buddhist World*

Vol. 14: *Gift and Duty: Where Grace and Merit Meet*

Vol. 15: *Sacred Moments: Reflections on Buddhist Rites and Christian Ritual*

Emerging Faith

Lessons from Mission History in Asia

Volume 16 in the SEANET Series

Paul H. de Neui, editor

Emerging Faith: Lessons from Mission History in Asia

Published by William Carey Publishing
10 W. Dry Creek Cir
Littleton, CO 80120 | www.missionbooks.org

William Carey Publishing is a ministry of Frontier Ventures
Pasadena, CA 91104 | www.frontierventures.org

Cover image: Kaleomokuokanalu Chock, flickr.com
Mike Riester, cover and interior design
Melissa Hicks, copyeditor

ISBNs: 978-1-64508-256-9 (paperback), 978-1-64508-258-3 (mobi), 978-1-64508-259-0 (epub)

Printed Worldwide

24 23 22 21 20   1 2 3 4 5   IN

Library of Congress Control Number: 2019955124

The cover art is a photograph taken by
Kaleomokuokanalu Chock
of a stained glass panel that graces the entrance to the
First Chinese Christian Church in Honolulu, Hawaii.
It symbolizes emerging faith with the cross rising out
of a lotus flower.

Contents

Part 2
Lessons of Emerging Faith from Key *Places* in Asian Mission History

DEDICATION

This volume is dedicated to Dr. Wilbert R. Shenk,
missiologist, mission historian, professor, and mentor.
His thoughtful teaching and grace-filled ability
to critique human participation in the missio Dei
has developed hundreds of his students to think missiologically
and become more effective reflective practitioners.
I count myself privileged to be one of those.

As Dr. Shenk has taught us, there is much to be gained
from the study of those who have gone before.
May we put into practice the lessons drawn from these lives,
ministries, and even mistakes. May we, with God's grace and Spirit-leading,
faithfully live our part in God's story for God's glory
and for our neighbor's good.

INTRODUCTION

God created the world out of nothing, and since then, he has continued to use that which he created. Part of the divine inheritance implanted in each human is the gift of creativity expressed in a dazzling array of cultural diversity, especially in Asia, but everywhere around the globe. These expressions are part of both the imago Dei and the impact of human influence. The mysterious work of the missio Dei is how God works within human expressions to bring God's purposes to reality (kingdom come), inviting the people of God to join in this global cause.

The ancient image of the cross growing out of the lotus flower, which dates back to the earliest days of Nestorian mission, exemplifies an Asian example of the diverse cultural emergent points of the Christian faith. God enters into every cultural form and transforms it for God's own purposes and for God's glory. The beauty of this symbol is that the former culture is not merely a jumping off point to be forgotten, nor a bridge to be crossed and perhaps burned behind, but rather it is a foundational place of beginning for further development—socially and spiritually, at every level of human existence. There is a profound deepening of meaning to the fully opened lotus that expands enlightenment beyond mere human understanding. In this way the Christian faith continues to emerge, and it must be freed to continue to do so in order to speak to the worldview and issues of every time in history.

So how well have we learned from the lessons of others who have come before us? Many have put their own spin on George Santayana's original quote, "Those who cannot remember the past are condemned to repeat it." But the sentiment is true. Are we learning or simply repeating the same mistakes in our own times and places? Each location where God calls us has its own history, and it is especially urgent that those desiring to serve interculturally learn as much as possible about the past before entering the context. No culture in the world is a blank slate; rather, we can look for the initiating, inviting work of the missio Dei already emerging out of every surprising source. As followers of Christ, we can be sure that God is already present and active even before outsiders arrive.

SEANET is proud to present *Emerging Faith: Lessons from Mission History in Asia*, the latest volume in its topical series specifically designed to equip those who are called to love the Buddhists of the world. This is no ordinary history book. What makes this book unique in comparison to other studies on mission history are the multiple perspectives presented here. Some of these chapters describe Buddhist missiology—lessons from which people of all faiths can benefit. Some authors will focus on the context, others on the content. Half of the authors are from non-Western cultural backgrounds. We are especially grateful to the three female scholars who participated in this work. In this volume sixteen reflective practitioners share their insights from a variety of historical perspectives.

Overview

I have divided this collection into two sections, the first dealing specifically with key people, who may or may not be well known in mission history. The second section deals with larger movements in regions of Asia from which lessons may also be drawn. For those looking for a quick overview, the following are brief summaries of each chapter of this volume:

Part 1

Lessons of Emerging Faith from Key *People* in Asian Mission History

Chapter 1: In "Lessons from the Buddhist Mission History of King Asoka," Indian scholar Bouvert Regulas discusses how King Asoka's personal commitment to Buddhism helped propagate Buddhism within and beyond his empire. As the first Buddhist emperor, Asoka contributed to the development of Buddhism in three important ways. First, he applied basic principles of Buddhism to his rule through government and foreign policies. Second, he sent and supported Buddhist missionaries throughout the kingdom and beyond. Third, Asoka was able to maintain Buddhism as a major religious tradition in the kingdom through interfaith dialogue. There are many lessons that all who desire to work in Buddhist contexts can learn by studying the missionary practices of this historic leader.

Chapter 2: Claire Chong presents "Learning from 'The Gentle Way' of 16th-18th Century Jesuit Missionaries." This study describes the Jesuit attempt to bridge the gap between theory and praxis. This controversial, yet much lauded, exemplar of cross-cultural engagement advocated a radical enculturation of the Christian faith. The Jesuits' motivation and methodology shed light on current practices of contextualization.

Chapter 3: E. D. Burns discusses "The Golden Lamp Hung Out of Heaven": Adoniram and Ann Judson's Bibliocentric Strategy for Reaching the Buddhists of Burma. Burns seeks to demonstrate that the Judsons' allegiance to the written word dominated their evangelism and disciple-making strategies, including Ann Judson's contributions, though cut short by her untimely death. This chapter reflects their legacy as primarily witnessed in the words and accounts of Adoniram. Much of Adoniram's lifelong devotion and bibliocentric ministry philosophy stemmed from the foundation laid with Ann in the first years of ministry together.

Chapter 4: Karl Dahlfred reminds us that nothing is done in secret in mission. His chapter, entitled "Missionary Communication When Locals Are Listening," describes how missionaries generally profess to love and respect the people they are working among, but sometimes the manner or content of what they communicate undermines that claim. Drawing upon brief historical case studies of missionary communication in Thailand that have been poorly received by Thai people, this chapter will identify causes of unintended offense in missionary communication and make recommendations for appropriate and discerning communication in the contemporary context of religious pluralism and digital media in Southeast Asia.

Chapter 5: Henry Steel Olcott's contribution to the Buddhist revival in Sri Lanka is presented by Sri Lankan historian Dr. G. P. V. Somaratna. Many Westerners know nothing about the contributions of this American theopholist to the revival of Buddhism in Sri Lanka. His story is one of great significance—working with the three main sects of Buddhism; uniting all castes under his leadership; contributing to popular Buddhist education; starting Buddhist Sunday schools; travelling throughout Ceylon to remote villages to propagate his plans for Buddhist revival; raising funds for the Buddhist national cause; and founding the Maha Bodhi Society and helping to organize Buddhism in India and several other countries.

Chapter 6: "Reaching Out to Karmic Monastic Communities: Lessons from the Life of Karl Reichelt" is presented by Scottish mission scholar Rory Mackenzie. He addresses the question of how the gospel of Jesus can be presented within the framework assumed by the Buddhist worldview framework that does not require the religious other to assume a Western worldview. In general, evangelical missionaries approach their adherents with the mindset that they can persuade local people to merely replace doctrines one for another without recognizing that such central defining elements are not merely doctrinal.

It is necessary for Western missionaries to move beyond their efforts at making the Buddhists see the world as they do, as was done in the work of Norwegian Lutheran missionary, Reichelt.

Chapter 7: Singaporean scholar, administrator, and practitioner, Lawrence Ko, presents "Traversing Buddhist Mountains and Translating Sutras: Timothy Richard's Quest for Souls in China." Ko tells the story of Welsh Baptist missionary Timothy Richard, who spent forty-five years reaching the Chinese with the gospel. His influence resulted in his appointment as the chancellor of the first university in Shanxi province in 1902. His quest for souls saw him engage with social concerns such as famine relief. He visited abbots and scholars in order to study and translate Buddhist sutras. This chapter examines Richard's creative attempt to bridge the gospel with the religious beliefs of China and contextualization of the gospel in a holistic manner.

Chapter 8: Austin House familiarizes us with "Three Shining Stars: Lessons Learned from Thai Missionaries to Buddhists." House presents the stories of Chai Ma's work among the Kamu in French Laos, Lin's work in the Shan State of Burma, and Kru Muang's work in Yunnan, China. Each of these stories includes high and low points of their ministries in the context of their times, and lessons that can be learned from the lives and mission settings of these Thai missionaries.

Part 2

Lessons of Emerging Faith from Key *Places* in Asian Mission History

Chapter 9: This section begins with Stephen Bailey's overview chapter, "Christianity in Theravada Buddhist Southeast Asia." Bailey traces the historical interaction of Protestant Christianity in four Buddhist societies: Cambodia, Laos, Myanmar, and Thailand. He considers the way in which Protestant missions followed and was shaped by the general pattern of Southeast Asia's engagement with globalization. The backdrop to this study is the reality that only about 1 percent of the members of the dominant Buddhist groups are Christians after nearly 200 years of Christian witness. This chapter concludes by identifying characteristics of the engagement of Protestant faith in these Buddhist societies with the goal of shedding light on the general failure of Protestant missions among Theravada Buddhists.

Chapter 10: "Historic Highlights from Protestant Missions to Asian Buddhists" is the title and focus of Alex G. Smith's chapter. Smith presents the mission challenge of the twenty-first century to apply adequate methods, productive means and effective strategies to reach majority Buddhists, including most Chinese. Lessons from past missions to Buddhists over the last two centuries reveal both affirmations and alarms, encouragement and warnings to assist future church-planting efforts. This chapter highlights and illustrates mission flaws, as well as inspiring stimuli from Asia, in the progress of modern mission.

Chapter 11: Japanese historian, scholar, and missionary practitioner, Eiko Takamiza, presents her chapter, "Is Japan a Mud Swamp? Exploring Causes of Kirishitan Persecution in Japan's Edo Period." In the historical novel *Silence*, author Shusaku Endo describes the cause for the Japanese resistance against the Christian mission as Japan's cultural soil of "mud swamp" that withers all the roots planted. Eiko's work examines what caused such long and atrocious persecutions against Japanese believers. Three periods—under Nobunaga Oda, Hideyoshi Toyotomi, and Ieyasu Tokugawa and his successors—are explained, with special focus on their interactions with missionaries and believers.

Chapter 12: How many know of "The Lasting Impact of Christianity Upon China from the Taiping Uprising?" In this chapter Cristian Dumitrescu presents four critical lessons for those learning about or serving in China. Over time, most aspects of this particular historic rebellion have been forgotten, but one legacy from it lives on in the memory of Chinese leaders today: the relationship of revolution with missionary Christianity. Although the resulting religion had very little to do with Christian or biblical beliefs, this powerful rebellion against the government is still perceived as the outcome of Christian missionary activity. The Taiping movement did, however, attempt to contextualize Christianity for the Chinese and this chapter reviews some of the successes as well as lessons contemporary workers in China need to learn in order to avoid the mistakes of Hong Xiuquan and his "Heavenly Kingdom."

Chapter 13: In this chapter, "Christianization Lessons from Mission History in China," David Lim discuss nine instances when China was almost evangelized to become a Christian-majority country. We are now living in the tenth opportunity for its national evangelization and transformation. With the return of a strict anti-religious regime under President Xi, could the Chinese church effectively return to the revival movement that will fulfill the potentials of "gospel explosion" through implementing the historical lessons learned especially in the Mao and post-Mao era?

Chapter 14: James E. Morrison shares "Christianity's Journey to the Roof of the World," giving an overview of work in Tibet. The land of Tibet seems to have a certain mystique about it and is often seen as one of the last remaining strongholds for missionary endeavor. This chapter seeks to briefly explore the journey of Christianity to the Roof of the World, tracing the major players involved and the various mission strategies employed. An evaluation of these pioneering efforts is also given by considering the lessons that can be learned and drawing some possible missiological conclusions.

Chapter 15: "Lessons from Barriers and Bridges to Mission in Cambodia: An Historical Perspective" are covered by Paul Ka-Ming Au. This chapter traces Christian missions in Cambodia from the first Catholic missionary in the sixteenth century to present practices in the twenty-first century. It follows the efforts of missionaries during the turbulent history of Cambodia, from wars to colonization, independence, Khmer Rouge, and post–UNTAC era. Currently there are more Christians in Cambodia than at any other time in the nation's long history. Reflections on how this happened and the failures of the past are combined to identify bridges and barriers to the gospel in Cambodia.

Chapter 16: The final chapter of this volume brings up a crucial topic for anyone working with Asian Buddhists, one that has not been dealt with adequately. In this chapter Sheryl Takagi Silzer discusses "The Definition of the Person as a Family: Lessons Learned from the History of Christianity to Buddhists." Historically, in Buddhist countries, Christianity has been viewed as the religion of foreigners. This chapter briefly reviews the history of Western Christian missionary methodology among Buddhists and describes how the definition of the person as an individual lessened the receptivity of the gospel message in Buddhist countries where the person is defined as a family. With this difference in mind, missiological reflections on the different definition of the person are made.

May this be a work that has historic value. May we learn from the lessons and mistakes of others and with God's grace be better equipped to become more effective communicators and embody the good news for all people. May our faith emerge stronger and more insightful as we learn from the lessons of those who have gone before us. May we paraphrase the words of the writer of Proverbs 24:32, "I applied my heart to what I observed and learned a lesson from what I saw in life—and in print" for God's glory and our global neighbor's good.

"These words I speak to you are not incidental additions to your life,
homeowner improvements to your standard of living.
They are foundational words, words to build a life on.
If you work these words into your life, you are like a smart carpenter
who built his house on solid rock.
Rain poured down, the river flooded, a tornado hit—
but nothing moved that house. It was fixed to the rock.
But if you just use my words in Bible studies and don't work them into your life,
you are like a stupid carpenter who built his house on the sandy beach.
When a storm rolled in and the waves came up,
it collapsed like a house of cards."

Matthew 7:24–27 (The Message)

PART 1

Lessons of Emerging Faith from Key *People* in Asian Mission History

CHAPTER 1

Lessons from the Buddhist Mission History of King Asoka

Bouvert Regulas

Asoka the Great ignited the most massive Buddhist missionary movement in human history. His reign over most of the Indian sub-continent from 268–232 BCE proved to be one of the most expansive periods of the teachings of Buddha not just in that region but throughout Asia. Asoka's personal commitment to Buddhism propelled a small localized movement into a world religion that spread peacefully across the face of the continent, where it remains strong today. His missiology as a Buddhist scholar and mobilizer can teach much to those committed to seeking and sharing truth in Buddhist contexts. This chapter explores Asoka's mission movement and lessons that can be learned from it.

Asoka became the first Buddhist emperor and contributed to the development of Buddhism in three important ways. First, he applied basic Buddhist principles to his rule through government and foreign policies. Second, and most significantly, he sent and supported missionaries throughout his kingdom and beyond in order to spread the teachings of Buddha. Third, Asoka was able to maintain Buddhism as a major religious tradition by maintaining positive interfaith dialogue with other religions.

The Conversion of Asoka

Asoka (b. 304 BCE) was the son of King Bindusara and the grandson of King Chandragupta, the founder of the Maurya dynasty (321–187 BCE). His father reigned twenty-eight years and his grandfather reigned twenty-four years. Known as a violent warrior, Asoka was anointed as a king over an older brother when he was thirty-six years old. At the commencement of his reign, he murdered his ninety-nine half-brothers. Asoka came to the throne 268 BCE and died approximately 232 BCE (Gantam 1992:152).

Vincent Smith writes that the consequences of the Kalinga War completely changed Asoka, leading him to embrace the concept of non-violence. The Kalinga War may not have been his first, but certainly was the last war he led voluntarily. His grandfather had attempted to subdue this productive, artistic region (today known in India as Odisha) but had failed. Asoka's victory came at a devastating cost. Over ten thousand of his own men were killed, while one hundred thousand Kalingan soldiers fell. One hundred fifty thousand people were displaced and the Daya River ran red with blood. The violent process of claiming this area as part of his empire became a radical turning point in his own life and Asoka sought out a new personal path through the non-violent teachings of the Buddha.

After the triumphant conclusion of the Kalinga War and the annexation of the kingdom, Asoka issued two special edicts prescribing principles of how both the settled inhabitants and wild jungle tribes of the conquered provinces should be treated. These edicts were preserved in recorded form at two sites, Jaugada and Thauli (Smith 2002:25). Asoka had recorded that for more than two and a half years he had been a lay disciple, but that for more than a year prior to the publication of the edict he had become a member of a Buddhist order of monks (Sangha) and devoted himself with utmost energy to the winning of immense heavenly bliss for his people by his teaching.

Asoka developed a close association with many famous monks and began to exert himself to promoting the dharma. Asoka gave presents to monks of all levels. He admired the teachings of the Buddha and identified his own favorite texts which he recommended to clergy as well as to laity. One innovation brought by Asoka was the fixing in writing of the two-and-a-half-century-long orally transmitted Buddhist traditions.

Asoka expressed a desire to visit the holy places of his religion and went on pilgrimages to visit these sites. The first place he visited was Lumbini garden, the birthplace of Buddha. He erected his first consecrated monument or stupa there in honor of the Buddha. Stupas became important in the popularization of Buddhism because of the relics they contained and the locations on which they were built. His next visit was the Boddhi Tree at Boddh Gaya (Smith 2002:251). He later introduced the ceremony of bathing the Boddhi Tree. Asoka also visited the sites of Buddha's first sermon and Parinirvarna (the place of Buddha's death). During his pilgrimage Asoka erected 84,000 stupas.

Records of Asoka's life are chiefly inscribed stone pillars which are found scattered in various parts of India and provide important information about his reign and policies. Asoka built shrines and monasteries, inscribing Buddhist teachings on pillars in many places (Smith 2002:27). The memory of Asoka's twenty-first regnal year (249 BCE) is preserved on the Remindental and Nieliva Pillars in Trarai, now part of Nepal. These records prove that Asoka visited the "Lumbini garden," the traditional place of the birth of Gautama Buddha, and also paid reverence to the Stupa of Konakamans for Kanakamuni, the "Former Buddha" which he had enlarged six years earlier (Smith 2002:39). This record states that Asoka erected thirty or more monuments at the expense of much labor from a distance of 120 miles. Ten of these inscribed pillars still exist; one is known as the Delhi Topra Pillar (Smith 2002:123).

Asoka built stupas, temples, and stone pillars engraved with his edicts everywhere in his kingdom. These were visible Buddhist teachings available to the public. In this way, people were impacted by Asoka's witness to the faith. Asoka showed how to live the Buddhist life correctly according to the ethics of Buddhism and influenced people to adopt Buddhist teachings as an ethical way of life. Perhaps the most significant impact Asoka left on his community was his personal conversion from a violent murdering individual to a life of Buddhist ethical standards.

The redirection of Asoka's life through his conversion to Buddhism is clearly evidenced in an inscribed stone pillar known as Minor Rock Edict II, erected soon after the Kalinga War. The evidence of personal transformation is striking when compared with Minor Rock Edict I, created a few months earlier. The earlier edict appears to be that of a zealous blood-thirsty leader boastfully displaying his powerful political pursuits forever in stone. After the Kalinga War, Minor Rock Edict II provides the most concise summary of what would become the driving force of Asoka's life: the Dharma Law of Piety. It details the duties of compassion, almsgiving, truth, purity, gentleness, and saintliness. No student of the edict can help but be struck by the purely humane and practical characteristics of the teaching (Smith 2002:29). Many summaries of the Dharma Law of Piety are found in subsequent edicts that survive on carved pillars today.

Asoka the Buddhist Ruler

Asoka's purpose in life evolved to propagate the Dharma Law of Piety to all levels of society. David Burnett describes that Asoka, in his edicts, defined the main principles of dharma as non-violence, tolerance of all sects and opinions, obedience to parents, respect to Brahmins and other religious teachers and priests, liberality toward friends, humane treatment of servants, and generosity towards all. It suggests a general ethic of behavior to which no religious or social group could object. It also could act as a focus of loyalty to wield together the diverse strands that made up the empire. The importance of non-violence was repeatedly stated in Asoka's edicts. His respect for life was based on the belief that all beings had feelings. Needless killing was prohibited and laws were passed against the butchering of pregnant and nursing animals.

Asoka demonstrated how the previously inconsistent roles of monk and monarch could be reconciled in practice. Vincent Smith writes that Asoka was both monk and monarch at the same time (2002:5). It was during this period that the Buddhist tradition began to reflect the ideal of a Buddhist emperor known as Cakkavattin or Dhammaraj (Dharma King) (Hazra 1982:36). Asoka regarded administration as his sacred duty where he was always on duty as the Dharma King.

Asoka believed Buddhism to be the way of spiritual development for all and had the Buddhist scriptures translated into many dialects.

Dharma for the people

Asoka visited scholars and encouraged them to teach people to keep the dharma (Burnett 1976:82). He contributed to the expansion of Buddhism through maintaining the Law of Piety as a significant religious tradition in the Mauryan Empire (Hazra 1982:46). He instructed people about Buddhism through stone edicts for the educated, stories and symbols for the uneducated, and as mentioned earlier, numerous stupas and shrines. This allowed everyone in the Mauryan Empire, regardless of religion, status, or education level, to have access to the teachings.

Asoka believed Buddhism to be the way of spiritual development for all and had the Buddhist scriptures translated into many dialects. During his administration he established a set of special officers acquainted with the Buddhist teachings on the sources of happiness and pain to exhort the people of the provinces along with the learned faithful, so that they might attain happiness in this world and in the next.

A fundamental principle of his belief was that all people are essentially equal and should observe the dharma, including himself. This meant avoiding sin and seeking to do good. All people were encouraged to have compassion for all living beings, to speak the truth, to act with forbearance and patience, and to help those in need. Asoka spread his views on the dharma in two ways, through regulations concerning the dharma and quiet contemplation of the *sadharma* (good deeds). He trusted the virtue of kindness, generosity, truthfulness, obedience to parents, and justice (Burnett 1976:82).

Asoka demonstrated his zeal for Buddhism by his promotion of the Dharma Law of Piety, his references to the canon of Buddhist teachings, the tone of his language, his pilgrimage to holy places and by his active control over the Sangha. His personal devotion to the teachings of Buddha, however, did not negate goodwill to other sects. His edicts repeatedly encouraged the duty of almsgiving to Brahmin as well as Buddhist ascetics. The king declared that all people were his children. He proclaimed his impartial consideration for all faiths, including Jains and Ajivikas, and he implored people to abstain from demeaning the faith practices of neighbors. He was well versed in all creeds and impacted many religions. From Rock Edict XIV (257–256) it is clear he understood that he was commanded to perform rightly towards all faiths. The Pillar Edict of 243 BCE goes further and insists on the necessity for every person to have a definite religious creed, "I devote my attention to all communities, for all denominations are reverent to me with various forms of reverence" (Smith 2002:60).

The well-known statement that "all are my children" occurs frequently in the edicts, as well as the simile that the officers of the state are to subjects as nurses are to children, looking after their well-being. He emphasized judicial procedures and the need for impartiality before the law and introduced a respite of three days for those condemned to death. Doubtless the administrator in him did not permit the abolition of capital punishment in spite of the precepts of dharma (Madan 1999:149).

It was his humanitarian and paternal administration which made Asoka among the noblest of kings. The prime objective of Asoka was to promote the material and spiritual welfare of all in this life and the next. For material welfare, he ordered liberal charity for the needy, protection of the interests of all people, protection against injuries, reduction of punishment to criminals, and release of old men or fathers of many children from prison. Asoka declared freedom for prisoners twenty-five times within the twenty-six years of his reign.

Sangha unity

Asoka played a leading role, through his new administrative machinery of *Dharmama-hamatras,* to prevent schisms in the Buddhist Sangha (Smith 2002:22). During King Asoka's time the assemblies of Buddhist monks were held and unity of the Sangha was central.

Asoka endeavored to bring discipline into the Sangha and tried to purify it as far as possible. In lending his authority to the expulsion of dissidents, Asoka was acting as the Dharma king who enabled the Sangha to keep itself pure. Although Asoka remained a lay follower, he was eager for the purity of the Sangha. Buddhist texts claim that he carried out a massive purification of the Sangha at Pataliputra, expelling many false monks (Burnett 1976:81). Asoka's generosity to the Sangha attracted a growing number of novices to the order, but some entered with false motives, seeking a life of leisure. Some monks began to speak their own deviant doctrines so that others refused to associate with them. Divisions grew. Asoka tried to restore harmony to the community and eventually called for a council meeting at his capital at Pataliputra in an attempt to reconcile the differences. This was the Third Council according to the Pali tradition (Burnett 1976:88).

Royal and private donations by way of land and money were made to the Sangha for the worship of Lord Buddha and for its maintenance. G. R. Madan wrote that Buddhism was then the popular religion and it satisfied the demands of the people. Gradually a number of monasteries grew up where monks and nuns lived and carried on their studies and meditation. The Sangha institution with monarchial discipline was the most remarkable contribution of Buddhism. Numerous images of Buddha, standing or seated, proved the great popularity of image worship (1999:148).

Buddhist teachings were the basis for Asoka's government and foreign affairs. Asoka used Buddhist principles as a strong foundation for government as he dealt with foreign policy peacefully and diplomatically. His internal affairs were based on toleration and acceptance of differences such as providing social welfare, support of the Sangha, and dealing with criminals. This made Buddhism grow due to its revolutionary and peaceful manner in dealing with all issues in life, which was modeled through Asoka's leadership. The emperor protected all faiths. He gave evidence that the dharma meant something much more generally acceptable than Buddhist doctrine. Asoka assumed the titles "Dear to the gods," "His Sacred Majesty," and "His Grace of gracious Majesty" (Smith 2002:22).

Through Asoka, the Sangha and lay people were able to unite in public worship at temples and shrines. If it was not for construction of Buddhist buildings funded by Asoka, the *Viharas,* people would not have been able to unite together and worship in their religious tradition. Construction of Buddhist temples and public Buddhist worship trace back to Asoka's contributions.

Asoka the Mobilizer of Buddhist Mission

According to David Burnett, Asoka played a major role in the propagation of Buddhism both within and outside his empire. He used the state machinery of Rajjukas and Mahamatras—adding a new specialized cadre of Dharma-Mahamatras—to disseminate simple everyday ethics culled by himself from his favorite Buddhist texts which he recommended to both clergy and laity. There is an inscription in which Asoka says that he had won a dharma victory by sending messengers to five kings and several other kingdoms. Asoka's ambassadors of righteousness would certainly not have travelled alone. Such a mission could well have included monks and many other assistants. Even his son, daughter, and younger brother went as Buddhist missionaries (Burnett 1976:81).

The secret of Buddhism's missionary success was the relevance of the doctrine preached. At a time when ideas of religion and liberation were confusing and segregated, Buddhism presented a simplified view of religion and liberation that was easy to understand and precise enough to follow. The nobility of Asoka's family background was also a contributing factor; many kings, rulers, and wealthy men gave generous support (Fernando 1985:17). According to Buddhist literary sources, Asoka was the ideal Buddhist ruler, extending generous and devout patronage to Buddhism in every possible way. Specifically mentioned is his initiative in both internal and foreign missionary endeavors after the Third Buddhist Council. It was from India under Asoka that Buddhist missionaries and traders travelled outside of India to many Asian countries and spread the Buddhist religion wherever they went (Loseries 2009:ix).

Contemporary Greek sources claim that Asoka sent Buddhist envoys to them. More proof comes from the fact that the edicts bearing this information were found in places like Kandahar, Afghanistan, Mansehra, and Shahbazgarhi, Pakistan, and in Greek territories. At the end of the nine months of the Third Buddhist Council, groups of Buddhist missionaries, supported by Asoka, were sent all over India and nine other countries to preach the dharma. Stories are told of monks being sent to the successors of Alexander the Great in Greece, Syria, and Epirus. Not much is known of the impact of these ventures, but a mission to Sri Lanka in 240 BCE was notably fruitful (Hazra 1982:38). From several inscriptions we learn that Asoka extended the influence of Buddhism from Bengal in the east, to Nepal and Kashmir in the north, from Gandhara and Camboja in the northwest, to Saurashtra in the west and to Tamaperm (Ceylon) in the south. He also sent religious missions to Egypt and Syria in the west, and Burma in the southeast (Hazra 1982:37).

Asoka made Buddhism an international religion. The dissemination of Buddhism proper with all its doctrinal and practical complexities was an initiative of the Sangha. Asoka's role in this endeavor had been to extend his patronage and support. His major contribution appears to have been in the form of exploratory missions to prepare the receptivity of host countries for missionary monks.

Asoka made Buddhism an international religion.

Rock Edict XIII published in the fourteenth regnal year (236 BCE) gives a detailed list of all the countries to which imperial missionaries of the Law of Piety had been sent. We are told that Asoka sought the conversion of even the wild forest tribes and that missions were sent to the nations on the borders of his empire, such as Yonas, Kambojas, Andhras, Pulindas, Pitenikas, and others who occupied the slopes of the Himalaya, as well as to the regions beyond the Indus, and parts of central India. Envoys were also sent as far as the Tramrapra Barni River to the independent Pandyan kingdom of the extreme south of the Peninsula. Beyond the boundaries of India, Buddhism reached the dominions of Antioch, Syria, Western Asia (261 to 245 BCE), Egypt (285 to 247 BCE), Cyrene in Northern Africa, and Macedonia. Asoka sent his son and daughter with missionaries to Sri Lanka and the impact was that Sri Lanka was converted to Buddhism (Hazra 1982:39).

Asoka's enormous imperial power highly influenced one of the most comprehensive religious missionary enterprises in recorded history. Buddhism quickly became the dominant religion throughout India and Ceylon and ultimately in Burma, Siam, Laos, Cambodia, the Indian Archipelago, China, Korea, Japan, Mongolia, Tibet, and other countries of Asia. In some of these places Buddhism did not enter until centuries after Asoka, but the diffusion of the religion in them was due to the impact of the great Buddhist emperor of India who transformed the creed from a local sect into a world religion (Smith 2002:46). Asoka as a missionary paid his supreme attention to preach a universal code of moral conduct which was beneficial to all. As a Buddhist, he laid emphasis on the ethical side of Buddhism more than its formal aspects. The most remarkable feature of Asoka's missionary activity was his attempt to spread Buddhism outside India.

One of the most important teachings of Asoka's missiology was his insistence upon enlightened religious toleration. Asoka's policy of toleration, however, must be understood in its context. We must remember that in his day there were no diverse religions in India. The teachings of Christ, Zoroaster, and Muhammad did not yet exist. When Asoka spoke of the toleration of other creeds, he was not thinking of exclusive militant religions like Islam nor of institutionalized religions like Christianity, but of Hinduism and Jainism, all connected by many links of common religious sentiment (Smith 2002:61). The Dharma Law of Piety which he propagated had the distinct features of benevolence and toleration. The emperor protected all faiths and interpreted dharma to mean something much more acceptable than simply Buddhist doctrine (Smith 2002:59).

Under Asoka's policy of religious tolerance, the Buddhist religion was respected and expanded to other neighboring kingdoms. While Asoka enforced pious regulations, he put his trust in the promotion of the Law of Piety among the populace. He continuously extolled the merits of almsgiving, and attached much importance to practical works of benevolence, for which he set a personal example (Hazra 1982:65).

Asoka the Buddhist Social Worker

Another important legacy left by Asoka was social welfare and the care for others. People witnessed Asoka's rule as being a true example of what Buddhism should be. This significantly impacted the people of his and of neighboring kingdoms who became Buddhist because of him.

Asoka instituted many social development projects. Medicinal plants were planted and cultivated on either side of roads for healing of the sick. Wells were drug and rest-stops built for travellers. Asoka's concept of dharma has been acclaimed as the fountainhead of social welfare which generations of Indian rulers followed. Asoka established a social welfare system because he believed it was important to support all his people. Asoka believed that everyone should be treated with friendliness (Hazra 1882:144).

Rather than a religion, Buddha Dharma became a path, a way of life for the evolution of society in general. In his compassionate liberalism, Asoka made his officers as gentle and kind as possible. Though an ancient king, Asoka's large-scale public works resembled the works of a modern welfare state. He constructed inns for pilgrims and roads for travellers. For the thirsty, he dug wells. For shade, he planted trees. For men and animals, he laid out orchards. He sought to minimize bodily pain of both humans and animals and established centers of medical treatment for both (Madan 1999:156). Considering the gigantic size of the Maurya Empire, one would imagine this was a time of hectic activities in the service of humanity.

Asoka's Dharma Law of Piety provided an ideology of persuasive assimilation. It arose as much from his personal conviction of Buddhist teaching as from the wider discussion of ethical precepts and imperial policy. It is reasonable to conclude that Asoka's claim that "every proclamation by beating of drums has become the proclamation of dharma" applied to the propagation of Buddhism through both administrative mechanisms and missionary operations. Asoka used the symbols of Buddhism but saw his role in the context of a broader ideology. Such an argument requires the historian to look beyond the symbols. Thus donations, *dana,* were at one level pious voluntary offerings for the acquisition of merit, *punya.* At another level, through donations institutions were supported and administered. An inscription which mentions Asoka's missions says that he had won a dharma victory by sending messengers to five kings and several other kingdoms. Asoka did this repeatedly with his dharma. Other kings had military victories; he had dharma victories. Other kings went on hunting expeditions; he got much more pleasure out of dharma expeditions giving gifts to the needy, as well as touring the country giving instruction in the dharma (Hazra 1982:37).

A legend of King Asoka was that he had determined to distribute one hundred million gold pieces to the Sangha. Towards the end of his life he realized that he had only given ninety million and so resolved to complete his donation. Asoka sent his personal furniture to the Sangha, down to his last silver plate. He was reduced to poverty and according to the legend he donated the last thing he had to the Sangha, some myrobalan fruit, a type of cherry plum (*Terminalia chebula*). Asoka made a will leaving his entire empire to the Sangha. After his death, his heir was obligated to pay the remaining four million pieces of gold (Burnett 1976:89).

Lessons from Asoka's Buddhist Missiology

No student of the history of religion can ignore Asoka. He stands beside St. Paul, Constantine, and the Khalif Omar as one of the few who raised religions founded by others to positions of prominence in the world. In comparison to Constantine, Asoka's influence was far more personal. Constantine's official promotion of Christianity was an act of political submission to an already unrelenting force rather than that of willing devotion by an enthusiastic believer (Smith 2002:21). If Constantine had not adopted Christianity his successors surely would have because of the impact it was having throughout the Roman Empire, but if Asoka had withheld his promotion of the teachings of Buddha there is no reason to suppose that this doctrine had enough strength to spread throughout all of India and to half of the civilized world. Asoka championed Buddhism when it was confined to a small weak sect within India and enabled it to grow into a world religion.

The symbols for India are another legacy of King Asoka. The ornate carved capital atop one of his stone inscriptions, the Sarnath Pillar, inspired the use of back-to-back lions that is the Indian national emblem. The twenty-four-spoked Asoka-chakra, which has found its way into the Indian national flag, was a fine artifact of Asoka's period (Madan 1999:156).

What can Christian missionaries learn from the missionary work of Asoka? We must understand the nature of the people whom we serve and tangibly demonstrate our commitment for development in all of life. They should not feel that Christianity is foreign or that we are strangers; rather we must be for each other and together work with God's initiative for the good of all. Paul the Apostle said in Romans 1:14, "I am obligated both to the Greeks and non-Greeks, both to the wise and the foolish."

Is King Asoka's Buddhist missionary legacy a challenge to modern Christian movements in Buddhist contexts? Christians have often attempted to preach the gospel in many parts of the world without giving any thought to the richness of the religious traditions already present in those lands. Even if past mistakes could be pardonable, Christian missionaries living in Buddhist contexts today can no longer be excused if they do not try to investigate the message of the Buddha and how it compares with their own beliefs (Fernando 1985:19). There may be some surprising points of commonality.

In light of Asoka's legacy, what is the relevance for Christian missions today? There are many Christians who are asking whether evangelistic missionary work serves a meaningful purpose in contemporary society. The study of Buddhism is far from undermining the Christian missionary position, but could rather enhance it by bringing Christians to a new realization of the contemporary relevance of their mission. Missionary work does not serve a valid purpose in the modern world if it is misconstrued as solely converting a person from one religion to another. The purpose of missionary work is also to bring an individual from a state of mental childishness to a state of mental adulthood. The work of the missionary is thus the work of helping people to be mature, technically called in Buddhism *Arahats,* and in Christianity, saints. In Colossians 1:27–28, we read that "To them God has chosen to make known among the Gentiles the glorious riches of this mystery, which is Christ in you, the hope of glory. He is the one we proclaim, admonishing and teaching everyone with all wisdom, so that we may present everyone fully mature in Christ."

If missionary work is seen in that perspective, how critical is it to modern society? If the goal of missionary work is personal transformation, then there has been no era in the history of humankind in which it was more urgently needed than today. For missionaries to be effective, they must be guided by a broader vision. They cannot claim to have a monopoly on truth or an individual path to spiritual nobility. They must be teachable and flexible when others have various valid techniques. God revealed himself to all human beings in the universe. In Romans 1:19–20 we read, "Since what may be known about God is plain to them, because God has made it plain to them. For since the creation of the world God's invisible qualities – his eternal power and divine nature – have been clearly seen, being understood from what has been made, so that people are without excuse."

Is dialogue possible between Christians and Buddhists? We need not compete with each other; instead we can seek collaboration. Missionary work, or the work of educating human beings to adulthood, is a task Christians and Buddhists can labor at together. The very extensiveness of the task in the contemporary world would justify such collaboration. Modern Christian missionaries should not be taken aback if as a result of such collaboration they would one day come across an individual who, after successfully benefiting from the techniques of both religions, should consider themselves Buddhist Christians or Christian Buddhists. It is quite possible that Christian and Buddhist traditions have elements that are complimentary to each other (Hazra 1982:35). People need both peace of mind and self-fulfillment, achieved through the commitment to societal development, both a sense of self-dependence and sense of relationships, both a life of self-control and correctly oriented emotional lives.

Religion is not an end in itself. This is a fact often overlooked, but which Christians would do well to remember. Dialogue and multi-logue are possible and even tools for missionaries to extend the kingdom of God. We read at the end of the book of Acts that Paul discussed many things regarding the kingdom of God with people. "They arranged to meet Paul on a certain day and came in even larger numbers to the place where he was staying. He witnessed to them from morning till evening, explaining about the kingdom of God, and from the Law of Moses and from the Prophets he tried to persuade them about Jesus" (28:23).

Asoka left permanent legacies to influence the future. His contributions to civilization are of lasting value. Two thousand three hundred years after his death world leaders of the twenty-first century are still recognizing what Asoka did for humanity. The peace missions of Asoka to various other kings were the first experiments in that effort. Jesus implied that religion should serve humanity, not enslave it. Human beings, not religion, were important to him. The mission of religion mattered most to Christ, not religion itself. If that was a view of the founders of these religions, would it be right for their followers to think differently? If there is an affinity among the religions with regard to mission, would it not be a desire of the founders that their adherents collaborate in its execution? In James 1:27, we read that "Religion that God our Father accepts as pure and faultless is this: to look after orphans and widows in their distress and to keep oneself from being polluted by the world."

Not long ago some believed that for a Christian to study another religion would compromise their faith. Any religion apart from Christianity was considered pagan and contacting it was to be avoided. That extreme view no longer prevails. But the age-old Christian unconcern for other religions and philosophies is not totally dead. For many the study of another religion, even though not harmful, is not a necessity; at best it is a worthwhile pursuit for those who have time for it. In contrast, we should remember that missionaries like David Livingstone and William Carey were able to successfully enter into the culture of the people groups they served because they had studied them. Because of their special ability to understand, they were heartily welcomed by those communities.

Conclusion

Asoka's legacy is among the world's foremost missionary movements. Under his oversight Buddhism was effectively transformed from a minor movement to a world religion. Asoka's attempts to spread it outside India resulted in the benefit of humanity at large. He opened the doors of other countries not only to a mighty religion, but also to a tremendous force of civilization. Within a few centuries after Asoka, Buddhism was seen as the religion of Tibet, China, Japan, Ceylon, and the entire region of Southeast Asia.

Asoka was no founder of a religion. He was no prophet. But among those who propagated religions, he was one of the greatest. It was his advancement of Buddhism which paved the path to make that religion one of the largest in the world. Buddha lived, moved and died within a small territory (Burnett 1976:8). There is no indication that during the interval of the three centuries from the death of Buddha until the time of Asoka that Buddhist teaching made any great advances beyond a very narrow area. Asoka gave Buddhism a central place in his empire as much as the emperor Constantine did for Christianity. There is much we can learn from Asoka in carrying on the mission legacy today.

References

Ahir, D. C. 2010. *Buddhism in India.* Delhi: Buddhist World Press.

Basu, Ratna. 2007. *Buddhist Literary Heritage in India.* New Delhi: Munshiram Manoharlal.

Brown, David A. 1973. *A Guide to Religions.* Delhi: ISPCK.

Burnett, David. 1976. *The Spirit of Buddhism.* England: Monarch.

Fernando, Antony. 1985. *Buddhism Made Plain.* Indore: Satprakashan Sarehar Kendra.

Gantam, C. P. 1992. *Manual of Indian Buddhism.* Delhi: Bharatiya Kala Prakasam.

Hazra, Kanai Lal. 1982. *History of Theravada Buddhism in South East Asia.* New Delhi: Munshiram Manchandal.

Loseries, Andrea. 2009. *Buddhism and its Social Significance for the Asian World.* Delhi: Buddhist World.

Madan G. R. 1999. *Buddhism in Various Manifestations.* New Delhi: Mittal.

Nakamura, Hajime. 1975. *Buddhism in Comparative Light.* New Delhi: Islam and the Modern Age Society.

Smith, Vincent A. 2002. *Asoka: the Buddhist Emperor of India.* New Delhi: Asian Educational Services.

Thera, Narada Maha. 1973. *The Buddha and His Teachings.* Singapore, Singapore Buddhist Meditation Centre.

CHAPTER 2

Learning from "The Gentle Way" of 16–18th Century Jesuit Missionaries

Claire T. C. Chong

Heart to heart conversations with some non-Christian friends reveal raw and previously unspoken sentiments towards Christians and their way of converting others. "When the [foreign] Christians came to my village, it was very invasive. They talked so strongly and I felt like they were forcing us," one confided to me. "The Jesus group has a certain aura about themselves (*meern eriyabot m'yang;* Khmer), they think highly of themselves (*rert k'phuh*). The Jesus group often denounces us (*zhaod prokan*)," bemoaned an elderly Cambodian man. Our evangelistic methods today may not be brutal and bloody, but could we have subconsciously inherited the conquistador and colonial ethos that characterized Christian mission for so many centuries?

The Jesuit missionaries of the Society of Jesus, which was founded in the sixteenth century, were guided by a principle of gentleness. Their mission approach was called *Il Modo Soave,* translated as "the gentle way." This gentleness is not just referring to the softer qualitative tone of voice or a more tender manner of behavior. The Greek word in Philippians 4:5, *epieikes,* may expand and enrich our understanding of what it means to be gentle. Integrating definitions from Bible dictionaries, *epieikes* can be thought of as not insisting on the letter of the law or custom and exacting overly strict standards but being faithful to the spirit of the law. Other words that explain *epieikes* are: being reasonable, moderate, yielding, clement, tolerant, accommodating, gracious, and forbearing.

In this chapter, I seek to unpack this word in the context of Christian mission, through the lens of the Jesuits' interpretation. I focus on two particular Jesuit missionaries, Matteo Ricci and Ippolito Desideri, and study the ways they constructed "the gentle way" of mission in Confucian and Buddhist contexts respectively. I should say that the objective of this work is not to evaluate theological positions or scrutinize the correctness or weakness, precision or inaccuracy of the Jesuits' use of terminologies. This writing is penned for a broader purpose: it seeks to invite mission practitioners to reflect on our current approach, to consider practical implications of how we may "provide reasons of our hope with gentleness and respect" (1 Pet 3:15), and reflect the character of Christ who is "gentle and humble in heart" (Matt 11:29).

Il Modo Soave

Il Modo Soave, "the gentle (or sweet) way," was a model of mission that was developed to counter the prevailing *Tabula Rasa* ("blank slate") principle of the imperialistic and conquistador approach (Pomplun 2010:135–140; Hsia 2005:199–216). According to the latter, there was nothing compatible between Christianity and non-Christian cultures, every aspect of the indigenous culture was evil and had to be wiped clean leaving a blank slate in order to establish an authentic Christian faith. In practice, the *Tabula Rasa* mission approach was confrontational, unyielding and—sadly—cruel. The Jesuit missionaries had witnessed the failure of this method in Japan. They realized that if Christianity were to make any in-roads in the Far East, in particular China which had the reputation of being impenetrable, a totally new approach had to be employed. *Il Modo Soave* was thus conceived. It advocated kind and temperate persuasion borne out of a deep regard for "The Other." The process of conversion should be invitational and not impositional; the missionary should be winsome and not forceful.

Although *Il Modo Soave* was conceptualized by Alessandro Valignano (1539–1606), which was in turn based on a vision cast by Ignatius of Loyola (1491–1556), the founder of the Society of Jesus, this signature approach of the Jesuit Mission is often associated with Matteo Ricci (1552–1610). This is because of the remarkable success of evangelization of the Chinese in 16–18th century China which pivoted largely on his methods. During this time, Christianity flourished, and an "Imperial Edict of Tolerance," licensing and protecting Christianity, was issued in 1692 by the Qing Emperor Kangxi, who himself supposedly professed faith in Jesus Christ.

This chapter presents the work of Ippolito Desideri (1684–1733) who served in Buddhist Tibet. Unlike the famed Ricci, Desideri, until more recent years, has been largely unknown. His short mission of five years was abruptly interrupted by political reasons—national and ecclesiastical—and was hardly prized as a success; there were few souls won and his written works, largely unread, languished in the archives for almost two centuries. However, recent English-translated publications of his biography (Sweet 2010; Pomplum 2010) and his Tibetan catechisms (Stucco 2016; Lopez and Jinpa 2017) have alluded to the erudition of this Jesuit scholar. Comparing the evangelistic catechisms of Ricci and Desideri, Lopez and Jinpa described the latter's work as displaying "a deeper understanding of ... doctrines and a greater philosophical sophistication than Ricci" (2017:10). Such an honorable commendation should pique the interest of mission workers committed to contextual theologies.

However, this "gentle" missional approach was not without contention. *Il Modo Soave,* which distinguished the Jesuit mission, was also the bane of the Society of Jesus. Its radical methods ran across the grain of the traditional approach. The Society became embroiled in an extremely polemical and bitter dispute and was temporarily dissolved by papal decree from 1773–1814 (Mungello 1994). Though restored, its approach remains controversial, especially among non-Catholic communities.

Nevertheless, using a Buddhist metaphor quoted by Desideri, the bitter bark of the sugarcane should not deter the mind of the learned from benefiting from its sweet essence when crushed (Lopez and Jinpa 2017:43). I submit four characteristics of *Il Modo Soave* for consideration for a more incarnational approach to cross-cultural missions: profound respect, prudent accomodation, gradual progression, and thoughtful confrontation.

Profound Respect

How one treats another depends on how one views The Other. *Il Modo Soave* recognizes that all people, regardless of their faith professions, are still precious creations of God. This fundamental view cultivates a loving and respectful disposition towards The Other. Both Ricci and Desideri demonstrated a profound respect for the Chinese and Tibetans.

In the introduction letter of himself to the Emperor Wan Li, Ricci spoke of the "fame ... of the remarkable teaching and fine institutions with which the imperial court has endowed all its peoples" (Cronin 2011:168). Ricci lauded Confucius as a "great and learned man" who "surpassed in holiness" and was "excellent in virtue" (Ricci 1953:30). He did not spurn Chinese customs such as *kowtow, guanxi* through gift-giving and reciprocity, or coming under Chinese patronage. His highly positive assessment of Chinese wisdom was evident by his assiduous study, "day and night to the perusal of their literature" (ibid. 5). In addition to learning through reading, Ricci engaged himself in numerous dialogues. From the time he stepped onto Chinese soil, he maintained the posture of a learner and listener. It is apparent that the more Ricci learned about the Chinese, the higher his esteem was for this ancient civilization. He was captivated by the sophistication of Chinese civility, impressed by the intricacy of the Chinese script, and marveled at the Chinese technology including their methods of printing and astronomical instruments (ibid. 19–59). In describing the Chinese to the West, Ricci penned, "the Chinese possess high intelligence—innate and sharp" (Shelke and Demichele 2010:101). It was this extraordinary esteem for the Chinese and the adept acculturation and embrace of Chinese culture that won Ricci and his band of missionaries the confidence of the Emperor Kangxi who appreciated how "the Westerners admire our sacred culture" (Fu 1966:105).

Desideri also spoke highly of the Tibetans. In *Historical Notices of Tibet (HNT)* which was written with the Italian audience in mind, he described Tibet as a "peaceful kingdom" (2010:II.13.79) and her people as having "lively spirits, good intelligence and ... very capable ... rarely idle or lazy" (II.15.91,95). He expressed admiration of their "very good character... great propensity towards piety ... and their greatest virtue beyond all else was their inclination towards mercy" (II.16.101). He commended certain aspects of their religion as "most praiseworthy ... as they not only prescribe avoidance of vice and inculcate victory over all the passions ... they lead man to a humanly sublime and heroic perfection" (III.20.292). Like Ricci who also commented on the good model the Chinese can be for European Christians, Desideri also remarked, "how these things practiced by this blind people ... can serve as a reproof to Christians who at times do not manage to do the same to the true God whom they adore" (II.16.102). What is particularly significant was Desideri's faith in what may be called God's prevenient grace over the unbelieving Tibetans. Despite the "erroneous and foul" (III.20.292) aspects of their religion, Desideri believed that the Tibetans were "truly worthy of deepest compassion from our hearts" (III.20.291) and recognized the "operation of the divine grace that was secretly animating and inciting them" (I.13.194). He affirmed that,

> It is true that God has provided sufficient reason to man even in his natural state—and not merely a sufficiency but abundantly—to incline him to flee from evil and urge him toward love of the good and the acquisition of virtue, so that even these

> blind pagans, who to some may appear to be entirely abandoned by God, have also been abundantly supplied with reason and with impulses to travel the path to which they have been directed. If they are not faithful to this same God in using that unique gift that he has placed in their hands that it might bear fruit, then he is not only justified in not entrusting them with the fuller and more precious gift of the supernatural light of faith, but even more, he is justified to cast them away from him forever (III.20.292–93).

Indeed, Ricci and Desideri were compelled by a fervent passion to "save souls" but their *approach* was shaped by a profound respect towards the people they were serving. Their missionary endeavor was not driven by a messianic pity for the less fortunate. They did not view their role as one more accomplished and refined, trying to teach and civilize "the tribal other." Their approach was one of engagement between equals, on their terms in the light of their culture, history, and traditions.

Prudent Accommodation

Viewing The Other honorably as fellow creations of God compelled the Jesuits to minister the gospel to people in such a way that it did not bring "violence to souls long accustomed to another way of life" (quote by Ignatius of Loyola in Young 1959:384). This practice of accommodation in which missionaries adapted themselves to the indigenous customs was encapsulated in a Jesuit maxim: "It is not that they must [become] like us but we like them" (Criveller 1997:35). In expounding this rule of accommodation, Valignano explained,

> Do not attempt in any way to persuade these people to change their customs, their habits, and their behavior, as long as they are not evidently contrary to religion and morality. What could be more absurd, indeed, than to transport France, Italy, or some other European country to the Chinese? Do not bring them our countries but the faith (Hsia 2005:210).

Matteo Ricci is known to be the one who developed this "pastoral principle of accommodation ... to its utmost expression" (O'Malley 1993:342). While some of his methods were lauded, others came under severe scrutiny.

One striking application of accommodation was the allowance of the customary practice of honoring the deceased. The ancestor rite, for the Chinese, is "the embodiment of reverence for the past... It is the reason for a Chinese being a Chinese" (Lin 1959:37). Ricci understood this. He realized that this practice from antiquity expressed the most cherished and deeply ingrained Confucian value of *xiao,* filial piety; the Chinese identity was founded in the adherence of this enduring teaching and the bedrock of national governance is anchored on this cultural doctrine (Lakos 2010). Ricci also recognized that the ancestral rite bore a pertinent civil agenda of maintaining social harmony and order, and hence national security of a vast and highly populated nation. Ricci respected and willingly accepted the emic rationalization of the Chinese and did not repudiate the tradition nor considered the rite an abomination. However, among the peasantry, Ricci recognized that many practiced the ancestor rites with elements of superstition. They believed that by appeasing the dead spirits, the living might receive blessings and protection. Still, Ricci did not see the need to abolish ancestor rites in their entirety; it only needed pruning off the aspects inconsonant with Christian scripture. Furthermore, Confucius had taught that the true gentleman sacrificed to his ancestors because it was the proper thing to do; lesser men did so to serve the spirits, and according to the ancient classics, the ancestor spirits could not invoke blessings because all rewards and punishments were entirely the jurisdiction of the omnipotent God, *Shang-ti,* and in accordance with God's laws. Ricci therefore drew up specific directives forbidding converts to offer petitions to the dead and burn paper money, denouncing the belief that the dead received nourishment from the food offerings (Rule 2010). However, regarding the practice of *kowtow* (bowing on knees), the offering of food and drinks, the presentation of candles, incense and flowers at spirit tablets, Ricci harbored no grave concern. He did not see them tantamount to idolatry, but simply Chinese forms of remembrance and exhibiting deference.

The other notable application of accommodation was the way Ricci and Desideri represented the gospel. These two remarkably learned missionaries crafted their evangelistic catechism by accommodating, or contextualizing the Christian message, to local wisdom. Having assiduously studied and translated the ancient Chinese texts, Ricci found that "the teachings of the academy, save in some few instances, are so far from being contrary to Christian principles" (Ricci 1953:98). His favorable judgement of Confucius' philosophical doctrines led him to construct a "Confucian-Christian synthesis" (Mungello 1989:55–67); Ricci's erudition is evident in his *magnum opus Tian Zhu Shi Yi, The True Meaning of the Lord of Heaven* and a second catechism for catechumens, *Tian Zhu Jiao Yao, The Essential Doctrines of the Lord of Heaven* (Ricci 1953:448–50; Hsia 2010:224–44; Dudink 2002). Desideri similarly devoted much time and effort into learning and mastering Tibetan Buddhism and the Madhyamaka philosophy that undergirded it. He ploughed through the Tibetan Canon, an enormous collection of 5000 texts compiled in two huge anthologies, namely the Kanjur which consists of 108 volumes of the teachings of Buddha and the Tanjur which comprises 224 volumes of commentaries on the Kanjur. The result of this onerous feat was two now increasingly well-known catechisms, *Inquiry Concerning the Doctrines of Previous Lives and Emptiness* and *The Essence of the Christian Religion* (Lopez and Jinpa 2017). The former parallels Ricci's *True Meaning,* while the latter compares with *Essential Doctrines.*

While Ricci's and Desideri's renditions of the Christian gospel both reflected the scholarly conventions and local wisdom of their respective traditions, these outstanding works demonstrate subtle differences in the methodologies of contextualization employed. In Ricci's Confucian-Christian synthesis, he imbued the Christian message with qualities that were congruent with the Chinese moral philosophy undergirding Confucianism. Hence, the tenets of self-cultivation such as filial piety (*xiao*), virtuosity (*de*), righteousness (*yi*), and humanity (*ren*) were central in Ricci's Christian rhetoric. Ricci also astutely employed philosophical metaphors and cited passages from the classics, such as those pointing towards the notions of an immortal soul, heaven and hell, and the omniscient Creator (elaborated below), and hermeneutically wielded them to bolster his Christian argument. Ricci praised and affirmed the Chinese for the good and noble aspects and employed them as "redemptive analogies" and "hermeneutical bridges" for the gospel. However, as poignantly noted, "Ricci, the great champion of missionary adaptation, shrank back from adopting Chinese terms to translate theological notions, and he contented himself with transposing in Chinese characters the corresponding Portuguese sounds" (Dudink 2002:47). Some of the Chinese words that Ricci did use ironically, according to Mong, were borrowed from Buddhism, a religion that Ricci intensely denigrated (2015:391–2). Ricci also relied on neologism, and the evolution of his neologized variants in the several editions of his catechisms reflected the struggle and complexity of cross-cultural translation. Furthermore, Ricci heavily depended on the philosophical framework of the Western tradition, namely Aristotle. So, although Ricci's rhetoric was punctuated with Chinese analogues, his neologism, transliterations and frequent reference to Greek thought made the reading of Ricci's catechisms still feel somewhat European and foreign.

By contrast, the tone and texture of Desideri's catechisms was unashamedly Buddhist. Desideri translated the gospel inside out, using Buddhist vocabulary, conceptual categories, metaphors, allegories, and syllogisms; the whole reading felt Buddhist. Desideri refers to the Christian God as the "self-existent jewel," "jewel" being a highly revered Buddhist term of reference. Desideri declared this "crown jewel" as "relying on nothing, independent, spontaneously present and changeless," and as the singular "object worthy as a place of refuge" (Lopez and Jinpa 2017:192, 207–8). In apophatic fashion, which is a typical Buddhist manner of portraying the supramundane, Desideri described the self-existent jewel as peerless, boundless, unrivalled, immeasurable, inexpressible, inconceivable (ibid. 208–9). Desideri introduced the person of the Holy Spirit as the "unsurpassed perfect mind" and together with the Father and the Son, "the three are established as a single indivisible unity" (ibid. 210–1). Lopez explains that there was no Tibetan translation for "spirit" (even in Khmer, the word rendered for spirit, *vinyan,* comes from one of the five aggregates, consciousness); Desideri chose to render the word "spirit" as *yid,* which refers to the "mind" and often used interchangeably with "heart" and "consciousness" (ibid. 174). Beyond the construction of specific Christian terms, the exposition of the tenets of the Christian faith in *Essence* was delivered in distinctly Buddhist thought categories. Desideri described the conversion process as "[entering] the path of the stainless Christian faith, the pure religion" by "[meditating] again and again from the depths of the mind on the existence of something that is intrinsically established" and "[believing] not simply in words but with all your thoughts" (ibid. 208). After explaining the Trinitarian nature of God and person of Jesus Christ, Desideri again described the process of coming to faith was to contemplate and benefit from "two cherished special objects": the "unsurpassed nature of the self-existent jewel is three" and the "immeasurable compassion" of Jesus Christ (ibid. 212). The power of the immeasurable compassion is able to subdue the "chains of the root defects," dispel the accumulation of faults, "eradicate misdeeds," deliver beings from the "noose of affliction" and from the "inexhaustible sufferings of hell" (ibid. 221–2). Lopez and Jinpa comment that Desideri's teaching methodology is reminiscent of the Buddha's *upaya*—the skill of rendering profound concepts in terms that the listener can understand (ibid. 173). It is for this reason that Desideri won himself the reputation of having profoundly penetrated Buddhist concepts and having achieved "full possession and skilled comprehension of all that subtle, sophisticated and convoluted material" (Bargiacchi 2008:36).

It is evident that while Ricci and Desideri immersed and enculturated the Christian message to Confucian wisdom and Buddhist terminologies respectively, Christ and the crux of the Christian faith was plainly preached in their syntheses. Analyzing the contextual methods of both these two Jesuits, it may be summarized that Ricci's method is characterized by his erudite wielding of content, while Desideri's exhibited his proficiency of language and concepts. In either way, these methods fulfil St. Ignatius' vision of "[entering] through the other's door but [coming] out our own" (Young 1959:52).

Gradual Progression

Central to the accommodative method of *Il Modo Soave* is the conviction that people should not be treated as imperial subjects, bound to immediate compliance. The Jesuits endeavored to convert the locals gently and deferentially. Ricci wrote, "We do not want to force them to become Christians, and we are satisfied laying the foundations of a grand work when His Divine Majesty opens the way" (Hsia 2010:165). For the Jesuits, it was vital to use the appropriate means of bringing about the Christianization of society, and this approach is one of gradual progression.

> For the Jesuits, it was vital to use the appropriate means of bringing about the Christianization of society, and this approach is one of gradual progression. ”

Although Ricci was not dismissive of the ancestor rite, his position on this Chinese practice was more of acquiescence than of total embrace. Ricci, who was described as "tolerating prudently" (Rule 2010:2), deemed this accommodative act as "intentionally transitional but indispensable" especially for the early phase of the mission (Song 2002:13). It was Ricci's hope that "in time the faithful would be able to modify [the ritual] in a Christian fashion" (Criveller and Guillen-Nuñez 2010:43) and "replace this custom with alms for the poor" (Ricci 1953:96). Ricci was mindful that certain flexibility had to be permitted and change of a three-millennium old custom had to be ushered in gently and respectfully. Ricci's method focused on people, and not, heretical as it may sound, on theological orthodoxy. He did not subscribe to compromising on the truth but he was concerned about how they could journey towards the truth through small minimally abrupt transformations that would not alienate their soul from everything they were familiar with *a priori.* This person-centered and compassionate disposition is evident in the opening paragraph of the chapter describing the Chinese rites and customs, in which Ricci pleaded for sympathy, patience and grace towards the people because they had been "obscured in pagan darkness for some thousands of years" (Ricci 1953:82). Ricci exemplified an extraordinary attitude that was rare, in those days as in these.

Similarly, *True Meaning* (and Desideri's *Inquiry*) was another remarkable application of the principle of gradual progression. Ricci deliberately did not give his unbelieving audience the full measure of the Christian faith—an approach vehemently criticized by his opponents (Criveller 1997:81–4). They judged this publication as blatantly deficient because it did not give a complete presentation of the Triune God and the Incarnate Christ. Ricci defended his method and explained that this first catechism was based on general revelation that could be more readily "understood with the light of reasons" (1985:43). He had hoped that this introduction to some rudiments of the faith could "prepare the way for those mysteries which depend on faith and revealed wisdom" (ibid. 43). Ricci did not regard it helpful to present the gospel to first time listeners with special revelation as the starting point, because listeners may have legitimate reservation about the authority of scripture and thus find it hard to accept.

By contrast, in a second book in Ricci's serial, *Tian Zhu Jiao Yao, The Doctrines of the Lord of Heaven* (and *Essence*), Ricci spelled out all the main tenets of the

Christian faith, including the doctrines of the Trinity and of Christ, the scriptures, and the sacraments—articles based on special revelation that could only be accepted by the exercise of faith. It is apparent that Ricci did not deem it wise to unload lock, stock and barrel all of Christology, soteriology, and the likes, on his listeners.

Ricci's seemingly restrained two-step method of engagement should not be mistaken as being ashamed of the gospel. The Christianization of China was undoubtedly Ricci's fervent passion. He was intensely committed to the mission, but Ricci was not in a rush for results. Ricci wrote,

> Know that I and all those who are here dream of nothing else day and night. For this we have left our country and dear friends, and are dressed in the clothes and shoes of China; and we speak, eat, drink, and dress in nothing but the manners of China. But... our time in China is not yet one of harvest, nor even of sowing, but of opening wild forests and combating wild and poisonous snakes. By the grace of God others will come and write of conversions and the fervor of Christians (Fontana 2011:176–7).

It is evident that Ricci's timeframe for the Chinese mission was not measured in terms of years but in decades.

Thoughtful Confrontation

One might ask: Were the Jesuits pandering to the locals and presenting a compromised and palatable gospel? No! Ricci and Desideri categorically repudiated ideologies incompatible with scripture. Ricci denounced the practices of divination and idolatrous rituals and encouraged neophytes to destroy religious objects of worship (Ricci 1953:83–92). He denigrated certain customs that he deemed as "barbarous" and "serious evil" (ibid. 86–7) and even withheld baptism of those not ready to give up their harems (Hsia 2010:219, 285). He spoke firmly against the pantheistic elements of Neo-Confucianism, atheistic notions of Buddhism and the rampant idolatry of Taoism (Mungello 1989:68–72; Ricci 1953:337–42; 1985:99–121). Even as Ricci affirmed the nobility of the Confucian ethical system, he underscored the insufficiency of human effort alone in attaining the Confucian ideal; "it is for this reason that one so rarely sees a man whose virtue has been cultivated to perfection" (391).

Desideri too was hardly acquiescent towards ideologies inconsonant with his Christian convictions. His refutations against rebirth, emptiness and the non-existence of the Creator were far more extensive than Ricci's (Lopez and Jinpa 2017:78–149; 192–206). The Jesuits cannot be inculpated for indiscriminate accommodation. It cannot be sufficiently underscored that the Jesuits did not turn a blind eye to the fallacies of Confucianism or Buddhism. They courageously confronted erroneous beliefs, and how they did so was striking. Instead of demonizing the philosophical system of The Other and reckoning that their whole intellectual tradition had to be abandoned and replaced in its entirety by a new and foreign "revelation," they gently, yet powerfully, reasoned with the Chinese and Tibetans in persuasive discourse. In the following paragraphs, I illustrate Ricci's and Desideri's methods by analyzing their confutations against the non-existence of God.

> "The Jesuits did not turn a blind eye to the fallacies of Confucianism or Buddhism. They courageously confronted erroneous beliefs, and how they did so was striking."

Ricci employed a distinctive three-pronged strategy. Firstly, using natural reasoning, Ricci argued that the inherent yearning of all humans to seek spirituality, even in the form of superstition, provides evidence for God. Delving into a deeper treatment of rational argument, Ricci relied on the scholastic philosophy of Aristotle: employing the teleological argument and the essence-accident distinction, he contended for the necessary existence of an external intelligence and an uncaused Creator Being. Secondly, Ricci strategically allied himself with Confucianism by countering Buddhism and Taoism which were regarded as heterodox sects by the imperial court. He thus criticized the Buddhist conception of "voidness" (*kong*) and Taoist ideology of "non-being" (*wu*). He also categorically rejected the Neo-Confucianist doctrine of the "Supreme Ultimate" (*Taiji*)—the cosmological energy believed to be the source from which the universe and all of life came to be. Finally, and probably the *tour de force* of his three-pronged method, Ricci referred his readers to Chinese history and pointed them to "the testimony of their own ancient philosophers" (Ricci 1953:95). By quoting from the Confucian classics, including *The Doctrine of the Mean, The Book of Odes, The Book of Changes, The Book of Rites, and The Book of History,* Ricci reacquainted his Chinese audience with the monotheistic faith of the Chinese in antiquity and the supreme Lord of Heaven who is called *Shangdi* in Chinese (Ricci 1985:121–7). Ricci further explained that the understanding of the immanent and personal *Shangdi* had been subverted by kings and literati in the subsequent ages, replaced by philosophical concepts and ambiguous metaphysics, and adulterated by the advent of other religious and cultic sects.

Desideri too was unapologetic in pointing out his differences with his Tibetan audience. He explicitly stated, in the introductory paragraph of *Essence,* that he found the Madhyamaka philosophical doctrine of all things without exception being dependently originated and therefore empty of any absolute intrinsic nature, ultimately delineating the existence of any intrinsically established entity (an uncaused first cause, i.e. God), to be "unreliable and false" (Lopez and Jinpa 2017:192).

Desideri's rhetorical method bore a distinctive feature. Like Ricci, Desideri utilized the forms and structures of local scholastic conventions. However, unlike Ricci who referred—not unfrequently—to the wisdom of the European philosophical tradition, Desideri constructed his discourse from within the Madhyamaka philosophical framework that undergirds Tibetan Buddhism, and relied minimally on points of argument external to it. Desideri challenged the internal logic of Buddhist conception and questioned its tenability by systematically examining each line of reasoning and investigating each bifurcating possibility. He exacted this treatment to all the foundational pillars of what he termed as the "pernicious error... of extreme monstrosity and irrationality"—the denial of the existence of God (Desideri 2010:III.10.194). So, the conceptions of dependent origination, emptiness, "beginninglessness," conventional and analytic consciousnesses, and also commonly used metaphors such as the chariot and the moon's reflection on water were subjected to meticulous scrutiny. Each intellectual surgery culminated in the necessity for an intrinsically established foundation (an uncaused first cause, i.e. God) upon which all dependently arisen phenomena could rest. Leveraging on an idea precipitated by the renowned Buddhist scholar, Tsong Khapa, Desideri expounded on how the doctrine of emptiness itself is dependent and arises from certain terms and conditions and hence questioned its validity and integrity.

It is necessary to note that Desideri, in his refutations, did not express objection to the general ideologies of dependent origination or emptiness; he employed these conceptual categories and assumed certain aspects of these doctrines and made them the basis of his argument. What he categorically rejected was the final inference of not having a single entity that is intrinsically established and therefore the exclusion of God. It should also be said that although Desideri did not make any specific reference to European sources of argument, a few of his persuasions were reminiscent of Aquinas' arguments for First Cause and of Degree and Augustine's story of a boy wanting to fill a sand-hole with the ocean. Desideri's thesis obviously arose dependently from his pre-conditioned paradigms.

It is noteworthy that both Ricci and Desideri did not quote Christian scriptures nor deliver their message in Christian jargon. Their persuasive apologetics were delivered in languages and in thought categories familiar to the local people and importantly in a manner that pulled their heartstrings. The Jesuits spoke in The Other's terms and engaged them by tuning into their own frequency, esteemed the wisdom of their own sages, and astutely wielded their teachings and weaved them into winning arguments for the gospel.

A Pauline Approach?

St. Paul of the New Testament does not strike us as a conventionally gentle character. However, referring back to the Greek understanding of *epieikes,* one might arguably draw some similarities between Paul's evangelistic approach to that of the Jesuits' *Il Modo Soave.* Acts 17, read in comparison with Acts 13, demonstrates how Paul, in trying to communicate the spirit of the Christian message, endeavored to moderate his message and accommodate it to the Hellenistic mindset, in an *upaya* manner. Instead of condemning the Athenians for rampant idolatry for which Paul felt greatly distressed (Acts 17:16), he addressed them honorably (Acts 17:22), in the same way he did with his fellow Jews (Acts 13:16) and commended the Greeks for their pursuit of spiritual matters (Acts 17:22). Instead of recounting the history of Israel, proving that Jesus is the one the prophets spoke about, and speaking in terms of baptism, forgiveness of sin and salvation (Acts 13:24, 26, 38), Paul engaged with the Greeks in the language of Hellenistic philosophy, speaking on the beginnings of the universe and man (Acts 17:24–6). Instead of citing scriptures (Acts 13:33, 35, 40), Paul quoted from the sacred poems composed by a semi-mythical seer-philosopher, Epimenidus, and another poet, Aratus, in honor of the Greek god, Zeus (Acts 17:28). Paul might very well have been denounced for sacrilege by the opponents of the Jesuits' *Il Modo Soave* approach.

The testimony of the Jesuits, appreciated in the light of scripture, has shaken the foundations of how I have been schooled and trained to evangelize. Could an *upaya* gospel narrated in Buddhist terms, conceptual categories and metaphors be more comprehensible in the minds of Buddhist seekers? Could faith expressions crafted from and with traditional non-Christian rituals resonate more in the hearts of worshippers and thus encourage Christian faith? Could allowance of a more generous liminal, and grey space—for gradual progression from an old faith without Christ to one with Christ—be gentler on "souls of those long accustomed to another way of life"? I submit this chapter for prayerful deliberation and godly counsel.

References

Bargiacchi, E. G. 2008. *A Bridge Across Two Culture: Ippolito Desideri S.J.* (1684–1733) A Brief Biography. Presented at the XVth Congress of the International Association of Buddhist Studies, Atlanta: Firenze.

Criveller, G. 1997. *Preaching Christ in Late Ming China, Jesuits' Presentation of Christ from Matteo Ricci to Giulio Aleni.* Taipei: Taipei Ricci Institute.

Criveller, G. and C. Guillen-Nuñez. 2010. *Portrait of a Jesuit: Matteo Ricci.* Macau: Ricci Institute.

Cronin, V. 2011. *The Wise Man of the West: Matteo Ricci and His Mission to China.* London: Random House.

Desideri, I. 2010. *Mission to Tibet: The Extraordinary Eighteenth-Century Account of Father Ippolito Desideri S. J.* (L. Zwilling, Ed., M. J. Sweet, trans.). Boston, MA: Wisdom.

Dudink, A. 2002. "Tianzhu Jiaoyao, The Catechism (1605) Published by Matteo Ricci." *Sino-Western Cultural Relations Journal.* 24 (1) 38–47.

Fontana, M. 2011. *Matteo Ricci: A Jesuit in the Ming Court.* London: Rowman & Littlefield.

Hsia, R. P. C. 2005. *The World of Catholic Renewal, 1540–1770.* New York: Cambridge University.

________. 2010. *A Jesuit in the Forbidden City: Matteo Ricci 1552–1610.* Oxford: Oxford University.

Lin, Y. 1959. *From Pagan to Christian.* Cleveland, OH: World Publishing Company.

Lopez, D. S. L., and T. Jinpa. 2017. *Dispelling the Darkness: A Jesuit's Quest for the Soul of Tibet.* Cambridge, MA: Harvard University.

Mong, A. I. R. 2015. "The Legacy of Matteo Ricci and his Companions." *Missiology: An International Review.* 43 (4) 385–397.

Mungello, D. E. 1989. *Curious Land: Jesuit Accommodation and the Origins of Sinology.* Honolulu: University of Hawaii.

________. 1994. *The Chinese Rites Controversy: Its History and Meaning.* Nettetal: Steyler Verlag.

O'Malley, J. W. 1993. *The First Jesuits.* Cambridge, MA: Harvard University.

Pomplun, T. 2010. *Jesuit on the Roof of the World: Ippolito Desideri's Mission to Tibet.* OUP USA.

Ricci, M. 1953. *China in the 16th century: The Journals of Matthew Ricci, 1583–1610* (L. J. Gallagher, trans.). New York: Random House.

________. 1985. *The True Meaning of The Lord of Heaven* (E. J. Malatesta, S.J., ed., D. Lancashire and P. K-C. Hu, trans.). Paris: Institut Ricci.

Rule, P. A. 2010. "Directives of Matteo Ricci Regarding the Chinese Rites." *Pacific Rim Report.* 54 (1) 1–8.

Shelke, C. and M. Demichele, eds. 2010. *Matteo Ricci in China: Inculturation through Friendship and Faith.* Rome: Gregorian & Biblical.

Song, M. 2002. "Apologetics of Matteo Ricci: Lessons from the Past." *Journal of Asian Mission.* 4 (1) 79–95.

Stucco, G. 2016. *When Thomas Aquinas Met Nagarjuna: Two Works by Ippolito Desideri, S.J.* CreateSpace Independent Publishing Platform.

Young, W. J. 1959. *Letters of St. Ignatius of Loyola.* Chicago: Loyola University.

"The Golden Lamp Hung Out of Heaven": Adoniram and Ann Judson's Bibliocentric Strategy for Reaching the Buddhists of Burma

E. D. Burns

The first American Baptist missionaries to Burma, Adoniram Judson, Jr. (1788–1850) and Ann Hasseltine Judson (1789–1826), were equally devoted to spreading the good news of Jesus Christ to the Buddhists of Burma. The foundational source of the Judsons' perseverant mission was the supreme and sufficient word. This chapter will seek to demonstrate that the Judsons' allegiance to the written word dominated their evangelism and disciple-making strategies, and it will demonstrate Ann Judson's contribution to the mission, though cut short by her untimely death. Much of the Judson legacy credits Adoniram for his ministry, which lasted twenty-four long years after Ann's death, primarily due to the decades of records and volumes of sources available related to Adoniram. This chapter, the content of which chiefly derives from the author's book (Burns 2016:64–93), will consequently reflect their legacy as mostly witnessed in the accounts of Adoniram. Much of Adoniram's lifelong devotion and bibliocentric ministry philosophy stemmed from the foundation laid with Ann in the first years of ministry together. This chapter will illustrate the Judsons' bibliocentric strategies for reaching the Buddhists of Burma.

To issue a missiological synthesis and analysis of Adoniram and Ann Judson's strategies, academic responsibility and historical judiciousness requires us to remember that their theological and historical contexts were much different than ours. Merely critiquing their strategies through the filters of twenty-first century priorities and sentiments would prove to be historically myopic. If the chief end of the Judsons' engagement of Buddhism was that both parties could have a mutually affirming interfaith dialogue, as though they were serving in the globalized twenty-first century, then Adoniram and Ann Judson's strategies might seem intolerant and antiquated. But since their *telos* for engaging Burmese Buddhists was to make Buddhist-background believers who trusted in Jesus Christ's work alone as their atonement and righteousness and who went on to independently plant and shepherd their own indigenous churches, then the Judsons' Bible-centered strategy was a dynamic success, the spirit of which all Bible-centered missiologists should heed and seek to emulate.

" What a Christian truly believes about God, sin, salvation, humanity, and the Bible will directly determine how he/she conceives and executes ministry strategy. "

Methodology is always derivative of theology; simply put, what a Christian truly believes about God, sin, salvation, humanity, and the Bible will directly determine how he/she conceives and executes ministry strategy. For the Judsons, the work of sowing gospel seed was slow and not as socially acceptable as other humanitarian efforts, but Adoniram and Ann were certain that the written word required proclamation through publication and preaching. They were not dreadfully depressed when growth was slow, because the overriding purpose of their Bible-proclamation was for the glory of God. They were generally hesitant to grant assurance to new "professing believers" until those believers had showed a degree of submission to scripture.

Similar to the articles of agreement adopted by Judson and two other missionary companions (Wayland 1853, 1:184), the Judsons' missiological convictions and practices were: the importance of personal faith and believer's baptism, evangelism and contextualization, linguistic and cultural acquisition, and the establishment of self-supporting indigenous churches (Eitel 2012:129–48). Or stated another way, the Judsons' methods were learning the language and culture proficiently, publicly preaching the gospel, translating the Bible and distributing tracts, planting churches, and training indigenous pastors (Neill 1986:249). "Literate and civilized as they were" (Anderson 1987:56), the Burmese were ready for the written word of God, thought Judson initially. Though their literacy was high compared to other parts of Asia, because their literacy level was insufficient for reading the scriptures, the Judsons "opened a school for teaching adults to read" (Wayland 1853, 2:11). Adoniram later said it was his "intention to place [three Karen] men in the adult school and qualify them to read and interpret the scriptures to their countrymen" (2:12).

Strategic Model 1: The Judsons Practiced Bible-Centered Conversionism

Judson's theology of baptism greatly influenced his view of Christian conversion. His passion for the conversion of the heathen was not satisfied with mere tract distribution or immediate professions of faith. Judson recorded that when a Buddhist would begin considering Christianity, all his relatives and acquaintances would rise up to prevent him. It would have been tempting to soften the exclusivity of the gospel and thus promote religious multi-perspectivalism and ecumenical dialogue, but Judson's adherence to biblical convictions prevented him from settling for inoffensive and socially acceptable theological minimalism.

In a journal entry in February 1820, Judson recorded a conversation he had with the Buddhist teacher, Moung Shwa-gnong, which illustrates his convictions. Moung Shwa-gnong insisted that he held to the fundamentals of the Christian religion, but Judson was not convinced that he was a genuine convert. Moung Shwa-gnong said, "I believe in the eternal God, in his Son Jesus Christ, in the atonement which Christ has made, and in the writings of the apostles, as the true and only word of God." Yet, Moung Shwa-gnong claimed he tried avoiding persecution by going along with people to the pagoda for worship so that he did not look out of place, but he was sincerely not in agreement with his former ways of worship. Judson observed that Moung Shwa-gnong was progressing in the direction of discipleship, but he contended that Moung Shwa-gnong still lacked full devotion to Christ's commands in scripture. Judson said, "Teacher, you may be a disciple of Christ in heart, but you are not a full disciple. You have not faith and resolution enough to keep all the commands of Christ, particularly that which requires you to be baptized, though in the face of persecution and death" (1853, 1:263). Moung Shwa-gnong consequently left without pursuing baptism any further.

But five months later, Moung Shwa-gnong found Judson and confessed his desire to be publicly baptized, despite the likelihood of persecution, convincing Judson of his submission to Christ's written command to be baptized and corresponding evidence of spiritual life.

"Judson sought to train up the church through the regular teaching of the word. When he was not translating, he was teaching and training."

Strategic Model 2: The Judsons Made Disciples with the Word

Judson sought to train up the church through the regular teaching of the word. When he was not translating, he was teaching and training. Judson developed biblical/theological education for the Burmese ministers-in-training. The Bible courses covered both the Old and New Testaments, but the teachers prioritized the New Testament, teaching "verse by verse, with comparison of parallel passages made in the recitation room. It was the constant aim of the teacher not only to unfold the sense of the scriptures, but also to show the pupils practically how to make the Bible [*sic*] its own interpreter" ("Intelligence from Missions" 1854:8).

Ann played an indispensable role in discipling young believers. Where Judson was a linguistic genius, mastering grammar and syntax, Ann was a social magnet, as it were, that attracted language skills. Her language acquisition emerged from her dynamic intuition and lively personality. Other than being the source of their home's warm hospitality, Ann contributed significantly to translating Judson's first tract—*A View of the Christian Religion* (Judson 1860)—and her own evangelistic/ discipleship tract—*The Catechism* (Judson 1909)—into Siamese. Ann's *Catechism* also underwent translations into Talaing (Mon) and Karen. Within eleven years after Ann's death, by 1837, the Judsons' mission station had distributed a copy of the *Catechism* to every family in Rangoon. By 1890, the printing press had printed 273,000 copies of it.

Just as Judson saw the dictionary as indispensable for the ongoing propagation of the scriptures, he also viewed Bible-based discipleship as the vehicle for the ongoing sustenance and maturity of the indigenous church. Two of his main works for Bible-centered discipleship illustrate his ability to synthesize doctrine for the sake of discipleship: "A Burman Liturgy" (Wayland 1853, 2:467–75 and *A Digest of Scripture* Judson 1838).

Judson's "A Burman Liturgy" provided doctrines useful for discipleship. Judson prepared this liturgy in 1829 for new missionaries who had not yet learned the language and for his Burmese assistants whom he trained for ministry. Judson's copious devotion to biblical detail influenced his commitment to systematize the biblical commands for the sake of obeying scripture rightly.

More extensive than his liturgy, Judson's *A Digest of Scripture* is a compendium of doctrinal assertions using the language of scripture in order to teach the basic doctrines of the Bible. Judson did not write a thorough systematic theology textbook, but he compiled the scriptural evidence necessary for producing such a larger work. Grounded in the infallibility and sufficiency of the Bible, Judson sought to use the Bible's own language to explain its doctrine. *A Digest of Scripture* exemplifies his conviction of the perspicuity of scripture and its power to convert and revive the soul. In nearly two hundred pages of biblical text upon text, Judson outlined what he saw as the whole of scriptural doctrine for the sake of training the church to think and live biblically (Judson 1838:i-iv).

Strategic Model 3: The Judsons Prioritized Proclaiming the Word

Judson contended that gospel proclamation is not comprised only of oral communication, though proclamation is certainly not less than oral communication. Proclamation, moreover, essentially involves distribution of the scriptures. Judson scolded those who were indifferent to the universal dissemination of the Bible. At the ninth annual meeting of the American and Foreign Bible Society, held May 15, 1846 in New York, Judson gave an address (Judson 1883) that unpacked his theology of gospel proclamation and his word-centered piety. Judson argued that the Greek word for *proclaim* has the idea of oral preaching and literature distribution, just as a king's ambassador could proclaim a pardon to the inhabitants of a city through both oral declaration and printed publication, and just as Paul could equally proclaim the gospel through both preaching in the synagogues and publishing gospel truth through his epistles. Judson's intention was not to demote the power of preaching, but to promote the efficacy of the biblical text.

Judson further explained that when a missionary first goes to a heathen people, the missionary's communication is largely oral; however, "he will have very imperfectly fulfilled his commission if he leaves them without the written word." Judson maintained that such neglect results in the kind of "mischievous consequences" that are evident in mission stations "conducted by the Man of Sin," that is, Roman Catholic missions. He went on to caution that among some Protestant mission stations, there had recently been "a tendency to promote the oral communication of the gospel, not, indeed, to an undue pre-eminence, but in such a manner as to throw a shade over the written communication by means of tracts and scriptures." He went on to explain that though the initial indiscriminate, evangelistic preaching of the gospel and tract distribution might initially seem more successful, "all missionary operations, to be permanently successful, must be based on the written word. Where that word is most regarded and honored, there will be the most pure and permanent success." He said that the written "word of God is the golden lamp hung out of heaven to enlighten the nations that sit in darkness, and to show them the path that leads from the confines of hell to the gates of paradise." Judson upheld the Bible, in its original languages, as comprehensively containing all existing revelation from God to the world. The written word is "just *the book,* the one book, which Infinite Wisdom saw best adapted to answer the end of a written revelation." He charged that God entrusted his perfect word as "the sacred deposit in the hands of the church." Judson issued woes to those who deny others to partake in such a treasure and to those who seek to snuff out the light of the gospel of heaven. Judson wished to see the Bible translated and broadcast in every language and to be "deposited in every palace, and house, and hut inhabited by man" (Wayland 1853, 2:235–8).

Eight years earlier, he had uttered similar sentiments in a letter to the American Baptist Board. He said that he had hoped to complete the Bible and deposit it in every village and township across Burma. Though it would require great endurance and much expenditure, once Bibles were positioned in the places of influence and prominence in each town, the seed sown "would spring up in abundant fruit to his [God's] glory." He observed that the townspeople would often gather at the houses of the educated leader, whether it be a priest or principal, in each village for the purpose of listening to the leader read from a religious book. Consequently, he said that he sought to introduce and leave the Bible at the chief location in every town in order that the light of the gospel would efficaciously pervade the dark corners of the Burman empire where no missionary could reside (Judson 1883:410–1).

In the letter, he went on to say that Protestant missions of his era differed from Roman Catholic missions by "honoring and sounding out the word of God." He asserted that those missionaries who esteem the proclamation of scripture higher than any other charitable venture would "be most owned of God, and blessed with the influence of the Holy Spirit." Seeking to contextualize by donning priestly garments of a monk, he would refer to an analogy he used for contextualization in evangelism. He likened the Bible to "only one golden lamp which God has suspended from heaven" to guide sinners to heaven. He warned that missionaries dare not obscure its light by preventing its indiscriminate and universal circulation. He cautioned against perceiving this goal as somehow devaluing the role of gospel preaching, because preaching is "the grand means instituted by Christ for the conversion of the world." However, he explained that all evangelism and discipleship "must be based on the written word." Even if the preacher were to move on from a village, the gospel witness would not depart with him, since "the inspired word may still remain to convert and to edify." From his bibliocentric perspective, preaching the gospel and the written word were inseparable. Together they are, he said, "the two arms which are to pull down the kingdom of darkness, and build up the Redeemer's. Let us not cut off one of these arms, for the other will by itself be comparatively powerless." He was convinced that the history of the church testified to the fact that one of these arms alone is powerless without the other (Wayland 1853, 2:126–7).

Publishing the Word

Two very important events marked the year 1816: the arrival of a printing press and the appointment of a professional printer from Philadelphia, George H. Hough (1757–1830), to operate the press. As the strategies and capacity of the mission station developed, their most productive and intensive years were from 1836–1837 during which the mission station, under Judson's visionary leadership, and with the enthusiastic assistance of six indigenous preachers, disseminated over ten million copies of tracts and evangelistic literature in three different languages. The tract distribution teams blanketed Rangoon and the vicinity three times to ensure every family received the literature. Judson would meet every morning with his indigenous evangelists to pray and debrief on the previous day's work, which provided opportunity for constructive feedback and encouragement. By 1839, because of this broad-sowing initiative, several hundred were seeking baptism, and only a few years later, the Rangoon mission station recorded 774 Burmese members. Seven years after Judson's death, one village chief said that the study of the scriptures and tracts, received twenty-two years earlier from Judson himself, had led his whole village to forsake their idolatry (McElroy 2013:21–2).

For Judson, the work of translation, Bible distribution, and proclamation were the chief work of missions, and if a door were shut in one region, he did not agree with employing some other socially acceptable platform for the purpose of staying in the region. Rather, he contended that the missionary ought to continue trying to enter other locations in order to broadcast the Bible to as many people in as many nations as the Lord wills.

Regarding the possibility of expanding translation and literature distribution into China after he had finished his Bible translation, for example, Judson wrote of his passion to see the Bible dispensed in other languages for the conversion of the nations, and he described his potential strategies for introducing the Bible to China and beyond. From his activistic evangelical perspective, there was no other alternative to such missionary work. Because of the indomitability of the proclaimed word, he said his duty was to scatter gospel seed, letting the scripture do all the work. He charged, "But we must all go forward, preaching the gospel, and distributing Bibles and tracts in every possible way, and in every language under heaven. If one door is shut up, we must push in at another" (Middleditch 1854:312).

Translating the Word

Judson admitted that he had a different translation philosophy than many missionaries: "to ascertain the exact meaning of the *original text,* and to express that meaning as exactly as the nature of the language into which they shall translate" (Wayland 1853, 2:146). The labor of many missionaries, he said, had been "dreadfully misdirected." He said that it was the duty of a man to spend his whole life to produce "a *really good* translation," and this required working "*slow* and *sure,* and to see to it that whatever we do, in regard to the inspired word, is *well done*" (Judson 1883, 408). His third and last wife, Emily C. Judson (1817–1854), described him as "very strenuous about his Burmese version, and would no doubt have persevered in his translation if the whole world had been against him" (1883:408).

Regarding his work ethic and duty of translation, Judson wanted to express the biblical meaning in a way so accurate and understandable that his translation would need little revision in the future (Wayland 1853, 2:165). His eminent biographer, Francis Wayland (1796–1865), claimed that he mastered the Burmese language "to a degree never before attained by a foreigner" (Ibid). Though Judson availed himself to the best of exegetical commentaries and scholarship (Ibid), he would not let the publications of scholars do the work for him. He ever insisted on going to the original biblical texts themselves and only using the critical commentaries as references. Thus, he would not canonize an interpreted verse until he was certain of its meaning in the original language and in the Burmese language (161–3). Wayland recorded that an eminent linguist in India who was an expert in Burmese said of Judson's translation, "We honor Wickliffe and Luther for their labors in their respective mother tongues; but what meed [*sic*] of praise is due to Judson for a translation of the Bible, *perfect as a literary work,* in a language so foreign to him as the Burmese" (1853, 2:167).

Approximately one hundred years after Judson's death, the Burma Christian Council invited the Prime Minister of Burma, U Nu (1907–1965), to attend a tea. The Christian leaders were discussing whether to publish a new Burmese Bible translation. U Nu, though a devout Buddhist, was quite familiar with the Christian scriptures (i.e., Judson's translation), and he retorted, "Oh, no, a new translation of the Bible is not necessary. Judson's translation captures the language and idiom of Burmese perfectly and is very clear and understandable" (Brown 1962:24).

Preaching the Word

Adoniram and Ann were at times tempted to despair for lack of noticeable "success" in their proclamation and translation efforts. Francis Wayland established how Adoniram and Ann valued the preaching of the gospel in missions as opposed to doing other "fruitful" ministries, albeit good ones, which seemed to bring in more immediate "fruit." Wayland said that the letters of the Judsons never suggested regrets or doubts about the seeming fruitlessness of their labor. They did, however, indicate their concern that their friends in the States would grow weary of their lack of perceived success. Wayland said that the letters of Adoniram and Ann expressed "entire certainty" about the ultimate success of their work, though they might not see it till glory. He commented, "Their confidence rested solely and exclusively on the word of God... relying not at all on what they could do, but wholly on what God had promised to do for them" (Wayland 1853, 1:205–6).

Though famous for his labor of love in translation, Judson was a preacher at heart. His desire to see the gospel preached drove him to translate the Bible from which the missionary must preach. For Judson, preaching the gospel was ultimately "the great business of his life" (1853, 2:97). He gave himself to translation because he believed God's providence ordained such a responsibility to him and because the American Baptist Board requested it (122). Wayland recorded that whenever Judson's translation work intermitted, he would go to the *zayat* and preach heartily (97), which one colleague, Justus Vinton (1806–1858), described thus: "Every tone, every look, every sentence, spoke out in the most emphatic language, to tell us that the man was seriously in earnest, and himself believed the truths he uttered" (388–9).

At the close of 1827, Judson's journal entries describe the mission's proclamation efforts under his leadership. He recorded a few strategies "for the spread of truth": First, they met for public worship every Sunday at 10:30 in the morning, and the assembly numbered between twenty and seventy. Attendees included the missionaries, Buddhist scholars, native converts, truth-seekers, and occasional travellers. During the public meeting, they would sing songs of adoration and praise, followed by a casual extemporaneous homily, which depended upon the nature of those gathered each time. Then the assembly would finally close in prayer. Though some would leave right afterwards, many would remain and engage in religious discussions for a significant amount of time. Second, they would practice regular evening worship. This was more of a gathering for the mission families, the scholars, and the local Christians. Approximately twenty people gathered for the daily evening worship. They would begin by reading scripture, then an explanation, and finally an exhortation. After concluding in prayer, Judson would spend the remainder of the evening with the new converts and host "instructive and profitable" conversations based on the scripture. The next day he would reason from the scriptures in the *zayat* with any truth-seekers who had attended the night before (Middleditch 1854:240–1).

Strategic Model 4: The Judsons Rested in the Infallible Word

Adoniram and Ann were convinced that the Bible, whether printed or preached, was an infallible evangelist. As such, they believed that the most faithful missionary strategy had to pattern itself after the model of the apostles in Acts who went about scattering the seed of the word. In order to see the power of God in missionary activity, the missionary must heed this pattern. Consequently, the Judsons sought to seize every opportunity in conversations with individuals to implore them to be reconciled to God in light of the love of Christ (Wayland 1853, 1:206–7). Since God blessed the apostles' obedience to Christ's final command, the Judsons devoted themselves to keep the proclamation of the word central to his missionary activity (2:167).

Many missionaries considered the Burmese men too impenetrable to reach with the gospel, so they opened schools for the native children in order to educate them from a civilized Western worldview. They started with proclaiming the gospel, but after many setbacks, they opted for more humanitarian ministries and social work (1853, 1:205–8). Adoniram, however, spent himself to evangelize instead of using other reputable social and educational platforms because he believed in the transforming power of the word. Moreover, Judson was adamantly "opposed to large missionary stations" (2:96) because he believed they became self-absorbed and unfruitful. Mission stations would distract missionaries from their devotion to God's work, and they would inevitably spend themselves on "indirect, subsidiary, and questionable modes of effort, such as indoor labor, school teaching, English preaching, bookmaking—things in themselves good, but not distinctively missionary" (Ibid). Even further illustrating the Judsons' convictions, in one of her early letters in August 1817, to a friend, Ann described the depravity of the Burmese hearts and illustrated how the Judsons viewed human depravity, which led them to the conviction that gospel proclamation is fundamental for conversion (Judson 1823:97–102). Even in his last year of life, Adoniram's commitment remained to preaching the gospel instead of educating natives in English schools and teaching English civility (Wayland 1853, 2:317–9).

Strategic Model 5: The Judsons Employed Bible-Centered Apologetics

Judson resolutely upheld the Bible as the supreme fountain of truth in evangelism and discipleship. A Buddhist teacher, Moung Shwa-gnong, was debating with Judson about the validity of the Christian gospel, and he told Judson that he could not adhere to a religion whose king would allow his son to undergo such humiliation. Judson's account of the controversy exemplifies his unswerving allegiance to the Bible, and it illustrates his own evangelistic method of Bible-based apologetics. After much debate over some tracts and the gospel of Matthew, Judson said in direct terms that the Buddhist teacher was not a true disciple of Christ. He reasoned, "A true disciple inquires not whether a fact is agreeable to his own reason, but, whether it is in the book. His pride has yielded to divine testimony. Teacher, your pride is still unbroken. Break down your pride, and yield to the word of God." Subsequently, the teacher later replied that he saw the error of trusting in his reason alone. He admitted his belief in Christ's crucifixion "because it is contained in the scripture" (Clement 1851:83–4). To Judson, this was a sign of life because it demonstrated spiritual awakening to the revelation of the scriptures.

Judson valued the written word so much that he refused to "waste" tracts by just handing them out without the recipients demonstrating interest. In 1831, he had given away ten thousand tracts, but only to those who requested them. People travelled for three months from Siam and China and from a hundred miles north of the capitol because they had heard that Judson was the man who gave away writings about how to escape the eternal hell. They asked him, "Are you Jesus Christ's man? Give us a writing that tells about Jesus Christ" (Middleditch 1854:273–4).

Of all Judson's tracts and literature, his *The Golden Balance* interacted the most with the Buddhist worldview (Judson 1836). In this tract he compared and contrasted Christianity and Buddhism, demonstrating which religion is true based upon the most excellent aspects of each religion. For instance, he would ask and then answer some questions such as these: Which religion has the more excellent God? Is not Jesus Christ more excellent than Gaudama? Which religion has the more excellent law? Which religion has the more excellent scriptures? He would say that the most excellent and most supreme of each category would underscore which religion is true, for both cannot be true because they are mutually exclusive (1836). The distribution of this tract (100,000 copies) during 1836–1837 by Judson's Burmese disciples proved to be pivotal for their mission efforts, arousing interest among hundreds of Burmese to regularly visit the mission station to hear Judson and his Burmese protégés preach.

Concluding Missiological Principles for Application

In the twenty-first century, when more people are educated and yet more are simultaneously distracted by social media than ever before, our remaining task of proclaiming the written word and making disciples of all *ethnē* is daunting. Though we have the providential blessings of immunizations, vaccinations, jet travel, and instantaneous communication, the geopolitical and cultural shifts in our day are just as unpredictable and volatile as nineteenth-century Burma. The Judsons never knew when a fever might claim their lives or a xenophobic monarch might imprison them on false charges, so they sought to impress upon the Burmese people that the written word is the golden lamp from heaven, which indeed would serve as the timeless source of eternal truth for the people even after the Judsons were gone.

As the Judsons would contend, the life-creating power is in the seed, the written word.

In terms of missiological strategies, we might differ in how we adapt culturally, learn languages, and establish relationships, but the long-lasting, life-producing power is neither in our pragmatic methods nor our unique strategies. As the Judsons would contend, the life-creating power is in the seed, the written word; when we uphold the dissemination of the word—whether through speaking or writing—as sufficient and central, then we can rest, knowing that the Vinedresser is in control and will cultivate his vineyard in his time, in his way.

Let us consider, finally, the witness of Adoniram Judson to the faithful work of God through his written word. Sensing dissatisfaction among supporters back home because of the Judsons' perceived lack of results, Adoniram pushed back in a letter and defended the slow growth of sowing the word: "If they ask again, what prospect of ultimate success is there?—tell them, as much as there is an Almighty and faithful God who will perform his promises, and no more" (Judson 1816:184).

This chapter has shown that the supreme and sufficient word was the burning and shining golden lamp from heaven that guided the Judsons' mission strategies. For Adoniram and Ann, the biblical message was a summons from the king that demanded earnest proclamation through oral preaching, translation, publication, and dissemination. Allegiance to Christ's command to be baptized was the first step of assurance of genuine conversion. Seeking to honor the word of Christ, the Judsons went "forward, preaching the gospel, and distributing bibles [*sic*] and tracts in every possible way, and in every language under heaven" (Middleditch 1854:312).

References

Anderson, Courtney. 1987. *To the Golden Shore: The Life of Adoniram Judson.* 2nd ed. Valley Forge, PA: Judson.

Brown, Russell E. 1962. "The Life and Work of Adoniram Judson." *Andover Newton Quarterly.* 2 (3) 9–33.

Burns, E. D. 2016. *A Supreme Desire to Please Him: The Spirituality of Adoniram Judson.* Eugene, OR: Pickwick.

Clemént, Jesse. 1851. *Memoir of Adoniram Judson, Being a Sketch of His Life and Missionary Labors.* Auburn, NY: Derby and Miller.

Eitel, Keith E. 2012 "The Enduring Legacy of Adoniram Judson's Missiological Precepts and Practices." *Adoniram Judson: A Bicentennial Appreciation of the Pioneer American Missionary.* Jason G. Duesing, ed. Nashville: B&H Academic.

"Intelligence from the Missions, Theological Training of Native Pastors." 1854. *The Baptist Missionary Magazine* 34:6–15.

Judson, Adoniram. 1817. "Extract of a Letter from Mr. Judson to Mr. Rice, Rangoon, August 3d, 1816." *The Baptist Missionary Magazine* 1 (1817):184.

________. 1836. *The Golden Balance.* 6th ed. Maulmain: American Baptist Mission.

________. 1838. *A Digest of Scripture, Consisting of Extracts from the Old and New Testaments: On the Plan of "Brown's Selection of Scripture Passages."* Maulmain: American Baptist Mission.

________. 1860. *A View of the Christian Religion in Three Parts: Historic, Didactic, and Preceptive.* 15th ed. Maulmain: American Baptist Mission.

Judson, Ann Hasseltine.1823. *An Account of the American Baptist Mission to the Burman Empire: In a Series of Letters, Addressed to a Gentleman in London.* London: J. Butterworth & Son and T. Clark.

________. 1909. *The Catechism.* Rangoon: American Baptist Mission Press.

Judson, Edward. 1883. *The Life of Adoniram Judson, By His Son, Edward Judson.* New York: A. D. F. Randolph & Co.

McElroy, Jack. 2013. *Adoniram Judson's Soul Winning Secrets Revealed: An Inspiring Look at the Tools Used by "Jesus Christ's Man" in Burma.* Shirley, MA: McElroy Publishing.

Middleditch, Robert T. 1854. *Burmah's Great Missionary: Records of the Life, Character, and Achievements of Adoniram Judson.* New York: E. H. Fletcher.

Neill, Stephen. 1986. *A History of Christian Missions.* 2nd ed. The Penguin History of the Church. Vol. 6. Harmondsworth, England: Penguin.

Wayland, Francis. 1853. *A Memoir of the Life and Labors of the Rev. Adoniram Judson, D.D.* 2 vols. Boston: Phillips, Samson and Company.

CHAPTER 4

Missionary Communication When Locals Are Listening

Karl Dahlfred

One of the keys to public speaking is knowing your audience. In the history of missionary communication, missionaries have had to contend with multiple audiences, crafting messages for widely differing groups, and sometimes multiple groups at the same time. Missionaries have written letters to their home churches or mission boards in one language while at the same time preparing tracts and sermons in another language for use in their host culture. They have spoken and written to win non-Christians to the faith and to solicit greater support from those already committed to the cause. When they have known their audiences well, correctly assessing their previous knowledge, assumptions, and sensitivities, much good has been accomplished. But when we look at the historical record, this has not always been the case.

Sometimes missionaries have simply misunderstood their listeners. At other times, statements meant for a sympathetic audience have come to the attention of an unsympathetic audience. And despite the professed love of many missionaries for the people in their host culture, attitudes of superiority have sometimes crept through. They were not intending to offend, but offense was taken. Criticisms that were not meant to be heard have been both heard and resented. Put simply, missionaries have time and again undercut their evangelistic goals with the content or manner in which they communicate. How does this happen? To what degree is it avoidable? What can be done to remedy it?

In this chapter, I would like to provide three case studies of missionary communication gone awry in order to highlight common causes of communication mishaps and suggest guidelines for minimizing such missteps among both foreign missionaries and local Christians in Buddhist cultures. To do this, I will recount two historical examples and one modern example of mishaps in missionary communication in Thailand that also bear relevance for cross-cultural gospel communication beyond the contexts of Southeast Asia and Buddhist majority cultures. After narrating the three case studies in some detail, I will use these incidents as reference points in identifying causes of missionary miscommunication and suggesting solutions for modern gospel communicators.

Prince Damrong Objects to a Tract

The year was 1931 and American Presbyterian missionary Paul Fuller regularly took to the city streets of Bangkok to preach the gospel and hand out tracts, together with his Thai co-workers Nai Kitch and Boon Mark Gittisarn. They spoke the gospel to many people and distributed large numbers of tracts that included the name and location of local pastors and their churches and offered free New Testaments for anyone who would read the four Gospels and Acts. They saw few tangible results from their efforts. Fuller was uncertain if the materials they handed out were ever read because even the catechumens in his own church were unmotivated to read the Gospels and tracts they had been given. Fuller suspected that those who criticized Christianity had never even read a single Christian tract. He estimated indifference and "loyalty to the national religion" to be the biggest obstacles to the advance of the gospel in Siam (Fuller 1931).

In the midst of this widespread indifference to evangelistic literature, an incident occurred which Fuller described as "not a pleasant one" but which "nevertheless revealed that our literature sometimes penetrates to unexpected depths" (Fuller 1931). One of the pieces of literature that Fuller and his team distributed in great quantities was a gospel portion that included the books of Genesis and Luke. Tucked inside this scripture portion was a tract about salvation that had been written thirty years previously by Dr. John A. Eakin, a long-standing and well-respected member of the American Presbyterian Mission (APM). Eakin had since passed away but his two sons, John L. and Paul A., had followed in their father's footsteps. Both were members of the American Presbyterian Mission in Siam, the latter holding the position of executive secretary for more than a decade. The tract in question had been approved for publication by the Literature Committee of the APM's Siam Mission and been used extensively for many years. Despite decades of use without incident, in 1931 the Literature Committee of the Siam Mission decided not to republish this title and had discarded it along with other older materials, at least some of which were retired due to "objectionable parts." Paul Fuller, however, was not aware of any potential problems with the tract and took it upon himself to reprint it for use in his own evangelism (Eakin 1931a).

However, a problem arose when this tract came to the unfavorable attention of Prince Damrong, a son of King Mongkut (r.1851–1868), and one of the senior princes of the Siamese royal family. The prince and the American Presbyterian missionaries had excellent working relationships and communicated frequently as they had a shared interest in the modernization and development of the Siamese nation. However, a tension existed between the prince and the missionaries since the latter also aimed at the conversion of Siamese people to Christianity, a goal not shared by the Buddhist royal family and government of Siam. Prince Damrong took exception to a particular passage of the tract which he felt disparaged Buddhism. In a letter to Cleland McAfee of the American Presbyterian Board of Foreign Missions, Paul Fuller quoted in translation the objectionable part of the tract, underlining the phrase that the prince found most distasteful:

> God (before the ten commandments were given) was pleased to teach the hearts of men and exhorted them to give up their sins. After that He came down to earth and gave the ten commandments which were to warn the hearts of men to know good and evil, but mankind did not obey the commandments of God. Several hundreds of years afterwards Somenakodom, that is the Lord Buddha came and proclaimed a new way of salvation: that man should make merit and accumulate merit for himself in order to be able to escape from sin; but God in Heaven observed and beheld that Buddhists were tempted into wrong and fell into perishing just the same (likewise). Then God was greatly distressed and <u>could not endure it</u> and He determined in his heart to come to this earth and provide the way of salvation for mankind according to the promise which He had proclaimed many hundreds of years before. Accordingly, He came to earth and was born as a man in the village of Bethlehem (Fuller 1931).

The missionaries first became aware of Prince Damrong's thoughts on this tract when he summoned Dr. George B. McFarland to the palace and asked whom he should deal with as a representative of the Mission "concerning the matter and method of propagating the Christian religion both in print and by word of mouth" (Eakin 1931b). McFarland in turn took the matter to Paul Eakin, executive secretary of the Siam Mission. Eakin immediately realized the seriousness of the matter and prepared a written statement of explanation and apology, with the assistance of Mrs. Bertha Blount McFarland and Mrs. Geraldine Fuller. Eakin, together with

Dr. McFarland, then secured an audience with Prince Damrong and presented the letter to him. Eakin wanted to reassure the prince that it was the "clear intention" of the Mission "to do nothing that could be construed in any way as unfair to the government or people of Siam" (Eakin 1931b).

Eakin reported that the prince was "very kind and gracious in his response" and was glad that the mission's policy had not changed. However, Prince Damrong took the opportunity to lecture the missionaries concerning the attitude of King Prajadhipok and the Government of Siam towards other religions and religious communication. The objectionable content in the tract reprinted by Fuller was not an isolated incident and the prince "cited several cases which had come to his attention, where there had been ground for the charge of unfairness and misrepresentation" (Eakin 1931b). The prince made clear that Siam's policy of religious toleration did not allow for what he termed "free-thinkers," namely people who tear down other religions in order to win adherents to their own. "The king," explained Prince Damrong, "is interested in other religions because He realizes that many of his subjects get real comfort from their own faiths" but would "grow very intolerant toward any attempt to defame or belittle Buddhism." Eakin reported that the Prince thus recommended that a "code should be prepared and submitted to each missionary who comes and every national worker in our Mission, making clear our message and a method of presenting that message that absolutely omits odious comparisons and misrepresentations." Furthermore, he asked that "special care be taken in the selection of missionaries that are sent to Siam to ensure that they will be willing to see this viewpoint and respect it in their preaching and work in the schools and hospitals" (Eakin 1931a).

The Mormons Who Sat on Buddha's Head

In July 1972, a much more unpleasant encounter occurred between American missionaries and Thai Buddhist authorities. Whereas the audience of Paul Eakin and George McFarland with Prince Damrong was private and concluded cordially, the "Sukhothai Incident" as it has been termed by Shane Strate, was neither (2016). In July 1972, a group of young Mormon missionaries were taken on an educational outing to the future Sukhothai Historical Park with the ostensible purpose of learning about Thailand's history and religious heritage. The Sukhothai site, consisting of large stone Buddha statues and ancient temple ruins, had not yet been designated as a historic site and was located at the end of an unpaved gravel road. During their outing, the young missionaries decided to have a photo competition to see who could produce the best picture to send back home. One popular photo pose was putting the book of Mormon "in the outstretched hand of a statue, making it appear that the Buddha was studying LDS scripture"

(Strate 2016:185). The photo that would subsequently capture public attention, however, was taken at Wat Si Chum. Various missionaries took turns sitting on the head of a stone Buddha statue, their legs dangling over the face. There were no signs prohibiting such action and other visitors to the site did not raise objections. After their day out, the missionaries all returned to their work locations in different cities.

Returning to Nakon Sawan, missionary Joseph Wall, a twenty-year-old from California, took his film to be developed at a local photo shop where he knew the owner and had begun teaching him about Mormonism. An employee developing the film saw a photo of Wall sitting on the Buddha head and made an extra copy of the photo to send to a local newspaper. On July 9, 1972, the photo of Wall appeared in *Siam Rath,* a national Thai newspaper, with the following caption:

> Before [Thai] government officials or scholarship students travel abroad, they receive considerable instruction and training regarding the customs and manners of the farang countries so they know how to behave properly in foreign countries ... meanwhile, look at the insulting and disrespectful way that they treat the things that we worship. (*Siam Rath,* 9 July 1972; translation by author) (Strate 2016:186).

In 1972, there were few foreigners in Nakon Sawan and it did not take long for local people to identify Wall as the one in the photograph in the newspaper. Local Thai who had been studying Mormonism with the missionaries canceled their appointments and people let the air out of their bicycle tires. Those who knew the missionaries did not want to be seen with them. Although Nakon Sawan Police Colonel Sawai Intaravut denied that there were any street protests, newspapers carried reports of protestors carrying signs reading "Send farang Christian missionaries out of the province immediately!" (Strate 2016:187, 199). The Thai term *farang,* meaning "white foreigner," is commonly used by both Thai and foreigners. The police colonel confirmed, however, that people came to him demanding that Wall be arrested. On July 13, Thai police arrived at the residence of Joseph Wall and arrested him along with fellow missionary Kimball Larson, who had taken the now infamous photo. Immediately arraigned in a local court, the pair claimed they did not know the stone Buddha statue was a sacred relic, nor that their action was illegal. Without the benefit of a lawyer, the two were questioned by the judge who then lectured them about the offensiveness of the action:

> Thais are free to worship whatever religion they choose, but most choose to worship Buddhism. Religion is necessary for mankind. If a person has no religion, that person is a Communist. Thais worship Buddhism. If someone insults that religion it is an attempt to undermine the structure of society. This is especially true of educated people such as you, who are teachers of religion. If this court did not punish you, the sin would be on the court. (*Thai Rat,* 15 July 1972; translation by author) (Strate 2016:188).

After the lecture, the judge found them guilty and sentenced them to one year in prison, which was later commuted to six months because they had signed a confession admitting guilt. The two young men claimed that they had acted out of ignorance, but the judge determined that their act was done with malicious intent, not ignorance. Since they were religious teachers, they should have known better. They intended to insult Buddhism. After sentencing, they were handcuffed and taken immediately to Nakon Sawan provincial prison to begin serving their terms.

This incident touched off protracted outrage and public debate in the Thai media, and served as a case in point for various nationalist, anti-Western, and anti-Christian narratives (Strate 2016). Mormon leaders instructed their missionaries in Thailand to stay inside and not evangelize (Hamblin 2008). Mainstream missionary groups sought to distance themselves from the Mormons, fearing that the negative publicity would impact their own work. Speaking on behalf of the Southern Baptists, Ronald Hill told Thai media that Mormons are not Christians and real Christians are just as appalled as the Thai are. The really insulting part, Hill asserted, is that a church would send teenagers to preach the gospel without proper cultural training (Strate 2016:196–7).

Porn Is Now Your Friend

The third case study for this chapter takes us from the analog era of the printed page and photographic film into the digital age of the internet and social media. The speed and reach of communications have increased exponentially in the past thirty years such that the potential fallout of communication mishaps is greater than ever before. A brief illustration from the popular social media platform, Facebook, serves to illustrate this point. In early 2018, a foreign missionary in Thailand, who will remain unnamed, posted a light-hearted photo in a closed Facebook group for foreign missionaries in Thailand. It was a picture of a social media notification reading "Porn is now your friend." His comment on the photo was "Just got this notification. A not-so-subliminal message from the devil." Both the missionary who posted the photo, as well as everyone who participated in the lengthy comment thread discussion that followed, understood that "Porn" in the context of this notification was the Romanized transliteration of a common Thai nickname. However, the vast majority of native English speakers associate the word "porn" with "pornography," hence this missionary's tongue-in-cheek commentary that this notification was the devil tempting him to look at pornography.

The particular Facebook group where this was posted was started by, and intended for, foreign missionaries working in Thailand, and the majority of group members are foreign missionaries. However, a small number of Thai Christians are also members of the group. With one exception, the first handful of comments on this photo were foreigners pointing out that "Porn" is actually a Thai name that means "blessing," lamenting the chosen transliteration of "Porn" and Thai unwillingness to spell it differently, or blaming the poor English skills of Thais for this particular transliteration choice. The implication in a number of these comments was that Thai people should choose a different transliteration of this name because spelling it as "porn" causes a negative association in the mind of non-Thai speakers. Following on from these initial comments from foreigners, some Thai jumped into the discussion, defending this common transliteration, arguing that it is not the problem of Thai people that "Porn" has a different meaning in other languages. From the comments of some Thai, it became apparent that the chosen Romanized transliterations of their names were just as sacrosanct to them as the spelling of their names in Thai script. They took exception to the suggestion that they change the Romanized spelling of their names to fit the sensibilities of foreigners. The fact that foreigners thought that the name "Porn" was funny was seen by some Thai as evidence of an attitude of cultural superiority and ridicule of Thai culture. One Thai commenter pointed out that since English speakers wouldn't laugh at their friend named "Dick" even though they knew the vulgar double meaning of that name, they also should not laugh at the name "Porn." After more discussion over the course of a few days, including reasoned and animated commentary by a few Thai members of the group, a moderator closed the thread to further comments. What was intended as a light-hearted post had turned into a cause of offense and the moderator judged that allowing further discussion was unlikely to be beneficial.

Causes of Offense in Missionary Communication and Suggested Solutions

In each of the case studies above, communication went awry and offense was taken due to error and ignorance rather than intentional maliciousness. In order to help Christian communicators avoid such mishaps in the future, I would like to extrapolate from these examples some causes of unintended offense and suggest preventative measures.

The first major cause of problems is expanded and unintentional audiences. The American Presbyterian missionaries had no idea that their tract would come to the attention of Thai royalty. The young Mormons took photos for people back home, never imaging that Thai newspaper readers would see them. The missionary who became friends with Porn posted his photo for fellow missionaries who would understand the joke. In each of these cases, an audience that was never supposed to see did exactly that. And they did not like what they saw.

On the one hand, we can never be certain that something we say, write, or photograph will not fall into the "wrong hands." But on the other hand, some forethought as to the potential reach of our words and images should help us to evaluate how our communication might be perceived by different audiences. Thinking through the potential audiences of our communication might lead to a revised version of what we intended to express, or a change of format, such private message or phone call instead of public post or group email.

A second cause of offense is biblically unchangeable content, and the changeable manner in which that is shared. For Christians who adhere to the Bible as God's unchangeable and authoritative revelation in matters of life and faith, there are truths that sometimes cause offense even when presented in a winsome and culturally sensitive way. The Old Testament many times speaks of the folly of worshipping idols and the New Testament makes clear the exclusivity of Christ and salvation in Him alone. These truths are offensive to the sinful nature. As people read the Bible and Christian leaders teach the scriptures, these truths will come up, sometimes in a mixed setting that includes people of other religions. These truths can be handled sensitively or insensitively. In the Thai Buddhist context, and other contexts where honor and shame or saving face are concerns, direct communication is not always appreciated. Denouncing idols and pointing out the failings of local religious beliefs and practices may serve to turn listeners away from considering the gospel more than it draws them to consider Christ. In the case of Prince Damrong's objection the American Presbyterians' tract, he may not have taken offense had the tract not named Buddhism directly. Although the tract writer's attempt to relate Christian truths to local circumstances is commendable, it may not have been necessary to implicate Buddhism in order to make the point that our human efforts to obey God fall short of what is required.

Although there are appropriate times and places to discuss the relationship of Christianity to other religions, discernment must be used, especially in evangelism. As the Apostle Paul did in Athens (Acts 17:22–34), positively acknowledging his audience's religiosity as a bridge to proclaiming gospel truth, a positive statement of the Christian faith today is more likely to gain listeners than denouncing local beliefs. On this point, Paul Eakin's concluding thoughts on his audience with Prince Damrong still bear consideration today. Writing to Cleland McAfee of the Board of Foreign Missions of the American Presbyterian Church, Eakin recommended that

> the Candidate department should be warned to be very careful in selection of missionaries that come to Siam. There is certainly no place for any missionary that so feels the superiority of Christianity that disparaging remarks about Buddhism are natural to him in his presenting of the Gospel. As someone has said, "One can have back-bone without bristles" (Eakin 1931a).

A third source of offense is lack of linguistic or cultural awareness on the part of the communicator. Although this is not always completely avoidable for those working outside their native language and culture, a proper attitude on the part of a missionary and attentive guidance on the part of leadership can go a long way to preventing problems. In the case of Prince Damrong, there was a gap between Thai Buddhist and American Christian sensibilities as to how one may speak of another's religion. A similar lack of awareness was a major factor in the Mormons' desecration of a Buddha statue. In the case of the social media notification about Porn, a number of foreigners did not have the same level of sensitivity about names, either Thai or foreign, as some Thai did.

"Missionaries need to think carefully about why they are in a given culture and whether it is their place or not to comment on certain practices around them."

A fourth and final factor in this non-comprehensive list is a lack of understanding one's place or role in relation to the host culture. There are simply some things that look or sound worse coming from a cultural outsider rather than a cultural insider. In the media debate over the photo of Joseph Wall's act of desecration, Thai journalist Matcha Phitsadara asked why there was such outrage over the photo of this foreigner when similar acts committed by Thais are overlooked, for example, "urinating on temple walls, knocking the heads off Thai Buddhas, [and] producing and selling artificially aged relics" (Strate 2016:197). Foreign missionaries and other Christians working cross-culturally need to think about how their words and actions will be received when coming from them, not from locals. Criticism of local culture and beliefs may be accepted by locals when coming from locals, but not from a cultural outsider. For this reason, missionaries need to think carefully about why they are in a given culture and whether it is their place or not to comment on certain practices around them. American Presbyterian missionary Loren Hanna, for example, unintentionally hurt the feelings of a Thai pastor in 1934 by commenting on how much better the roads were in his native California when compared to Thai roads (Hanna 1934:17). Even if what missionaries say may be true, their words may create an impression of cultural superiority and undercut their primary goal of making Christ known. Jesus knew that commenting definitively on Roman taxation would not further his ministry (Matt 22:15–22), and Christian communicators today must discern whether commentary on particular local affairs will help or hinder their own ministries in the master's service.

Conclusion

In the history of cross-cultural communication, there have been innumerable mishaps, many more than the few case studies mentioned here. And there will certainly be more this side of heaven. But offenses and miscommunication can be reduced when we give attention to the errors of the past. Occasional trip-ups need not turn into colossal failures if missionaries and other gospel messengers commit themselves to developing sympathetic relationships with those in their host countries, to learning local languages and customs, and attuning themselves to assumptions and sensitivities.

References

Eakin, Paul. 1931a. "Letter to Cleland McAfee, July 6, 1931." Philadelphia: Presbyterian Historical Society (Collection RG84).

________. 1931b. "Letter to the Members of the Mission, July 16, 1931." Chiang Mai: Payap University Archives (Collection RG001/78).

Fuller, Paul. 1931. "Letter to Cleland McAfee, September 1931." Philadelphia: Presbyterian Historical Society (Collection RG84).

Hamblin, Kedrik. 2008. "Proselytizing History Repeats with Recent Missionary Gaffe." *BYU NewsNet,* March 24, 2008. http://www.freerepublic.com/focus/f-religion/1991107/posts.

Hanna, Loren S. 1934. "Abdication and Succession." *Mission Opinion,* September 1934: 16–21. Margaret and Kenneth Landon Papers (SC-38). Wheaton, IL: Wheaton College Special Collections.

Strate, Shane. 2016. "The Sukhothai Incident: Buddhist Heritage, Mormon Missionaries, and Religious Desecration in Thailand." *Journal of Religion and Violence.* 4 (2) 183–203.

CHAPTER 5

Henry Steel Olcott's Contribution to the Buddhist Revival in Sri Lanka

G. P. V. Somaratna

Colonel Henry Steel Olcott (1832–1907) was a key contributor to the nineteenth-century Buddhist revival in Sri Lanka. He incorporated much from his Protestant Christian upbringing in his contribution to modernize Buddhism. This is a reason that many scholars have referred to modern Buddhism in Sri Lanka as "Protestant Buddhism" (Blackburn 2010:197–201; Bond 1988:80; Malalgoda 1976:246; Obeyesekere 1970:46–7). Born and raised in a Protestant Christian tradition, he was able to introduce much of the Protestant Christian spirit into modernizing the Buddhist movement which had already begun in the western and southern provinces of Sri Lanka (Malalgoda 1976: 256–62).

In 1875 Olcott, Helena Petrovna Blavatsky (1831–1891), and several other spiritualists formed the Theosophical Society in New York City, USA (Lewis and Petterson 2005:259). Later in 1878 Olcott and Blavatsky, began work in India initially in Mumbai and moved to Adyar near Chennai. Olcott's stay in South Asia lasted nearly thirty-two years. From there he made sporadic visits to Sri Lanka to encourage Buddhists. He first arrived in Colombo on May 16, 1880 as a Theosophist interested in founding branches of theosophical societies, but the cheerful welcome with flattering ceremony he received from Buddhists everywhere he visited modified most of his plans in favor of Buddhism. As a result, he had a special affection for Buddhists in the island. Eventually he was drawn into the Buddhist movement wholeheartedly. From his first visit to his death in 1907 he visited Sri Lanka thirty times, virtually every year. Olcott and Blavatsky stayed five months on this first occasion. Buddhists placed their confidence in this white "Buddhist" to champion their ambitions and aspirations to counter the Christian missionary challenge.

Olcott's Christian Upbringing

Olcott was born August 2, 1832 in Orange, New Jersey, the oldest of six children, to Presbyterian businessman Henry Wyckoff Olcott and Emily Steele Olcott (Agarwal 2003:4; Prothero 1996:13). As a child, Olcott lived on his father's New Jersey farm. The Olcotts were descended from the line of English Puritans that had settled in the United States for many generations. His publication on the genealogy of his family shows that it extended back to Thomas Olcott, one of the founders of Hartford, Connecticut, in 1636. During his teens he attended first the College of the City of New York and later Columbia University, where he joined the St. Anthony Hall fraternity.

His marriage to Mary Epplee Morgan in 1860 who was a daughter of the rector of Trinity parish, New Rochelle, New York, also contributed in many ways to stabilize his Protestant Christian association (Proch 2009:13). Olcott was raised as a Presbyterian, in the Calvinist tradition. Even though Olcott had been raised in a pious Presbyterian home, he became a leading figure in one of the most unconventional and dominant forms of spirituality in the nineteenth century (2018a:19; 114–36). Olcott was a Republican involved in Freemasonry, Spiritism, and the Anti-Slavery movement (Proch 2009:13).

He came to Sri Lanka with the language and culture that Christianity had produced. The powerful symbiosis of Christian rituals, art, music, literature, and philosophy dominated his thinking. He embraced all the symbols and methodologies of Christianity of his day. It is impossible to understand his activities without some knowledge of the Christian faith and the culture of nineteenth century American Christianity.

> "Despite his anti-missionary stance, Olcott shared with Christian missionaries an imperialist confidence in his ability to define and determine the character of Asian religions—a warning for practitioners today."

He was successful in winning the Buddhist lay elite, those educated in the British Christian schools, to lead this modernizing movement (Obeyesekere 1979:308–9). However, it is noticeable that despite his anti-missionary stance, Olcott shared with Christian missionaries an imperialist confidence in his ability to define and determine the character of Asian religions—a warning for practitioners today (Blackburn 2008:107; Prothero 2010:177). He became an agent in facilitating the interaction between Buddhism and Protestant Christianity. At the same time Olcott played a significant role in bringing knowledge of Buddhism to western countries, as well as in enhancing the cultural confidence in Sinhalese Buddhists.

Theosophical Society

In 1875 Olcott and Blavatsky founded the Theosophical Society of New York with Olcott serving as president and Blavatsky as corresponding secretary. Theosophy is a pluralist movement with a heavy component of occultism which began in the nineteenth century. The defining theme in Theosophy is the unity of all religions. It grew out of interest in the occult generated previously by Spiritualism, in which both Blavatsky and Olcott had participated. The society promoted an attention to philosophical attitudes drawn from Eastern religious teachings as well.

In December 1878, they left New York in order to move the headquarters of the Society to India. They landed at Mumbai on February 16, 1879. Olcott set out to experience the native country of Buddha whom he considered his spiritual leader. The headquarters of the Society were established at Adyar near Chennai.

For some time Olcott had corresponded with well-wishers in Sri Lanka; this prompted his first visit to Colombo on May 17, 1880. Olcott had read the report of the debate between Buddhist monks and Christian ministers at Panadura in 1873 (Malalgoda 1976:230). Report of the debate was published by John Capper of the *Ceylon Times* and later published in book form in English. The book had a wide circulation in England and America. On the twenty-fifth of the same month, Col. Olcott, and Madame Blavatsky met with Buddhist leader Damodar Mavalankar (1857–1885) and other Buddhist leaders in Galle.

Olcott was welcomed by the Buddhists as an ally who could guide them politically as well as culturally in their struggle against western domination. He soon became aware of the larger role that Sri Lankan Buddhists expected of him. Wherever he went, he was given an enthusiastic welcome, which Olcott noted with some irony. Olcott stated,

> The Asiatic people have certainly perfected the art of feeding the vanity of public men and their public men seem to like it. The Maha Bodhi journal reported, "No king ever received that homage of a devoted people as these two when they landed on the shores" (quoted in Bond 1992:48).

Olcott enthusiastically accepted this role as a Western champion of Buddhism against the Christian missions. Shortly after its founding, the Theosophical Society became the Buddhist Theosophical Society.

Buddhist Theosophy has hardly any theosophy in it (Goonatilike 2005:143; Malalgoda 1976: 246; Obeyesekere 1972, 1976). It incorporated a good deal of Buddhism, but not of the traditional type. In fact, this Buddhism had very high doses of Protestant missionary philosophy in it. Some have even stated that "theosophy is the natural child of the marriage between Christianity and Buddhism" (W. T. Stead quoted in Gombrich 2012:62).

The contribution to the Buddhist revival in Sri Lanka

Olcott strongly criticized Christianity and held that there is truth found in the spirituality of the East. His knowledge of Buddhism or Hinduism was meagre, yet the Theosophists preferred them to Christianity. When he came to Sri Lanka for the first time in 1880, he noticed that in the time they arrived influential Sinhalese families were "ashamed to acknowledge the Dharma of Buddhism...for fear of Christian opinion in authority." (*The Buddhist,* Feb. 14, 1890). However, within a period ten years Olcott found that a remarkable change had taken place. Olcott stated, "we were the first white champions of their religion, speaking of its excellence and its blessed comfort from the platform in the face of the missionaries, its enemies and slanderers" (2018a:178). Buddhists expected Olcott to lead their religion on the path to modernity (Obeyesekere 1995:53).

Olcott's Presbyterian upbringing persuaded him to view all religions individualistically, that each person can and should seek his or her own spiritual goal without intermediaries. He viewed the role of the priest in that venture as minimal. The Sangha were only teachers of traditional Buddhism, thus he stayed as far as possible from their educational and social programs.

One of Olcott's significant contributions to revival of Buddhist was the strengthening of the role of the laity and encouraging a reformist view of Buddhism (Bond 1992:48). Laity were not the primary actors in the revival of Buddhism until the appearance of Olcott in 1880 (Malalgoda 1976:237). Because it was a lay organization, the Buddhist Theosophical Society could easily permeate the life of everyday Buddhists. The Anagarika lifestyle that Dharmapala adopted was within this theosophical background. Olcott in his *Buddhist Catechism* stated, "The mere wearing of yellow robes, or even ordination, does not of itself make a man pure or wise or entitle him to reverence" (*Buddhist Catechism* 1887:45). Olcott promoted opening Buddhist schools and publishing Buddhist scriptural texts to open up religious knowledge to the laity which hitherto had been monopolized by Buddhist monks (Obeyesekere and Gombrich 1988:216).

Known as a supporter of Buddhism

Olcott's tracts and writings against Christianity had been translated and fairly widely disseminated through the country prior to his arrival, contributing to his popularity upon arrival (De Silva 1981:341–2). Olcott's plentiful correspondence with Buddhist monks in Ceylon eventually culminated in travel to and a tour of the island in May of 1880. He and Blavatsky arrived in Colombo, Ceylon on May 16, 1880 to an exceedingly warm welcome led by Mohottivatte Gunananda. On May 19, Olcott and Blavatsky were perhaps the first Westerners who publicly "took pansil" (Prothero 1996:95) at Vijayananda temple of the Ramanna Nikaya in Galle (Caldwell 2000:113). To "take pansil" is a ritual wherein laypeople make a voluntary commitment to try to adhere to the rules and precepts of Buddhism, in essence to proclaim oneself publicly to be a Buddhist. A written record of this event signed and dated by Olcott is posted on the temple wall to this day.

United all castes under his leadership

Because of the dominant impact of Hinduism throughout the island, Ceylonese Buddhism and Christianity was, (and to a large extent continues today to be), ruled by the caste system. This, Olcott, with his anti-slavery background in America, could not tolerate. He abhorred the discriminations found in the caste system, especially within any schools, religious sects, or fraternities (Blackburn 2010:107). In India Olcott greatly supported the education of Tamil Paraiyar (Dalit) Buddhists. When Olcott met the founder of the Ramanna fraternity, a Celonese sect of Buddhism, he felt a great affinity with their liberal attitude welcoming individuals from all castes who sought ordination (Malalgoda 1976:166). It soon became public knowledge that the American supporter of Buddhism preferred members of that fraternity above others that segregated by caste. As a result, the profile of the Ramanna Nikaya was heightened greatly (Kariyawasam 1975:20–9).

He persuaded the several Buddhist sects to agree to Fourteen Fundamental Propositions forming a common platform to aid those from many different caste backgrounds.

> My neutrality with respect to difference of caste and sect made me welcome to all, and I passed from vihara to vihara, addressing now an audience of Willalas [*sic.*], now one of the fisher caste, and on one of great Cinnamon peeler caste, each time collecting money for the Common object (2018a:371).

Contribution to Popular Buddhist Education

Olcott and the Theosophical Society became a catalyst for the establishment of Buddhist schools for non-monastic children. The education that prevailed in Buddhist temples was for the Sangha and the Sinhala upper classes. His survey of the educational situation in the island showed him the value of a network of Buddhist schools to counter the influence of Christian schools (Jayasuriya 1976:225). Olcott threw himself heart and soul into the fight for the establishment of Buddhist schools. In 1880 there were only two schools in Ceylon managed by Buddhists (Kirthisinghe and Amarasuriya 1981:4). In Question 328 of his Buddhist catechism he poses the question, "Is Buddhism opposed to education and the study of science?" The answer given is, "Quite the contrary; in the *Sigalowadda Sutta,* a discourse preached by Buddha in the bamboo grove near Rajagriha, he specified as one of duties of a teacher that he should give his pupils instruction in science and lore" (Olcott 1902:77).

Schools

The Buddhist Theosophical Society undertook to open English medium schools for the upper-class Buddhist families following the system introduced by the missionaries. The schools they opened in rural areas were Sinhala medium schools. These schools were replicas of the Christian mission schools. The curriculum and school management followed the same pattern. The sports, societies, houses were not different from the missionary schools. They were named after Buddhist saints such as Mihinda (1898), Ananda (1886), Dharmaraja (1887) following the tradition of Catholics who gave the names of their saints for their schools. By the end of the year 1888 there were 142 registered at the government department of public instruction as grant-in-aid schools under Buddhist management. Due to the efforts of Olcott the number rose to 205 schools and three colleges in 1907, the year he passed away. It is noteworthy that he did not have a single school named after him.

Organization

Olcott's Christian background, his military career, and judicial experience helped the institutionalization of Buddhist activities. Olcott welcomed as a political and cultural ally any and all who could assist the Sinhalese in their struggle and also bring to bear the organizational skills of the West.

Olcott realized that American Protestant religious organizational skills could be utilized by the Buddhists who were already experiencing a revival. He stated,

> If you ask how we should organize our forces, I point you to our great enemy, Christianity, and bid you look at their large and wealthy Bible, Tracts, Sunday school, and Missionary Societies, remarkable agencies they support to keep alive and spread their religion. We must form similar societies, and make our most practical and honest men of business their managers (Karunaratne 1980:31).

They assisted Buddhists in their struggle to match the organizational abilities of the Westerners in Sri Lanka.

In order to organize the resources for education and other Buddhist activities he used the Theosophical Society, which came to be known as the Buddhist Theosophical Society, as the central organization. The enthusiasm among Buddhists to open schools was not easy. Their grants in aid were not available to non-Protestants.

In 1891 the government passed a resolution that "no new school will be aided within a quarter mile of an existing school of the same class excepting in towns with special claims aforesaid" (Sessional Paper 18, 1891). Olcott came in May 1894 to be at a convention of the Managers of Buddhist schools. They appointed Olcott to lay before the Secretary of State for the Colonies the grievance of the Buddhist in in regard to this rule. He went to England to seek a sympathetic hearing from the Secretary of State in December 1894. It is recorded that Olcott campaigned against the Christian character of government schools (Buddhist June 6, 1890).

Fundraising

In July of 1880, he established the National Education Fund as a scholarship fund to finance the expansion of the Buddhist school system. The cooperation of the Sinhalese was disappointing. There were many pledges and promises of support but very few converted their verbal pledges into fiscal practice (Karunaratne 1980:34–5). Factionalism became wild when there was money collected in the fund. Olcott stated:

> There was such petty jealousy, such contemptible intrigues to get control of money, and such ingratitude shown towards me that I was at one time so disgusted that I was ready to throw up the whole thing and let them make their funds and found their schools by themselves (Olcott 1967:85).

In fact it was the desire to raise money for this fund that the Theosophical Society in Adyar sent Olcott back to Ceylon in 1881, though his dedication to that trip created a rift between Olcott and Blavatsky who insisted that he remain in India to work on the editing of *The Theosophist* journal. Olcott continued nonetheless, amidst threats that the senior members of the Theosophical Society disapproved and would no longer assist him. Olcott reportedly testified that he would continue his campaign for Buddhist education, even at the expense of never communing with them again. This declaration signifies the degree to which his passion for the Buddhist cause had grown. Olcott was even willing to abandon the movement which he had helped to found and to which he had devoted years of his life.

Idea of fundraising for Buddhist national cause

Fundraising was hardly known in Sri Lanka before the arrival of Olcott. C.W. Leadbeater stated in May 1884 that he could not collect "a single penny for the

'Fund' as the use of money was scarcely known in these areas." School fundraising was the practice of raising money to support educational enrichment programs by schools or school groups mostly known from the United States. They used parent-teacher organizations, booster clubs, etc. for this purpose. Olcott stated that "the Christians spend millions to destroy Buddhism, we must spend to defend and propagate it" (Olcott 2018b 1931:120).

On the Vesak day of 1881, the Buddhist National Fund was inaugurated at the Kelaniya temple (Sumathipala 1985:28). The BTS journal, *The Buddhist,* was an instrument through which funds could be raised for various causes and the assistance of the Buddhist public could be mobilized. When an Education Fund was launched for Ananda College by P. de S. Kularatne (1893–1976), money was raised to finance the appeal to the Privy Council of the Gampola perahera case, *The Buddhist* was very useful in providing for the Woodward Memorial Education Fund and the fund to aid the Ven. Ananda Metteyya (1872–1923).

At first Olcott found it hard to collect funds. He stated,

> I began with the High Priest and Megittuwatte, and arranged for some lectures that the committee had asked me to give in Colombo. Then, at a Branch meeting, I explained the system of voluntary self-taxation and adopted by many good Christians, by which sometimes ten percent, of their incomes is set aside for religious and charitable work; I had seen my father and other pious Christian gentlemen doing this as a matter of conscience (Karunaratne 1980:35).

Lay leadership

Olcott's involvement in Sri Lanka Buddhism since the 1880s began to attract the local westernized laity in a bigger way. When the Buddhist Defense Committee was formed in 1884 after the riots, Olcott saw that only the lay leaders were in it (Kariyawasam 2009:81).

The process of laicization of Buddhism was enhanced in this period. The Buddhist Theosophical Society provided a platform for the increasing involvement of laymen in the roles of religious leadership which was hitherto the monopoly of Buddhist monks. Olcott also encouraged laymen to take an active part in Buddhist causes and social welfare work (Gombrich and Obeyesekere 1988:232; Kariyawasam 2009:81). The laity educated in the Christian missionary schools were able to introduce modern concepts and science.

Theosophists considered that monks were not suitable for this kind of work. When Olcott organized new branches of the Theosophical Society in other towns also, he followed the same policy of avoiding recruitment of monks to them (Kariyawasam 2009:83). The Buddhist Theosophical Society purposely avoided monks even though they had taken an active part in these religious activities. Segregating monks was purposely done in order to concentrate on social and educational affairs (ibid. 85). By the 1890s, the work of the Buddhist Theosophical Society was completely undertaken by laity.

Societies

The YMBA, or Young Men's Buddhist Association, was created in Sri Lanka in 1898. The main purpose was to provide Buddhist institutions as an alternative to the Young Men's Christian Association. The Young Men's and Young Women's Buddhist Associations was another branch of his education program that came with Olcott's initiative. They offered the same kind of activities that the YMCA and YWCA offered.

Buddhist publications

The propagandist work and polemical work mainly aimed at Christianity with Western tactics was introduced. Their newspapers were used for this purpose as there were two printing presses under the management of Buddhists. *Sarasavi Sandares*a (1880) was a Sinhalese weekly of the Buddhist Theosophical Society (Sumathipala 1968:28). The English counterpart, *The Buddhist,* began publication in 1888. Publication of *The Buddhist* was no easy task. There was often a conflict of opinion both from laity and from the Sangha. Amidst obstacles and handicaps, men like A. E. Buultjens, C. W. Leadbeater, C. Jinarajadasa and D. B. Jayatilaka who were editors of the journal, did not hesitate in the face of difficulties. It was at the time the only journal on Buddhism in English.

Buddhist Catechism

A key event in the revival of Buddhism was the publication of Olcott's *The Buddhist Catechism* in 1881. Olcott wrote in his diary,

> Finding out the shocking ignorance of the Sinhalese about Buddhism, I began after vainly getting some monk to do it, the compilation of a Buddhist Catechism on the lines of the similar elementary handbooks so effectively used among Christian sects" (Bond 1992:50).

The Catechism was endorsed by the High Priest Sumangala (Kirthisinghe 1981:12). It was inevitably a Catechism oriented to a Western intellectualist view of Buddhism through Western eyes. Question no. 205 in his Buddhist Catechism is an example.

Q: What does Buddhism teach about marriage?

A: Absolute chastity being a condition of full spiritual development, is most highly commended, but a marriage to one wife and fidelity to her is recognized as a kind of chastity. Polygamy was censured by the Buddha as involving ignorance and promoting lust (Olcott 1881:47).

He made this statement in this catechism even though he noted the existence of polyandry and also occasional polygamy in the Buddhist literature as well as in Buddhist societies. In its catechetical form it clearly shows the author's training in polemics in its moralist attitude and anti-ritual tendency. Olcott's Buddhist Catechism echoes nineteenth century Protestant polemics against Roman Catholics.

Vesak holiday

It was Olcott who put forward the idea of asking the British government to make Vesak (Buddha's birthday, enlightenment day and day of death) a public holiday. The Colonial Government granted this in 1885 so that the Buddhists were able to celebrate in grand scale. It was first hosted in public on Vesak day, May 28, 1885, at the Dipaduttamarama, Kotahena, by Migettuwatte Gunananda Thera. This was the first Vesak public holiday under British rule. The proclamation of the day as a government holiday has had a remarkable effect upon the feelings of the people (*Buddhist* 1889:22). In an obvious response to Christianity, Olcott worked to develop Buddhist carols modeled on Christmas carols for Vesak, as well as promoting the custom of sending "Vesak cards" (Gombrich and Obeyesekere 1998:205). The first carol party of the Buddhist Theosophical Society occurred in 1885, visiting the temples in the neighborhood of Colombo. They had carol parties, tolling of bells, and evergreens, on the Vesak day in 1886. In this way they Christianized the Vesak festival. They also erected pandals [decorated monuments] which the Catholics did during the time of Jacome Gonsalves (1676–1742) in Kandy.

Olcott played a part in designing the universal Buddhist flag (Bond 1992:49), though the extent to which he was involved in the creative process is disputed (Goonatilake 2006:146). The Buddhist flag was originally regarded as a symbol of unity among the local Buddhists. When Olcott died, his body was covered by the Buddhist and American flags. Olcott took a special interest in the invention of the Buddhist flag as he felt the need for a symbol to rally the local Buddhists (Gombrich and Obeyesekere 1988:204). It was the work of a committee headed by Olcott. Gunanada Thera hoisted the Buddhist flag at his temple at Kotahena for the first time on a public occasion on the first Vesak holiday. The flag was designed in size and shape so that it would be in line with national flags. The flag consists of "the six colors," blue, yellow, red, white, pink, and a mixture of the five colors in the sixth stripe, said to be in the aura shown around of the head of Buddha when he attained enlightenment (Kirthisinghe and Amarasuriya 1981:12).

Olcott continued to mention the opposition he faced from the missionaries as well as local Christians. The appearance of Olcott stimulated a Buddhist movement which the missionaries did not expect. Because of this, many missionaries went out of their way to vilify everything that was Olcott's (2018a:310–1). Olcott wrote "In truth, these Protestant Missionaries are a pestilent lot. With the Catholics we have never had a hard word" (ibid. 175).What does this say about the mission approaches of these two groups?

"In truth, these Protestant Missionaries are a pestilent lot. With the Catholics we have never had a hard word." (Olcott)

Conclusion

Olcott and the Theosophists were able to introduce a rationalist and systematic critique of Christianity so that the burgeoning Buddhist movement could move ahead with a greater finesse to counter the weakening of Buddhism due to the Christian challenge. Modern techniques of Christian organizations which came from Olcott enabled the Buddhist middle class to match the offensive that came from the missionaries. It was the leadership and guidance of Olcott that gave Buddhist lay leaders a self-assurance and confidence to overcome the inadequacy of their abilities in the presence of the perceived Western Christian threat. He modernized Buddhism by introducing Congregational worship, which was absent in Buddhism, in the form of Bodhi puja, and limited the Buddhist sermon to half an hour.

Olcott injected Western Christian methodologies as a challenge to the activities of Christian missionaries. Some Buddhist writing appreciating his work have concurred with Olcott's words, "Happy Karma that brought me to thy shores" (Amarasuriya 1981:24). Ponnambalam Arunachalam in his 1901 Census Report noted, "Previously it was considered among Sinhalese rather fashionable to be thought Christian.... This is no longer the case. They are rather proud of their religion" (Wright 1907:224). The fact is that modern Buddhism in Sri Lanka is much more Western than most Sri Lankans realize. Even as Western missionaries have been accused of exporting their own forms of Christianity abroad, this is the unusual history of the Westerner who brought "Protestant Buddhism" to Sri Lanka.

References

Amarasuriya, B. P. and Kirthisinghe, M. P. 1981. *Colonel Olcott—His Service to Buddhism.* Kandy: Buddhist Publication Society.

Blackburn. A. M. 2010. *Locations of Buddhism: Colonialism and Modernity in Sri Lanka.* Chicago: University of Chicago.

Bond, George Doherty. 1988. *The Buddhist Revival in Sri Lanka: Religious Tradition, Reinterpretation and Response.* University of Southern California.

The Buddhist. 1882. The Magazine of the Buddhist Theosophical Society.

De Silva, K. M. 1981. *A History of Sri Lanka.* Berkeley: University of California Press.

Gombrich, Richard. 2009. *Buddhist Precept & Practice.* New York: Rutledge.

Gombrich, Richard and Gananath Obeyesekere. 1988. *Buddhism Transformed: Religious Change in Sri Lanka.* Princeton University.

Goonatilake, Susantha. 2005. "'Prophet' Looking for a Nineteenth Century Future." *Social Epistemology.* 19 (1) 129–46.

________ 2006. *Recolonization: Foreign Funded HGOs in Sri Lanka.* New Delhi: Sage.

Jayasuriya, J. E. 1976. *Educational Polices and Progress during British Rule in Ceylon 976–1948.* Colombo: Associated Educational.

Johnson, Paul K. 1995. *Initiates of Theosophical Masters.* New York: State University of New York.

Kariyawasam, Tissa. 2009. *Religious Activities and the Development of a New Political Tradition in Sinhalese, 1852–1906.* Colombo: Godage International

Murphet, Howard. 1988. *Yankee Beacon of Buddhist Light: Life of Col. Henry S. Olcott.* Wheaton: Theological Publishing House.

Obeyesekere, Gananath. 1970. "Religious symbolism and Political Change in Sri Lanka." *Modern Ceylon Studies.* 1 (1) 43–63.

________. 1992. *Colonel Olcott's Reforms of the 19th Century and Their Cultural Significance.* Colombo: Ralph Peiris Memorial Lecture. Unpublished lecture.

Olcott, Henry Steel. 1881. *Buddhist Catechism.* London: Trubner and Co.

________. 2018a. *Old Diary Leaves,* volumes, 1,2,3, Create Space.

________. 2018b. *Old Diary Leaves,* volumes, 4,5,6, Create Space.

Prothero Stephen. 1995. "Henry Steel Olcott and Protestant Buddhism." *Journal of the American Academy of Religion.* 63 (2) 281–302.

________. 1996a. The *White Buddhist: The Asian Odyssey of Henry Steel Olcott.* Bloomington: Indiana University.

________ 1996b. "The White Buddhist: Henry Steel Alcott and the Sinhalese Buddhist Revival." *Tricycle: Awake in the World.* Fall. aryasangha.org.

________ 1997. *The White Buddhist: The Asian Odyssey of Henry Steel Olcott.* New Delhi: Sri Satguru.

Santucci, James A. 1985. *Theosophy and the Theosophical Society.* London: Theosophical History Centre.

Sumathipala, K. H. M. 1968. *History of Education in Ceylon.* Dehiwela: Tisara Prakasakayo.

Tillett, Gregory. 1982. *A Biography of Charles Webster Leadbeater.* New York: Routledge.

Wright, Arnold. 1907. *Twentieth Century Impressions of Ceylon,* London: Laurier.

CHAPTER 6

Reaching Out to Karmic Monastic Communities: Lessons from the Life of Karl Reichelt

Rory Mackenzie

Karl Reichelt spent his adult life as a missionary in China. His critics said that his highly contextualized approach compromised the Christian message. His admirers suggest that his capacity to make and sustain cross-cultural friendships coupled with his ability to create a non-threatening environment in which to explore the Christian faith were significantly used by the Lord. Above all, Reichelt was a risk taker. Now, several decades after his death, we examine Reichelt's life and work to see what we may learn about reaching out to the Buddhist world.

Karl Ludvig Reichelt was born in 1877 on a farm near Arendal, on the south coast of Norway. His father, a sea captain, died when Reichelt was very young. He was brought up by his mother who opened her home for house meetings and visiting preachers. At age eighteen Reichelt studied at a teachers' training college in Notodden, where, according to Notto Thelle,

> [H]e encountered a more open, broadminded Christianity, which combined sound faith with a deep appreciation of humanity, nature, national traditions, and the culture of the people. Such attitudes certainly helped him later when he had to meet other cultures and learn to appreciate the other national and religious traditions of another people (1981:66).

Two years later he entered the Missionary Training College of the Norwegian Missionary Society (NMS) in Stavanger. He was ordained in Oslo in 1903, went on to complete a semester of medical studies in the capital and arrived in China in November 1903. After completing language study Reichelt worked in Hunan until 1911 when he returned to Norway after his eight-year term of service.

Call to Specialize in Reaching Out to Buddhists

In 1905, Reichelt made his first significant contact with Chinese Buddhists when he visited Weishan monastery, home to 400 Buddhist monks. Reichelt wrote home, "As never before I have been able to look into a unique world, a world full of deep religious mystique, but also full of deep spiritual poverty" (Sorik 1997:73). Reichelt and his companions spent one week in Weishan. They were treated with the friendliest hospitality he had ever experienced. This one-week visit proved to be a life-changing event for the Norwegian missionary. He wrote:

> Sitting with the monks, desperately eager to tell them of the gospel, he found that his words were not heard. They listened politely, but there was no echo. It was as if they lived in a different world; he could not speak to the framework of their thought. He realised that he was simply unprepared and from that time on he began to study Buddhism seriously (Ibid 1997:73).

Reichelt records another struggle he experienced on this visit. He was deeply burdened by the question, "Is it permissible for us to believe that God's Spirit can be at work within these bleak walls, where superstition and idolatry share space with the most exalted longings after truth, purity and freedom?" (Sorik 1997:73). Towards the end of his week in the monastery, Reichelt believed that God spoke to him.

> It was as if I heard the Lord's voice. It came to me in the form which St Paul expressed it in the Acts of the Apostles, 'God is not far from any one of us for in Him we live and move and have our being,' and 'God has not left himself without witness.' Long before missionaries came to China, God was in China. The glimpses of truth and points of contact you find he has placed there (Sorik 1997:74).

Reichelt concluded that what was necessary was serious study and noted "I need not say that it was a changed missionary who walked down from the Weishan heights. It was a missionary whose heart was full of holy power and joy" (Sorik 1997:74).

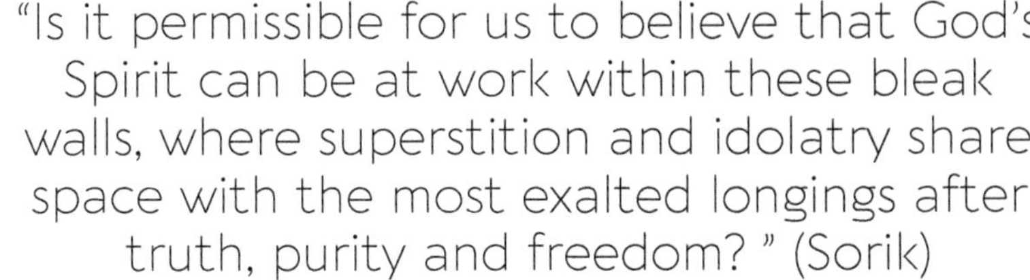

Learning on Location

Having decided to devote his life to work among Buddhists, Reichelt began to study and observe Chinese Buddhism. He developed friendships with Buddhist monks and learned lay people alike. Reichelt wrote that the greatest obstacle in building relationships was that Buddhist monks found Christ followers (both missionary and national) lacking in a sympathetic and gentle attitude towards others.

He returned to Norway in 1911 where he gave lectures on Chinese religion. These lectures were published in 1913 and later translated as *Religion in Chinese Garment.* On his return to China in 1913 Reichelt was appointed New Testament lecturer to the Chinese Union Lutheran Theological Seminary in Shekow. He taught there from 1913 to 1920 and used his vacations to visit temples and monasteries, making valuable contacts and collecting texts which he studied in order to gain deeper insight into Buddhism.

Reichelt's Ministry

In 1919, at the large Pilu monastery in Nanjing, Reichelt met several young monks who were interested in what he had to say. Kuantu, a twenty-two-year-old monk, who had a "deep religious spirit" responded to the idea of the Great Savior from the West (Paradise). Eventually, Kuantu got leave from the monastery and spent several months with Reichelt discussing the Bible and praying. He was baptized on Christmas day 1919 and was soon followed by a small group of others, including his teacher Penchong, and the abbot of the temple. On January 4, 1920, under Reichelt's leadership these new converts formed a "Christian Brotherhood among China's Buddhists," based on the understanding that "Our Buddhist *Mahayana* scriptures point forward to Christianity as their true fulfilment."

Clearly Kuantu's baptism and those who came to faith shortly afterwards must have seemed like the first fruits of things to come for Reichelt. True, others did follow but not as many as were hoped for. Kuantu, the first convert, while young and gifted did not fulfill Reichelt's expectations. Sharpe mentioned that Kuantu began to suffer from depression and wondered if the culture shock of living in close proximity with Westerners was not a trigger for his mental illness (1984:65).

Reichelt returned for home assignment to Norway in 1920, full of optimism. He lectured in Scandinavian universities on Chinese Buddhism. His best-known book, translated into English as *Truth and Tradition in Chinese Buddhism,* was based on his research and lecturing. In November 1922 Reichelt returned to China and with the support of the NMS, Reichelt started a Christian community called Ching Fong Shan, a half-way house organized along the lines of a Buddhist monastery. It functioned as a "Brother Home" or "Christian Monastery" for religious seekers, especially Buddhist monks.

> The monks usually stayed for a couple of days, but could extend their stay if they wanted to continue the study of Christianity. Every year an average of 1000 monks visited the Brother Home in Nanking. Here they could encounter Christianity in an atmosphere adapted to their own traditions, and talk about religious problems with Christians who were familiar with their religion and, moreover, regarded them as spiritual brothers, and 'Friends in the Way' (Thelle 1981:67).

Wandering monks and pilgrims were received and, if they were found to be "seeking," they were invited to stay for some weeks. Indeed, if they were also young and well-educated, they would be invited to attend the school attached to the Brother Home. During the first year of the school program there was a strong focus on religion. This study brought the students to a decision either to become Christian and generally to stay on, or to leave the school. Reichelt comments "We on our side plead with them not to make a decision before they are perfectly clear about the consequences" (1937:164). Following this there was a theological course which ran for three years. Reichelt went on to expand:

> In this way the baptized, gifted and promising men will get a training which in due time qualifies them for teaching, preaching, and pastoral work. In this course the ordinary theological curriculum is followed, special stress being laid upon the history of religion, the comparative study of religion and the psychology of religion (1937:164).

In addition to this formal training, many retreats were hosted at Tao Fong Shan. People from various religious backgrounds were invited to come and "sit down for earnest, religious talks and discussions" (Ibid).

Despite encouraging results from the outreach which took place at the Brother Home, the NMS had become uncomfortable with Reichelt's highly contextualized approach and what were said to be liberal ideas and syncretistic practice. "Reichelt was left to choose between complete co-operation with the NMS or complete severance. Reluctantly Reichelt chose to work independently" (Eilert 1974:14). In January1926, Reichelt formally parted company with NMS and started the Nordic Christian Buddhist Mission sometimes referred to as the Christian Mission to Buddhists. This organization adopted the Nestorian symbol of a cross rising out of an open lotus flower to signify the planting of the gospel in the heart of Buddhism. Eric Sharpe comments:

> To Reichelt—and this he had to explain time and time again in the next few years—the mission's symbol showed, first, that it was Christian, secondly, that it was directed towards Buddhists, and thirdly, that the 'new birth' comes only through the Cross (1984:81).

Reichelt's critics saw the juxtaposition of these two religious symbols as syncretism despite Reichelt's insistence that what was being signified was a missional approach. There were thirty-one registered "wearers of the cross" between 1920 and 1931. Indeed, the cross continues to be worn round the neck by present day members of the mission (now known as Areopagus).

Between Christmas 1924 and Whitsunday 1925, two Buddhist monks, eleven novices, and a Taoist monk were baptized (Sharpe 1984:84). This, however, was a turbulent time of escalating anti-foreign sentiment among the Chinese. In 1927, revolutionaries, in an anti-foreign rage, destroyed Ching Fong Shan; Reichelt and his Norwegian assistant Thelle narrowly escaped with their lives. Reichelt decided not to open a new center in China. After looking around a number of countries he thought it best to locate in Hong Kong. In 1930, a wooded hilltop was purchased from the government and Reichelt named it Tao Fong Shan, "The Hill of the Christ Wind." A Danish architect drew up plans based on Chinese monasteries and a beautiful complex was constructed that demonstrated a creative attempt to indigenize Christian expression.

Tao Fong Shan was where Reichelt researched Chinese Buddhism and developed his missionary thinking. He travelled extensively, from the borders of Tibet to other Asian countries. The primary focus of Reichelt's ministry, however, was sharing the Christian message with religious visitors. He and his assistants invited monks from China for visits. Some became Christian, a number becoming workers in his mission. Reichelt comments:

> One of the most interesting gatherings in our institute on Tao Fong Shan is the weekly evening meetings, when sometimes pilgrims and students from the different regions of East Asia tell how they were guided to come to this mountain. Their thrilling tales prove that our journeys, the distribution of literature, the wide correspondence maintained and, last but not least, the accounts given by the monks who have been here are all means in the hands of God for upbuilding the coming Kingdom (1937:163).

In his address to the 1938 Third International Missionary Council in Tambaram, Reichelt spoke of his experiences from the many years of his contextualized ministry. He had had close contact with thousands of ordained and lay Buddhists, Taoists, and Confucians. Many had stayed at Tao Fong Shan for months or even years. He remarked that many of these men were contacted on journeys to Buddhist centers and sacred mountains. Some of them, he said:

> [B]ecome baptized Christians, a considerably greater number have not joined the Christian Church but continue to feed upon the words of the New Testament and are bound to Christ our Lord in deep admiration, affection and love. These people have been acting as a vanguard for us in our work (Reichelt 1938:99).

Reichelt explained how Jesus Christ became the center of their lives. They were all searchers of truth and the experiences in their former religion prepared them for coming to faith. These converts heard Christ's voice because they were on the side of truth (John 18:37). According to Reichelt, in "many cases it was just the Gospel of St John which gave them the solution" as it pointed to the new birth which brought entry into the kingdom of God. After years of meditation in lonely cells, strenuous pilgrimages to holy mountains, and visits to great religious teachers, these pilgrims broke through and entered into the thrilling experience they longed for (1938:99–100). Reichelt concluded:

> What I have experienced through these many years in the sacred hours of conversation with these people has given me the profound conviction that Christ has been working everywhere through all the ages. We should, therefore, gratefully and joyfully use the material which He Himself has prepared for the coming of His Kingdom. That the result is genuinely right is also clear. For Christ Himself has given us the criterion 'Ye shall know them by their fruits' (Matt 7:16): a circle of people who through faith in the Lord have been set free from sin, fear and bondage and are now enthusiastically giving up their lives in service for Him (1938:100).

Between 1930 and 1952, 130 adults were baptized at Tao Fong Shan. There were seven baptisms at Shanghai between 1940 and 1947, and there was one baptism at the Yuen Chau branch recorded in 1946 (Sharpe 1984:204). Yet Reichelt's ministry was not restricted to "words," it also included deeds of compassion. Strandenoes points out Reichelt's practice of giving food and money to those in need (2009:136). He also sought employment for those out of work. His six months of medical and nursing studies provided him with skills to care for the sick, including suicidal opium addicts.

The Japanese invasion of China in 1937 put an end to monks visiting Tao Fong Shan. After Pearl Harbor the Japanese captured Hong Kong and a period of hardship followed. Reichelt was allowed to continue at the monastery with his family and carry on his ministry. At the end of the war Reichelt wanted to continue his work but he was 69 and not in the best of health. He returned to Norway, leaving his assistants to continue the ministry of the monastery. Political instability in China meant that travel was considerably restricted and a return to the old style of ministry became impossible. In 1939, Reichelt was awarded the St Olav medal by the Norwegian King (Hakon VII) for his meritorious work. Some two years later he was honored for his research on religious life in East Asia with an honorary doctorate at Uppsala University (Strandenoes 2009:129). In 1951, Reichelt returned to Tao Fong Shan on a short-term assignment and there, in March 1952, died of a brain tumor. Reichelt was buried in the Resurrection Cemetery at Tao Fong Shan.

Cost Associated with Reichelt's Ministry

In 1905, Reichelt married Anna Gerhardsen. The travelling involved in her husband's work and the political instability in East Asia meant they spent long periods apart. "It was not until after 1934 that she could be permanently with her husband and maintain a normal family life" (Thelle 1981:66). Reichelt returned by himself to Hong Kong for what was meant to be a brief period but died there in 1952. Separation must have involved considerable hardship for both of them.

Reichelt was severely criticized by many of his missionary colleagues. He was perceived by conservatives as being liberal. He drew fire not only from Westerners but also from Chinese Christians who did not wish to be reminded of their previous religion. A common complaint aimed at Reichelt's approach was "You go to the 'Brother House' to learn about Christianity but all you get is Buddhism!" Reichelt's missiological approach, although currently admired by some practitioners, did not go down well at the Tambaram conference.

"Reichelt's missiological approach, although currently admired by some practitioners, did not go down well at the Tambaram conference."

Henrick Kraemer's (1888–1965) book published in time for the conference, *The Christian Message in a Non-Christian World* criticized fulfillment theology, popular at the time. This theology described other faith systems as an effort to evade or placate God's wrath. Kraemer mentioned Reichelt by name twice in his book. He praised the Norwegian missionary for interpreting Christianity to Buddhist monks but condemned any notion of Christianity being a more refined expression of Mahayana Buddhism. Kraemer's critique was generally accepted and Reichelt's sympathetic approach to East Asian religion was viewed unfavorably by many missionaries. Reichelt felt frustrated that his careful defense of his mission to Buddhists was being damaged by this influential Dutch missiologist.

Providentially, the two met on the train to the Tambaram conference, and subsequently corresponded. Reichelt requested Kraemer to affirm in writing that his approach was "trying to present the positive Christian gospel in its full uniqueness to the Buddhist, not as a natural fruit of developed Buddhism, but as the unique and unspeakable gift from God" (Sharpe 1984:162). Reichelt felt that such a testimony would avert attacks Norwegian conservatives might launch on his mission as a result of Kraemer's earlier comments. Kraemer's response was friendly and he agreed. The "recommendation" made little difference, however, as by the time Reichelt received the letter Germans had invaded Norway.

It was not only Christians who criticized Reichelt. His work drew fire from Buddhists who accused him of trying to damage the Buddhist community. He accepted, however, that "the most violent opposition, the most biting outbursts of controversy and condemnation must be experienced by those who present the Christian message in Buddhist ranks" (quoted in Eilert 1974:144). Thelle comments that, "A paradox inherent in such a dialogical mission is that the moment it really succeeds, it will lead to failure—the conversion of a great number of Buddhist monks would inevitably create barriers of mistrust and animosity" (2005:175).

Reichelt's Missiology

The central tenet of Reichelt's approach to faith sharing is what he referred to as the "Johannine approach." This focused on the Prologue with its proclamation of the *Logos.* His position was that the second person of the Trinity is not to be restricted to the historical Jesus. There was never a time when the son was not. Reichelt followed the approach of Justin Martyr, Clement of Alexandria, and Origen. The belief was that the Eternal *Logos,* the Spirit of Christ has revealed some truths to men and women from other faiths as they sought it. These divine truths, or *Logos Spermaticos,* are found in other religions and need to be identified and used to help those in these traditions come to an understanding of Christ. Reichelt argued that the activities of the Son cannot be limited to the time since his incarnation. From eternity he has functioned as the *Logos.* He was in the beginning, both abiding with the Father and, at the same time, linked up with humankind and the whole cosmos.

> All that is true, good and noble in all nations and races, in all cultures and religions, has accordingly its origin in Him. What is the reason for this? The reason is that 'the light shineth in darkness' (verse 5). This is a permanent function on the part of the Logos through all ages, in all cultures and in all religions (Reichelt 1938:93).

According to Reichelt, as soon as the pre-existent Christ was recognized, Buddhists would acclaim their natural state as children of God. He "had witnessed that such a discovery caused 'an immense joy of recognition' among the converts" (Eilert 1974 135). There is a strong sense of optimism in Reichelt's missiology. He looked forward to a new era when the kingdom of God would come in fullness. Tao Fong Shan was for Reichelt a place where the kingdom of God could break through in the minds of those who visited (Ibid). There are traces of the bodhisattva concept of Mahayana Buddhism informing Reichelt's practice. But did he see himself and his colleagues as Christian bodhisattvas? He writes "The aim of mission, of world–salvation is therefore: to help all that belongs to Him to find its way back to Him again" (Eilert 1974:163). This is clearly in keeping with the bodhisattva's goal of striving for the liberation of all sentient beings.

"There are traces of the bodhisattva concept of Mahayana Buddhism informing Reichelt's practice."

Reichelt drew heavily on Buddhist concepts and terms. Reichelt believed that Pure Land Buddhism's focus on receiving salvation as a free gift as opposed to making merit through observing rituals was partly due to the influence of the Nestorian Christian mission in China and he was simply building on the good work God had done through that enterprise. Reichelt refers to this influence as

> '[T]he sacred golden inheritance' which had left traces on Buddhist views of God, the notion of the Trinity, the belief in a Western Paradise, and much more besides. Thus in pointing to Jesus Christ as the 'fulfiller' of Mahayana Buddhism's best insights, Reichelt's language clearly owes much to the fulfilment school of Christian missionary thought, at that time chiefly operating in India (Sharpe 1984:71).

Reichelt felt it essential to construct a liturgical space where the Buddhist visitor would feel comfortable. Thelle mentions "the most characteristic and perhaps also the most important testimony to Reichelt's devotional piety was his extreme preoccupation with establishing sanctuaries for worship wherever he arrived" (2005:133). Construction of these buildings received priority. Reichelt and his colleagues had the practice of taking their visitors "first to the sanctuary to worship, to share some sacred moments, to pray or just be quiet, before they were introduced to the rest of the facilities. It might have been inspired by Buddhist practices. But it certainly revealed the overarching importance of the sanctuary in Reichelt's religious life" (Thelle 2005:136).

In the West we are currently witnessing the forming of new monastic communities where people go and live in community in order to help those within that geographical area; usually the focus is on those at the margins of society.

There is a commitment to extending hospitality and living according to a rule of life which usually involves contemplative practice. Would it be possible to develop a ministry to Buddhists, either in the west or in Asia using the model of these new monastic communities?

Five Lessons from Reichelt's Ministry

First, Reichelt appears to have prioritized the keeping of Christ at the center of his life and ministry. He ends an article written entitled *Buddhism in China Today* with the following words:

> We have one great aim, namely, to give the full Christian message, the full positive gospel as it is revealed in the New Testament, using all the points of contact which psychologically may help the seekers after truth in East Asia to recognise Jesus Christ as the only way to the Father. We can afford to be broadminded because our work is through and through Christocentric (1937:166).

Reichelt found aspects of the cosmic dimension of Christ both attractive and biblical and allowed his Christological perspective to be influenced by some non-Christian views. That said, he refuted the view that the historical Jesus was separate from Christ. Part of reflecting on missionary practice for the evangelical is to ensure that we are faithful to both the biblical text and the missionary task. That is, between "the faith that was once for all entrusted to the saints" (Jude 3) and being "all things to all people so that by all possible means I might save some" (1 Cor 9:22) (Tyra 2013:12). Through dependence on the Spirit, reflection on scripture along with a critical reading of the writings of those from our audience, our capacity to communicate Christ in relevant ways can only be enhanced.

Second, Reichelt was genuinely interested in Buddhism but lived in missionary encounter with Buddhists. Reichelt's friendship with Buddhist communities was a new approach in the 1920s and 30s. He did not take a condemnatory approach toward Buddhists but engaged with them and learned as much as he could. Despite his high view of aspects of Buddhist teaching and affection for Buddhists he was able to live in missionary encounter meaning he did not always approve of everything. For example, he wrote of undercover black magic activities seen in Tibetan style monasteries he visited in Mongolia (Sharpe 1984:149). In 1937 he visited Siam (now Thailand) and found the Theravada tradition there "narrow and unimpressive" (Sharpe 1984:149). Clearly, the further Reichelt moved away from Pure Land Buddhism the less optimistic he was about Buddhist belief and practice.

A talk at Tambaram Reichelt indicates that despite his contextualized approach he had not parted company from the evangelical position:

> I also hold the view that in our witness we must never lose sight of the great truths in regard to personal salvation so strongly set forth by St Paul, such as sin and

> grace, redemption through Christ, the living faith which sets us free and makes us partakers of the Heavenly Kingdom, with its wonderful vision of life in time and eternity (1938:91).

More recently, Norwegian scholar Notto Thelle, son of the original assistant, describes Reichelt as a "pilgrim missionary":

> As a missionary he was convinced that he had a special calling to preach, with a particular vision of a mission to Buddhists. Whatever he did as a student of religion, a dialogue partner, and a preacher—he wanted to share his faith with others. He seemed to use every opportunity to deliver his message, expecting some of the monks to be prepared to grasp the gospel (2005:115).

Third, Reichelt took a contextual approach despite the risks of being misunderstood by fellow believers. Reichelt's monastery was a place where Buddhist monks were made welcome; he and his assistants wore a Buddhist type robe and the food was vegetarian. He developed forms of worship that would not be unfamiliar to Buddhist monks. There was the burning of incense, bells were rung and selected Buddhist scriptures were studied and related to the Bible, which was understood to be the supreme standard.

The Norwegian missionary wrote hymns and prayers that were couched in Buddhist terms. One example of Reichelt's boldness is found in a hymn to Christ included in a book of liturgy used at the Brother Home. In this hymn, Christ is worshipped as "The Great Tao without beginning and end (the eternal Word of God)," and the original face of all sentient beings (a Zen idea but alluding, at least in Reichelt's mind, to the concept of the imago Dei). Reichelt would often translate God for the Buddha and the "All Father" for Amida. Japanese Buddhist scholar and Zen practitioner D. T. Suzuki (1870–1966) commenting on Reichelt's center and the ethos of the worship there described it as a "refined, religious atmosphere indigenous to the religious soul of China" (1927:197).

Buddhist practice usually begins with the reciting of the Triple Gem:

> I take refuge in the Buddha.
>
> I take refuge in the *Dhamma.*
>
> I take refuge in the *Sangha.*

Reichelt believed that a Christian equivalent to the Triple Gem was necessary to help visiting monks understand that worship was taking place and proposed the following (a prototype of which he found in a Nestorian liturgy).

> I take refuge in the Father of all goodness and mercy.
>
> I take refuge in the mysterious, perfect Law (*Tao/Logos*).
>
> I take refuge in the shining pure Holy Spirit (Sorik 1997:76, Sharpe 1984:81).

Reichelt had a strong emphasis on the confession of sin and there were confessions each evening and in the Sunday morning service. Indeed, for Reichelt, "Saturday afternoons were often set aside for the preparation for Sunday, with strong emphasis on serious reflection on one's sins, contrition, and commitment to a new life" (Thelle 2005:153). Thelle cites this Tao Fong Shan hymn used prior to confession:

> Christ, give me a shining lamp.
> And remove the karmic hindrances, that [I may] obtain eternal life/birth.
> The sentient beings are innumerable, [my] vow is inexhaustible:
> I will dedicate myself to return the Lord's favour to innumerable lands (Ibid).

Here the confessor prays that the shining lamp of the Christian scriptures will remove all fetters which hold the believer back from spiritual development. Karmic hindrances refer to sin or unskillful action. The last two lines resonate with the bodhisattva vow. Thelle comments:

> Reichelt was impressed by the Buddhist vow to save all sentient beings, and adopted the expression as part of his own missionary urge: the flavour of forgiveness should be proclaimed to the whole world, or literally, to the innumerable lands (2006:154).

As already mentioned, Reichelt came under attack for his efforts at contextualization. He was well aware of the dangers of an over contextualized approach yet was prepared to take risks with "borrowing" from the other tradition. This is clear from his comment:

> Syncretism and compromises in mission work are a real danger which missionaries must continuously guard against. On the other hand it is equally certain that there is a great danger lest they neglect to make use of the sacred material which Christ through His Spirit has made available in the life of the peoples and in their historical heritage (Reichelt 1953:59).

He sometimes became more cautious as a result of the comments of his critics. That said, Reichelt was not overly concerned about the lines of demarcation between Christianity and other faiths. His first focus was making Christ known to Buddhists in terms they could best understand.

Fourth, Reichelt took the religious tradition of his audience very seriously and studied to understand it. Despite study and intellectual enquiry Reichelt always appeared to be missional. Moreover, we can see how Reichelt's interest opened up unusual opportunities for both himself and his colleagues.

"His first focus was making Christ known to Buddhists in terms they could best understand."

Fifth, Reichelt had what can only be described as a special gift for friendship with religious people from East Asia. He was often invited to speak at religious associations in temples and monasteries. In many cases some of the monks in a temple had already visited the "Brother Home" or rumors about the Christian "Master" had reached the temple in advance. Indeed, Gluer states, "The secret of Reichelt's success in his encounter with Buddhists was not in his theological principles but in his warm personality" (1968:56). Yet we cannot divorce Reichelt's theology from his personality. His openness to those of different faiths and his vision to offer generous hospitality on a "no strings attached" basis facilitated the creative experiment that we refer to as the Brother Home.

Conclusion

Missionaries from more theologically conservative traditions may experience a "calling" to reach out to those from another religious tradition and may wish to seriously study that religion. They may, however, feel that such serious study is not in keeping with a conservative position. To such, Reichelt offers "permission"! With Christ at the center of life and ministry one can be comfortable with a measure of openness at the circumference. We can in time, with God's help discover what is appropriate contextualization. Clearly, our approach will vary from situation to situation and the extent to which we feel able to contextualize may well vary as our understanding of the missional task changes.

Those who come from a background influenced by post-modern values or a less theologically conservative position may need to be encouraged to be more evangelistic as they engage with others. In terms of engaging with people of other faiths, Terry Muck suggests an approach of both "cooperation and competition" (2000:43–44). We cooperate because we have issues of common concern and can help each other achieve a particular outcome in holistic mission. Mission strategies compete because of distinct belief systems considered to be crucial for the "here and now" and "after death." Our friendships are not predicated on having the same religious beliefs but on relationships that have been built up over time.

In Reichelt's life and ministry we are reminded that if we maintain our relationship with Christ his love will be in our hearts. If Christ's love is in our hearts then the people we are called to will be in our hearts. If they are in our hearts then we will be in their hearts.

References

Eilert, Hakan. 1974. *Boundlessness: Studies in Karl Ludvig Reichelt's Missionary. Thinking with Special Regard to the Buddhist Christian Encounter.* Arhus: Forlaget Arcs.

Gluer, W. 1968. "The Encounter between Christianity and Chinese Buddhism during the Nineteenth Century and the First Half of the Twentieth Century." *Ching Feng.* 11 (3) 39–57.

Kraemer, Henrick. 1938. *The Christian Message in a Non-Christian World.* NY: Harper & Brothers.

Muck, Terry, 2000. "Missiological Issues in the Encounter with Emerging Buddhism." *Missiology.* 23 (Jan) 35–46.

Pierson, Paul. 2000. "Nestorian Mission." *Evangelical Dictionary of World Missions.* A. Scott Moreau, ed. Grand Rapids: Baker.

Reichelt, Karl L. 1937. "Buddhism in China at the Present Time and the New Challenge to the Christian Church." *The International Review of Missions.* 26 (1) 155–66.

________. 1938. "The Johannine Approach." *The Authority of Faith.* Tambaram Series 1:90–101.

________. 1953. *Meditation and Piety in the Far East.* (Sverre Holt, trans.). Cambridge: James Clarke and Co.

Sharpe, E. 1984. *Karl Ludvig Reichelt: Missionary, Scholar and Pilgrim.* Hong Kong: Tao Fong Shan Ecumenical Centre.

Sorik, A. 1997. "The Cross and the Lotus-The Story of the Christian Mission to Buddhists and KL Reichelt." *Areopagus.* 9 (4) 72–77.

Sunquist, S. W. (ed.). 2001. *A Dictionary of Asian Christianity.* Cambridge: Eerdmans.

Suzuki, D. T. 1927. *The Eastern Buddhist.* 4 (2) 195–97.

Strandenoes, T. 2009. "Contextualising the Commitments and Concerns of Dr. Karl Ludvig Reichelt in the 21st Century." *Swedish Missiological Themes.* 9 (2) 127–40.

Stanley, B. 2012. Http://www.ed.ac.uk/schools-departments/divinity/staff-profiles/stanley (Accessed 13.03.12).

Thelle, Notto R. 1981. "The Legacy of Karl Ludvig Reichelt." *International Bulletin of Missionary Research.* 5 (1) 65–69.

________. 2005. "A Christian Monastery for Buddhist Monks Part II." *Ching Feng.* 6 (2) 131–77.

________. 2008. "The Gift of Being Number Two: A 'Buzz Aldrin' Perspective on Pioneer Missions." *International Bulletin of Missionary Research.* 32 (1) 81–84.

Tyra, G. 2013. *A Missional Orthodoxy: Theology and Ministry in a Post-Christian Context.* Downers Grove, IL: IVP Academic.

CHAPTER 7

Traversing Buddhist Mountains and Translating Sutras: Timothy Richard's Quest for Souls in China

Lawrence Ko

Timothy Richard was a Welsh Baptist missionary who spent forty-five years in Qing China from 1870 to 1915. He helped establish churches and mission stations in the northern provinces in Shandong and Shanxi and trained local Christians and workers for the Chinese church. His quest for souls saw him engage with social concerns including famine relief and social reforms in China. His literary talents and passion for learning enabled him to reach the cultural elites and officials and engage in the modernization of China. Less known about Richard was the fact that he also visited with abbots and religious scholars in order to study and translate Buddhist sutras, traversing several Buddhist mountains, and even lived in residence in a Buddhist temple. His famous translations include *The Awakening of Faith in the Mahayana School of Religion, The Essence of the Lotus Scripture* and the Chinese classic *Journey to the West,* which he undertook to find effective means of evangelizing the Chinese. This chapter seeks to highlight his mission, motivation, methodology, and message in his missionary endeavors, as well as to measure the impact of his mission, especially his contribution in highlighting the Mahayana as the New Testament of Buddhism.

The Man and His Mission

Timothy Richard was born in Wales, the youngest son of a devout Baptist family of farmers and tradesmen on October 10, 1845. Richard became a schoolmaster at eighteen after his education. As the Second Evangelical Awakening was sweeping through Europe at that time, Richard was touched during the revival in Wales. During his baptism at the age of fourteen, he was inspired to become a missionary. In 1865 he entered Haverford Theological College to prepare for a missionary career. In 1869 he was accepted by the Baptist Missionary Society (BMS) and sailed for China, arriving in Shanghai on February 12, 1870. He moved to Shandong two weeks later to be based in Yantai (Qifu) in Shandong province where BMS had an established Chinese church of thirty-five members started by R. F. Laughton. Richard assumed responsibility of the Yantai church after Laughton died in June 1870 and after Dr. William Brown, the other BMS missionary, left in 1874. Richard would spend the first twenty years in Shandong and Shanxi in evangelistic and church work and then the next twenty-five years in literature ministry based in Shanghai.

His Mindset and Motivation

Richard's respect for China as an advanced ancient civilization, was evidenced in his application to the BMS when he stated that "the Chinese were the most civilized of non-Christian nations" and once converted, they would "help to carry the gospel to less advanced nations" (Richard 1916:9). He was eager to explore and enjoy the local culture and journeyed extensively in the northeastern provinces in his first two years. He went beyond the superficial adoption of Chinese dress, to devote himself to study Chinese language, customs, and Chinese religious beliefs in great depth.

Richard took great troubles to seek out and visit with leaders of the local temples and mosques as well as the gentry-officials of the community he was in. He was convinced by a sermon Edward Irving delivered to the London Missionary Society in 1824, which encouraged missionaries to "seek out the worthy" as described in Matt 10:11. Hence as Brian Stanley noted, Richard saw "the worthy" as the educated and powerful in Chinese societies from the religious leaders to the highly educated scholar-officials (Stanley 1992:180). The government officials if won over, could become less antagonistic towards the West and more sympathetic to Christianity and Christian missions.

His Methodology and Message

Richard's engagement in China was multifaceted and may be broadly categorized into the three categories: 1.) relief, 2.) reform, and 3.) religion. These complemented and shaped each area of his missionary endeavors. As Richard's accomplishments in the arena of relief and reform have been briefly highlighted above and are well documented elsewhere, we will focus here more on Richard's contribution to religion, especially in the translation of the Buddhists texts into English and spotlighting the importance of Mahayana Buddhism in the context of China if not East Asia.

The Grassroots strategy: Working through the local Chinese

Richard's evangelistic approach saw him adopt a two-pronged strategy, firstly reaching the grassroots and secondly in reaching the elites. In the former, Richard saw that it was more effective to recruit, train, and deploy local Chinese as Christian workers in the hinterland as this will reduce opposition and prevent conflicts due to growing *jiaoan* (anti-Christian riots). Training and unleashing the local converts to ministry work would also create a greater sense of ownership.

Elite strategy: Seeking the worthy

In the second strategy of reaching the elites, Richard would "seek the worthy" or what is commonly known as "the person of peace" in the local community. This constant motivation led Richard to actively visit and cultivate relationships with religious leaders and government officials as his strategic approach in his mission. He cultivated the friendship of scholar-officials whom he met during his famine work including Li Hongzhang, Zeng Guofan, Zhang Zhidong, and Zo Zongtang who were provincial governors and ministerial levels Qing officials. He visited scholars at the exam halls to distribute his publications and gained a following as a result as these were Chinese literati. Through his leadership of the Christian Literature Society (CLS) from 1890, his numerous translated works and publications were disseminated widely to the Chinese literati.

"Richard saw that it was more effective to recruit, train, and deploy local Chinese as Christian workers in the hinterland as this will reduce opposition and prevent conflicts."

Richard also intentionally met with religious leaders, the "religious elite" in his outreach. Desiring to learn about the indigenous religious faiths and how they were structured and organized, Richard took the initiative to visit with abbots of Buddhist temples and Daoist shrines and sought out several Daoist hermits who dwelled in mountain caves, who were surprisingly willing to meet him. He was perceptive to follow the protocol of inviting these religious leaders as respected guests and would ensure gifts were presented as was the Chinese custom (何菊 2014:163–170).

Traversing Mountains to Meet Abbots and Hermits

At Taiyuan, he was privileged to visit the largest Buddhist temple, and was invited to live in residence with a hundred Buddhist monks, which he accepted. He studied with them for over a month. Up close, he marveled at their devotion to Buddha and wondered if the Christians could surpass them. In 1888, when Richard was invited to present a paper on Daoism at an Asian religious conference held in Beijing, he took the opportunity to visit Beijing's famous Yonghe Gong and was received by the abbot of the temple as well as the top Buddhist abbot of Beijing.

In his attempt to learn more about Chinese Buddhism, also known as Mahayana Buddhism, Richard also took time and effort to traverse some of the famous Buddhist mountains of China including Wutai Shan and Tiantai Shan which housed important Buddhist temples. On a trip to Shandong's Laoshan, he visited many Daoist shrines and at Taiqing Gong, he met and conferred with the Daoist priests and the abbot (何菊 2014:168).

In June 1880, Richard ascended Shanxi's Wutai Shan. There he was welcomed by the abbots of the Buddhist temples and met for the first time, the Tibetan Buddhist monks and leaders. He accepted the invitation to observe the religious worship and rituals, which he noted included the use of masks which resembled faces of ferocious beasts used in Egyptian worship. The Tibetan worship music and dance reminded him of Russian Orthodox tunes while the Mahayana Buddhist chants and music reminded him of Gregorian chants. He also noted the prevalence of busy commercial marketplace right at the confluence where devotees gathered (菊 2014:193).

In May 1895, he ascended Zhejiang's Tiantai Shan. On his way there, passing by Hangzhou, he also took time to visit three of the important temples including Mituo Temple, Lingying Temple, and Haichao Temple and stopped by a shop selling Buddhist literature. On Tiantai Shan, Richard visited all the temples and made careful notes of the location, layout of temples and religious rituals he was invited to participate as an observer. At the top of the mountain stood Gaoming Temple, and he was met by the friendly abbot who took time to introduce to him the different schools of Buddhism and every statue of Buddha in the temple. But it was at Qingguo Temple which got Richard excited as he saw that there was no statue being worshipped. He thought of the possibility of non-idolatrous Buddhism as a bridge for sharing the Christian faith.

On his descent from the temple, Richard met a hermit reciting the *Diamond Sutra* and invited him to a dialogue. It was then Richard discovered the prophecy within chapter six which mentioned the emergence of a saint five hundred years after Buddha, who will pave the way for faith. Richard thus suggested to the hermit that the Sutra was alluding to the arrival of Jesus Christ. His trip to Tiantai Shan was a fruitful one for Richard and filled him with the excitement of not only learning about Buddhism and Buddhist texts, but also the possibility of translating Buddhist texts as a bridge to sharing the gospel (何菊 2014:190–1). As Scott notes, Richard was convinced of the need "to communicate the gospel cross culturally and through interlingual nexus (which) would ultimately lead more Chinese people to Christianity." This encouraged him to meet, study with and "to listen to local religious elites to see how they might share what he considered to be universal religious truths" (Scott 2012:13).

"His unique anthropological approach led him to new discoveries of what the Chinese believed and practiced. He discovered similarities and points of contact which could be a bridge for the gospel."

Through his travels, Richard sought to demonstrate how the gospel message is fulfilled in the religious aspirations of Asia in their search for savior and salvation. Richard's study of Chinese religions, both from live interaction as well as academic research were important for blazing a new trail in the new field of comparative religion. His unique anthropological approach led him to new discoveries of what the Chinese believed and practiced. He discovered similarities and points of contact which could be a bridge for the gospel.

Translating Sutras to Bridge Mahayana Buddhism with the Gospel

Throughout his life, Richard actively acquired knowledge about the culture and religion of China to help him preach more effectively to the Chinese. His religious articles and translations of Christian literature into Chinese continued in parallel with the writings and translation of Western works which influenced the political reforms of 1898. He also had a clear aim to influence and change the religions of China by demonstrating that the gospel was compatible with and indeed fulfills their religious aspiration. To accomplish this aim, Richard undertook the translation of Buddhist sutras into English.

Richard's publications on Chinese Buddhism include the following: *Calendar of the Gods in China, Guide to Buddhahood, Being a Standard Manual of Chinese*

Buddhism, The Awakening of Faith, and his final publication which was also his most comprehensive monograph on Chinese Buddhism, *The New Testament of Higher Buddhism.* This was his contribution to a growing list of titles on Buddhism published by missionaries in China and Sinologists from 1857–1920 (李新德 2007:17–18).

His *Calendar of the Gods* was written for missionaries as a practical guide to the religious festivals of China and translated from a Chinese source *Yueling Cuibian* to which he added annotations and materials from other sources. He also included commentaries on the "three religions" of China with their affinities to Christianity (Scott 2012:14). In his *Guide to Buddhahood,* Richard translated the works of a seventeenth century Buddhist monk Ouyi Zhixu entitled *Xuanfo Pu* (A Manual for Selection of Buddhas) which explains the Buddhist cosmological realms and levels of existence and different types of acts, good and evil. This selection of text for Richard's translation was interesting as it was neither an ancient Buddhist scripture nor a serious treatise but a popular book consulted by devotees among the Chinese Buddhist community. In his introduction, Richard explained his decision to translate an active source of the lived religious culture of China as he wanted to highlight the importance of Mahayana Buddhism as the "Advanced Buddhism" which has superseded Hinayana Buddhism (as Theravada Buddhism was known then), likening Hinayana as the Old Testament and Mahayana Buddhism as The New Testament. This was a preparatory work to his final work *New Testament of Higher Buddhism.*

Richard's New Testament of Higher Buddhism

In his *Higher Buddhism,* Richard incorporated his earlier translation of *The Awakening of Faith, The Essence of the Lotus Sutra, The Great Physician's Twelve Desires* and his introductory commentary to each. In the book, it is clear Richard was intentionally using Christian terminology to translate the Buddhist texts as he wanted to demonstrate firstly how Mahayana teaching had superseded the Hinayana and secondly how Mahayana was compatible with Christian teachings. This was evident in his translation of *The Awakening of Faith.*

Richard first encountered *The Awakening of Faith* when he chanced upon the book in Nanjing during his search for Buddhist scriptures. He met Yang Wenhui who owned Jinling Scriptural Press in 1884 and heard how Yang, a Confucian scholar, had converted to Buddhism after the reading *The Awakening.* In1894, Richard invited Yang to Shanghai to work with him in translating the text (Tarocco 2008:335–336). But Richard did not publish the translated text of *The Awakening of Faith* till 1900 when he learned of D. T. Suzuki's atheistic translation.

Richard's own reading of the book had excited him as he saw this as not merely a Buddhist book of Mahayana Buddhism but,

> An Asiatic form of the same gospel of our Lord and saviour Jesus Christ, in Buddhistic nomenclature, differing from the old Buddhism just as the New Testament differs from the Old... It commands a world-wide interest, for in it we find an adaptation of Christianity to ancient thought in Asia, and the deepest bond of union between the different races of the east and the west, namely the bond of a common religion (Tarocco 2008:323–43).

Scott notes that Richard was reading Ernest Eitel's B*uddhism* and his *Handbook of Chinese Buddhism,* as well as Max Muller's *Sacred Books of the East* among others in the field of comparative religion which was just reaching maturity then. With Richard's exposure to Chinese religions, a keen interest in comparative religions, and an intent to find an inroad for the gospel, he developed a genealogical theory of religion which aids the connection from Buddhism to Christianity through comparative religious study and the latest scholarship of the day, particularly in comparative philology. Consequently he "produced a theory of an ancient nexus of revelation to which all global expressions of religions could be traced" (Scott 2008:10). He drew on the scholarship of Max Muller's comparative philology tracing Indian religions to Persian influence and shared linguistic heritage. Following George Grierson's study of Nestorian influences on modern Hinduism, Richard postulated how Mahayana Buddhism must have been influenced by the interaction of the East and West in Babylonia during the time of the ancient trade routes. He argued how Mahayana teachings then developed by Ashvagosha must have incorporated the gospel of Christ and the theology of Apostle Paul to diverge from Hinayana Buddhism.

In *The Awakening of Faith,* Richard wanted to demonstrate the common message found in different texts by replacing Buddhist terms with Christian terminology especially with theistic terms. He also highlighted the distinctive turn in Mahayana Buddhism in adopting a concept of paradise, a Savior figure, the offer of grace for enlightenment which were not taught in Hinayana as evidence of Christian gospel influence. As Pfister notes,

> Richard argued that the essential doctrines and principles of this form of Buddhism with its Babylonian roots were consonant with Christian teachings and worth further exploration. Hoping his studies might lead to a quicker evangelization of Buddhists, Richard persisted in spite of public criticism by other missionaries, producing not only translations but also late in his life, an evangelistic appeal to Buddhists (2003:197–8).

The Measure of His Mission

In evaluating the impact of Richard's missionary efforts in China, we can briefly discuss the three areas of relief, reform, and religion to which he devoted his life.

Richard's participation in the famine relief first in the late 1870s in Shanxi and then again in 1889 in Shandong gained him great exposure to the needs and challenges of the two northern provinces. He also won a lot of converts and inquirers who were moved by his compassion and generosity. They responded to his gift of aid as well as tracts, catechism and hymn books (Wang 2015:179). The relief efforts also resulted in greater missionary collaboration as missionaries from different societies worked together in famine assistance (Ko 1990:30–2).

Richard started his involvement in reforms through writing for a leading newspaper *Shibao* at the invitation of Li Hongzhang, where he advocated his ideas for China's social, political, and educational reforms. His appointment as secretary of CLS, which he served for the next twenty-five years, provided him with the needed platform for him to broadcast his progressive ideas through hundreds of publications. His influence on the gentry and officials of the Qing government was evident from the impact on the Hundred Days Reform in 1898 and his service in the reparation negotiation after the Boxer massacre which resulted in his appointment as the chancellor of Shanxi university in 1902 as well as the conferment of an officialdom in the Qing court.

His contribution made him a household name in China in the late Qing era and his name was synonymous with the rise of modern China (Bohr 2000:75–8). At the end of his life, Richard would be conferred an officialdom ennobling his ancestors up to three generations and given the Order of the Double Dragon. Wong notes that since the 1950s, monuments and relics honoring missionary presence in late imperial China have been intentionally removed especially during the Cultural Revolution. The only exception seems to be that of Timothy Richard, whose tablet remains in the Taiyuan Normal University, which was the former Shanxi University (Wong 2000:27).

Scott highlighted Richard's pursuit of Mahayana texts as a divergence from orientalist mainstream tendencies to seek ancient texts and a new way of seeking understanding of Asian belief. His approach and construct of a "grand historical narrative of religious progress" including the undocumented Christian influence on Mahayana Buddhism can be attributed to his vision of global progress (2012:4–5, 20–1). Perhaps his vision was a reflection of the Edwardian era optimism and vision of progress prevalent at that time in Europe. As Kaiser noted, Richard's fulfillment theology was part of his eschatology and explains his novel way of interpreting Mahayana Buddhism (2014).

Even as Richard's translation appeared more as a speculative assumption with insufficient documentary evidence of Christian influence on the development of Mahayana teachings, Richard's work must be noted for his contribution to Sinology, especially in Buddhist studies. He continued the discussion on Mahayana teachings in the company of other missionaries and Sinologists in China ranging from T.W. Rhys David and Ernest Eitel to Samuel Beal and Joseph Edkins (李新德 2007:13–6). Garbe, in his review of Richard's approach, seems to concur with Richard's argument even though he agreed that more historical research is needed to attribute the sudden transformation in Mahayana tradition to Christian influence (1912:161–187).

Though his translations of *The Awakening of Faith* and the *Lotus Sutra* were considered unusual and startling and dismissed by both the missionary community and Buddhist scholars, Richard can be credited with a bold and creative attempt to bridge the gospel with the religious beliefs of China to win the souls of China and to encourage greater contextualization of the gospel in China. In fact, he was perceptive to identify the importance of Mahayana Buddhism as the faith of China and Japan and to highlight the radical twist of Mahayana teachings from the Hinayana Buddhism. His comparison of Mahayana as the New Testament of Higher Buddhism with the parallel notions of grace, savior, paradise, and enlightenment for the householder, will certainly resonate with the followers of Mahayana teachings in China (and now East Asia and the Chinese diaspora at large).

Conclusion

Timothy Richard was lauded by Kenneth Scott Latourette as one of the greatest missionaries sent to China. He was one of the few Protestant missionaries in China who could reach the officials and intellectuals of late Qing China and exemplified the first of a more holistic approach in missions. Richard's missionary approach was based on his eschatological vision of the kingdom of God which is not merely otherworldly but embraced the whole of life, including both human bodies and human souls (Wang 2015:174–6). His quest for souls saw him engage with social concerns, including the leadership in a famine relief effort in northern China as well as advocacy on social, political, and educational reforms in China. His intellectual bent and literary prowess led him to engage in literature ministry, including massive translation of Western works into Chinese through the CLS.

His research and translation of Mahayana Buddhist sutras into English was an important contribution to Sinology as well as Buddhist studies in China. It is hoped that Christian research into Mahayana traditions will continue which will further his legacy of Christian outreach towards not only China, but also the adherents of Mahayana Buddhist faith in East Asia as well as among the Chinese diaspora.

It was Richard's quest for the conversion of souls and transformation of China which inspired all his missionary endeavors over forty-five years. His legacy remains till this day. Despite his achievements, Richard would still remember clearly at the age of seventy, his initial calling to missions based on a sermon "Obedience is Better than Sacrifice," as he prided himself first and foremost as an ambassador of God (Wang 2015:190).

References

Bohr, P. Richard. 2000. "The Legacy Of Timothy Richard." *International Bulletin of Missionary Research.* 24:75–80.

Garbe, Richard. 1912. "Contributions of Christianity To Buddhism." 22 (2) 161–87.

Hsu, Immanuel. 1995. *The Rise of Modern China.* Oxford: Oxford University.

Johnston, Reginald Fleming. 1913. *Buddhist China.* London, John Murray.

Kaiser, Andrew T. 2014. "Encountering China: The Evolution Of Timothy Richard's Missionary Thought 1870–1891." University of Edinburgh. Unpublished dissertation.

Ko, Lawrence. 1990. "Protestant Missionary Co-operation in Late Qing China 1877–1890." Department of History, National University of Singapore. Unpublished thesis.

Lai Pan-chiu. 2009. "Timothy Richard's Buddhist-Christian Studies." *Buddhist-Christian Studies.* 29 (1) 23–38.

Pfister, Lauren F. 2003. "Rethinking Mission in China: James Hudson Taylor And Timothy Richard." In *The Imperial Horizons of British Protestant Missions, 1880–1914.* Andrew Porter ed. 183–212. Michigan: Eerdmans.

Richard, Timothy. 1907. *The Awakening of Faith.* Shanghai: Christian Literature Society.

________. 1910. *The New Testament of Higher Buddhism.* Edinburgh: T&T Clark.

________. 1916. *Forty-Five Years in China.* London: T. Fisher Unwin.

Scott, Gregory Adam. 2012. "Timothy Richard, World Religion, and Reading Christianity" In Buddhist Garb. *Social Sciences and Missions* 25:1–23.

Spence, Jonathan D. 1980. *To Change China: Western Advisers in China.* London: Penguin.

Stanley, Brian. 1992. *The History of the Baptist Missionary Society 1792–1992.* Edinburgh: T&T Clark.

__________ ed. 2003. *Missions, Nationalism, and the End of Empire.* Eerdmans.

Tarocco, Francesca. 2008. "Lost in Translation? The 'Treatise on the Mahāyāna Awakening of Faith (Dasheng Qixin Lun)' and Its Modern Readings." *Bulletin of the School of Oriental and African Studies.* 71 (2) 323–43.

Wang Wenzong. 2015. "Timothy Richard: A Missionary Who Impacted the Late Qing Dynasty." In *Builders of the Chinese Church: Pioneer Protestant Missionaries and Chinese Church Leaders.* G. Wright Doyle, ed. Eugene, OR: Pickwick.

Wong Man Kong. 2000. *British Missionaries' Approaches to Modern China, 1807–1966.* Oslo University. Seventh Special Session of the 19th International Congress of Historical Sciences, Presented at "Missions, Modernisation, Colonisation and De-colonisation." August 6–13. Unpublished paper.

Chinese Sources

李新德 2007. 亞洲的福音書」— 晚清新教傳教士漢語佛教經典英譯研究, 漢學研究通訊 26：1（總101 期）民國96 年2 月 pp 13–22.

何菊 2014. 传教士与近代中国社会变革： 李提摩太在华宗教与社会实践研究 （1870–1916）》 北京：中国社会科学出版社.

王树槐 2006. 《基督教与清季中国的教育与社会》 台北：宇宙光全人关怀机构.

陈建明 2006. 《激扬文字广传福音》 台北：宇宙光全人关怀机构.

Three Shining Stars: Lessons Learned from Thai Missionaries to Buddhists

Austin House

In most church history chronicles (particularly in SE Asian countries) there is a startling dearth of accounts about the kingdom-building efforts of indigenous Christians to Buddhist communities. In the late nineteenth century, the American Presbyterian Mission (APM) based in northern Siam began to take many expeditions into mission fields outside of Siam's formulating borders. Numerous accounts testify to the work of Presbyterian missionaries travelling into the regions of Laos, Burma, and China. APM missionary Daniel McGilvary's autobiographical account, *A Half Century Among the Siamese and the Lao,* documents his many tours (McGilvary 2003). McGilvary's book, like other missionary testimonies, is often amnestic about the significant role Thai Christians had in the evangelistic work accomplished on these tours and their planting of churches in foreign countries.

This chapter reveals the work of three northern Thai Christians who worked among Buddhist communities during the late nineteenth and early twentieth century: 1) Chai Ma was sent as a missionary to serve the Kamu in French Laos; 2) Lin toiled in the diverse communities of Tai Kün, Tai Nua, and Tai Lü in Shan

State, Burma; and 3) Muang taught and did outreach among the Tai Yai and Tai Yuan in Yunnan, China. All three men were sent and supported by their local churches to go and share the gospel cross-culturally in Buddhist communities. These three men left a lasting legacy built on effective biblical methods and lessons which can be utilized for Buddhist community outreach today.

1. Chai Ma to French Laos

In 1898, McGilvary, during one of his tours among the Kamu in northern French Laos, was informed by the French government in no uncertain terms that APM mission work was no longer welcome. When McGilvary departed the field, he left behind some northern Thai and Kamu diaspora evangelists. After six months of service, these men returned to Chiang Mai and reported how the Kamu in northern French Laos were open to the gospel, with eighty-seven being trained and ready for baptism. When the APM was locked out from French Laos, the northern Thai Church was given the challenge to find someone who could take on such a promising but challenging field. At the end of 1899, a well-respected northern Thai Reverend named Chai Ma, announced to the assembly and mission: "I will go to the Kamooh people beyond the Cambodia."

In January 1900, Chai Ma was fully supported and sent out by the Lampang Church as their missionary. His first six months of service had significant numeric success by his baptizing forty-one adults and twenty-three children, with interest shown in other villages as well. Unfortunately, at the end of Chai Ma's first year of service, an ill report was received by the northern Thai Church and the APM. While still married to his wife, who had remained in Chiang Mai, Chai Ma had taken on an additional Kamu wife in Muang Sai. Charges were brought up on his committing polygamy, and his salary was instantly cut off. An investigation confirmed Chai Ma's sin, and within a year the name of this stalwart of the northern Thai Church was severely tarnished. Sporadic attempts were made to continue the work to the Kamu in Muang Sai, but the trust the APM had in sending out other northern Thai Christians was severely damaged.

In 1915, fifteen years after Chai Ma's sinful lapse, he returned to northern Siam. Chai Ma came to request from the APM and northern Thai church to send a pastor to the Kamu to baptize ten families whom he had trained and shepherded. Missionaries who knew Chai Ma became advocates for his reinstatement. Dr. Samuel Peoples, an APM missionary, wrote an extremely revealing letter on Chai Ma:

> I have always had a warm side for Chai Ma: to my mind he has been more sinned against than we are disposed to take into account when passing judgment. The first transgression where we did it in the first instance. We had no business to

> send him off there alone: there was the first offense. Then when he transgressed, we held up our hands in holy horror and stood off; that was our second offense, and it seems we are still in that attitude. For my part I am sorry I did not inquire into the matter while Chai Ma was still on this side; but I myself am so far out of the was [*sic*] that we know very little of what is going on of ordinary affairs, or of affairs that are not brought up for general counsel. I certainly think it would have been wise to reinstate the man, of course doing it with the proper degree of impression upon the peculiar circumstances of the case. I believe Chai Ma is a thoroughly good man, and that he sees now his error, and, in fact, I am not quite sure that he is not now taking the right course. Whatever of stigma there would be upon him, there would be less of it in the Kamooh land than there would be at home, and there it would do less damage to his future usefulness, and he is more needed there than he is at home (Peoples 1915).

Chai Ma's sinful error, along with by Peoples' letter, reveals an essential lesson for local churches to consider when working in Buddhist communities.

A lesson from Chai Ma's service: Mutual hierarchy

Appraising Chai Ma's work, the repeated need to establish accountability systems to have a faithful witness rears its ugly head. When Jesus sent out missionaries into the field, he sent them out in pairs (Mark 6:6–7; Luke 10:1). Today, the sending of mission teams is not without critique often with two arguments made. First, a biblical interpretation is that when Jesus sent teams out, they were only for short-term periods. Second, these critiques are often based on the underlying issues of Western agencies sending homogenous Western teams (Zehner 2005; Ellis 2005). The first argument seems to have strength from a scriptural standpoint. Often in the Old Testament, prophets would have others alongside them. The Apostles Peter and Paul tended to follow Jesus' model of preferring to go out in teams (Acts 11:25–26; 13:2–5; 15:36–41; 18:18). The second argument for homogenous Western mission teams has some merit for further study (Hibbert and Hibbert 2017). However, this chapter will look further into the issues which multicultural teams might face as well as the issues which occur when the APM and northern Thai church sent missionaries and teams out into mission fields.

When Chai Ma was sent, he was not alone, but rather in a team as their leader. This team was made up of himself and some Kamu Christians, and the members most likely shared a strong cultural value for high-power distance. When Chai Ma, the leader of their team began a sinful relationship with a Kamu woman, perhaps the Kamu Christians within in this team believed they could not directly question or confront him. Therefore, the only way in which this team could resolve the issue was to report to whom they considered were their higher leaders back in Chiang Mai, who could provide the authority and accountability which Chai Ma desperately needed.

In this case one underlying issue was the need for the church to have effective witness and accountability over all its members. Unfortunately, it appears Chai Ma had little accountability to the members of his team which resulted in a devastating delay to bring about confession and repentance.

" Having systems of accountability among leaders and laity within the church allows for more significant and effective witness among one another and the world. "

Jeffrey A. Dukeman has proposed a compelling way for the church to operate. However, his proposal has critical applications for which multicultural mission teams may operate in the Buddhist mission field. Dukeman proposes a mutual hierarchy by writing:

> Mutual hierarchy means not having to decide against something just because it is more egalitarian or more hierarchical. Here [in a mutual hierarchy] each ecclesial member has hierarchies over the others in connection with his or her unique gifts, offices, and responsibilities. Recognizing this can help foster each member in using these hierarchies to serve the others and compliment them in the work of God's kingdom. Because of these advantages, this framework can foster the flexibility necessary for the complexities of God's kingdom and a sinful world. Each ecclesial member has unique powers, with varying levels of overlap and complementarity with the powers of others. Recognizing this can help foster flexible teams best adapted for unique problems and work (Dukeman 2017:322).

However, biblical accountability within the church is not one-directional. In Peoples' letter, he shares his belief on how Chai Ma had shown repentance. Just as important in this letter is that Peoples concedes that the APM also failed when they sent Chai Ma out to do work among the Kamu since they were well aware of his having severe problems with his wife. Sending a man away from his wife and family while the couple was in the midst of marital difficulty was inevitably doomed from the start. Years afterward, Peoples letter points for the desire to rehabilitate Chai Ma by receiving him again into the mission but also testifying that the APM shared culpability in his transgression. This is a vital lesson for the church living among and doing work in Buddhist communities today. Sin by the church and its members will inevitably be witnessed from within and by the Buddhist communities which surround them. It is imperative that the church, particularly in mission contexts, respond in a way that ensures the sin and its consequences are of consequence. In the same way, the church must reveal to the Buddhist communities they serve that the grace and mercy of God should not be disparaged. Having systems of accountability among leaders and laity within the church allows for more significant and effective witness among one another and the world.

2. Reverend Lin in Shan State, Burma

French Laos was not the only field in which the APM had interest. In 1904, after numerous attempts, the mission was authorized to start a station in Keng Tung, Burma under the leadership of Presbyterian missionary W. C. Dodd. Dodd for over a decade had pushed for work in Shan State and had sent and led many northern Thai and hilltribe colporteur teams into the region. When Keng Tung Station was to be opened, Dodd called upon Rev. Lin, a northern Thai pastor, and his large family of seven children to go along with him. Like Chai Ma, Lin too had a checkered past. During the early 1890s, Lin had shown a great promise by being ordained and serving as a teacher at the seminary in Lamphun then later Chiang Mai. While serving in Lamphun, Lin was accused of being "A lover of silver." He was then cast off and received no support from the APM and northern Thai church. When famine struck the area of Lamphun, Lin along with other Christians moved up to Papau village in Chiang Rai. While in Papau, Lin had a re-awakening and became a beloved shepherd for that community. When the opportunity to do work in a new field, despite the challenges of moving a large family to a new field, Lin took up the opportunity to expand God's kingdom.

A lesson from Lin's service: Evangelism methods

During the late nineteenth and early twentieth century, Lin was one of northern Siam's most well-trained pastors both academically and had a plethora of experience in the field. His work showed numeric success in three different fields in Siam and Shan State. One evangelistic method employed by Lin and other evangelists was to use Buddhist texts as a bridge to share the gospel to non-believers in an apologetic way. A Prince and Buddhist scholar among the Sam Tüen people challenged Lin insisting that the Pali sacred character have inherent merit. Charles C. Callender an APM missionary recounts the episode by writing:

> Lin asked, 'can we be delivered from sin and guilt by means of the Pali character?' and the listeners replied in the negative. (The Pali stands related to these people as Hebrew and Greek to Americans). Kru [Teacher] Lin then explained, 'There is no virtue in the character itself whether considered significant or insignificant, that which counts is faith and love and service in Jesus. He is the Redeemer of all who believe and trust in Him.' Kru Lin then told about the beginning of the world and many other things, talking till midnight, when the Prince asked about the extent of the Christian scriptures.
>
> When Kru Lin said there are 66 books in the Canon, the Prince remarked on the paucity of the Christian scriptures, and Kru Lin replies, 'With regard to the 66 books no one can add to them one letter or take from them one letter. They are not like the scriptures of Buddha. For example, take the single birth of

> *wethandaya* (last birth of Buddha before enlightenment). Anyone possessed with sufficient wisdom and artistic taste may rearrange this story to suit aesthetic taste. The story of P'ya Wethandaya has many versions, where in them can one find which is authentic? But this religion of Jesus is firm and reliable, for no one can add to it or take away from it.'
>
> To this the people listening gave assent saying, 'our neighbor speaks the religion of Jesus in the light, he does not talk in a hidden way like the religion of Buddha' (Callender 1907).

"One evangelistic method employed by Lin and other evangelists was to use Buddhist texts as a bridge to share the gospel to non-believers in an apologetic way."

A second evangelistic method employed by Lin and northern Thai evangelists to their Buddhist neighbors was to share and display the freedom which Christ gave. These types of power encounters have become popularly understood through the work of Charles Kraft and Alan Tippett (Kraft 2017). In a Buddhist village called Ban Tap, mission teams had found that there was a great deal of interest in the gospel. Interestingly, this village was set apart from others as it was a sanctuary village for those who were accused of witchcraft. Lin visited this village often and Dodd in one of his letters described the interest in this village:

> At Ban Tap (literally Soldier Village), the witch's village, the way was not opened up during this tour for a whole-village movement. Those who had formerly been interested, including the headman, called the Saja was open as ever to the gospel message. The Saja had us sleep in his house. He invited the villagers to his house every evening to listen. Crowds of men came, and some women. And every morning crowds of women and children came to our Christian services in the Saja's house, attracted by the hymn singing. We had no organ or violin with us this trip. The Saja urged his people to accept Christ. He insists that his house is free from demons. He had us write out in large script a form of prayer that God would drive out demons from any given place. Also the Lord's Prayer and a form for grace at meals. He wanted these prayers for use, and protests that he prays to Jesus every day. But he has not cut loose altogether from Buddhism. He almost promised to do so, but not quite. He would like to get the benefit of Christ's power over demons, witches, and sin, but is not quite ready yet to pay the price of full surrender and possible loss of official position (Dodd 1906).

Using both apologetics and power encounter as evangelism methods, the work in Shan State among Buddhists and other hill tribe groups began to show extreme promise. Whole villages were leaning towards accepting the gospel. Unfortunately, the question of geographical territory and denominational comity brought about devastating consequences which over time led the Presbyterian work in Shan State to come to an end. With the American Baptist Mission (ABM) employing different evangelistic methods and not having the resources and staffing that the APM had, an opportunity for great evangelistic outreach appears to have been lost (House 2017; Swanson 1982).

3. Kru Muang in Yunnan, China

As the APM ceded Keng Tung Station and most of Shan State to the ABM, it began to look further to the north. APM missionary W. C. Dodd, who had led the effort to open Keng Tung, made a new case for work in Yunnan, China. For over ten years, the northern Thai Church sent many colporteur and evangelism teams into this field. In 1917, a new APM station in Chieng Rung, Yunnan was opened and remained working until World War II. While many northern Thai pastors and evangelists served in this field, few stood out as much as Kru Muang.

Muang was a superstar in every sense of the word. As a young boy, Muang, came to the attention to the APM missionaries when he came to Nan hospital, bringing his father who had been attacked by a tiger. Kru Muang fought the tiger off with a machete. After his father recovered, Muang remained at Nan Station to get an education, and it was there he became a Christian. At Nan, Muang showed excellent potential, and after graduating from school, he went onto become a teacher in Nan. In 1922, a call was from Yunnan for the northern Thai church to send missionaries to aid in the work. Muang along with his wife, Tiam Tah, volunteered and went up to Chieng Rung to assist in running the school and the evangelism efforts there. It was during Muang's first year of service that Dr. Claude Mason, the only APM missionary stationed at Chieng Rung, grew desperately ill. Although it was during the rainy season and extremely dangerous to travel, Muang offered to make the trip by foot to Chiang Rai to seek medical help. He made the journey in an incredible eight days, practically running the entire journey through the jungle having to ford flooded rivers and streams. Muang returned with the doctor from Chiang Rai, and when Mason had the sufficient strength, he left Chieng Rung to seek further medical care. For over one year after this, Chieng Rung station had no APM missionaries, thus leaving Muang along with other northern Thai missionaries to lead the work successfully.

In 1926, Muang along with his wife and children returned to Nan for a well-deserved furlough. While at Nan, he was hired by a two-man film crew to serve as a manager and interpreter for the making of the silent movie "Chang" (Elephant.) While serving in this capacity, the crew saw Muang as the most adept to become the lead actor in the film. At the end of the filming, Kru Muang received a fine rifle and a new teak house for his work. The movie "Chang" went on to earn great commercial success worldwide, becoming one of the year's highest grossing films, and earning a special Academy award. From all the missionary accounts, there were concerns that after such great success, Kru Muang would become prideful with his newfound fame. This thought was unfounded as after Muang's work on the movie was complete, he and his wife Tiam Tah spoke with APM missionary Hugh Taylor and said: "The call of the Thai in South China is still ringing in our ears. We wish to go back to them" (Taylor 1942).

In 1928, Muang along with his family returned to work in Chieng Rung in Yunnan. At that time, the area was in a state of rebellion and Muang was at one point captured, accused of being a spy and was taken along with other prisoners to be shot and thrown into the Mekong river. Kru Muang gives his account of the event:

> I ran as fast as I could, but unfortunately I ran right into the advance guard of the northern army. They caught me at once and said that I was a spy from the southern forces. I protested my innocence and told them that I was a Siamese from Siam, but even my language did not seem to change their minds.
>
> They slapped me repeatedly and told me that I would be shot. For a while they kept me running ahead of them to act as a shield for the bullets of the enemy. They would not listen to my story that I was a Siamese. All they would say was that before long six or seven soldiers would shoot me as a spy. Thus, they drove me onward, beating me with the butts of their guns and shooting right past my ears at the enemy until I was deaf. Many of the soldiers near me were killed by the enemy bullets. It made me think of when Jesus was dragged along to the Cross and the thought that I might be asked to die as He had done brought courage to me. I prayed that whether I died or lived I would put my life in His care. When we arrived at the place where they were to shoot me, they removed my outer garments. It reminded me again of what they had done to Jesus Christ long ago and the thought brought me a little comfort. I prayed again, 'Oh God, do not leave me desolate.'
>
> I heard the captain say to the soldiers to wait for about five minutes, and if what I said was true, some of my friends would come and vouch for me. Almost four of the five minutes had gone when I saw a friend of mine, Dr. Galt, with the Commander of the army coming toward me. After answering the Commander's questions in a satisfactory manner, he gave me orders that I was to be freed but was to be constantly watched for the next ten days. This the soldiers did. They also took all our bedding and household goods that they wanted away, and what they did not want they destroyed. The fact that my life was spared was entirely due to the mercy of God (Muang 1933:111–2).

Kru Muang's composure and faithfulness by taking time to pray before his death sentence got the Captain's attention. This action set him apart from those accused alongside him. His faith gave witness, and by God's mercy, he was saved. After hostilities died down, Muang was then sent alone up to a new promising field at Muang Baw in northern Yunnan. Unfortunately, while in Muang Baw, Kru Muang fell into the temptation of drinking alcohol (most likely profusely) which severely impacted his witness in the field. When Kru Muang returned to Chieng Rung, he was confronted with these allegations. Instead of denying the sin, he repented and requested that he return to Muang Baw to confess his sins there as well. His witness was tarnished to be sure, but those around him believed that he was repentant of his sins. Muang returned to Muang Baw to help repair the damage he had done there. Then he returned to Chieng Rung, where he had more accountability mechanisms around him, including his family and peers.

Before and after this episode in Muang Baw, Kru Muang had a considerable role in another great work. As Kru Muang did evangelistic work, he also got the word out of an effort by Chieng Rung station to form a leper colony. While lepers were an ostracized people in Yunnan and tended to be outcasts from villages, they often remained in their family units. Typically, leper colonies during those days would attempt to keep the men and women separated from each other. However, Chieng Rung encouraged lepers to marry and remain within their family units. The caveat was that children born into these families who were uninfected would be forced to leave the colony for their physical protection. Chieng Rung's policy for attempting to keep families together was an effort to try and prevent further infections from spreading into Yunnan. By keeping families together, the mission saw fewer runaways from the colony. Within just three years, this leper colony had over one hundred members and in another three years, doubled to two hundred members. Kru Muang was instrumental in founding and shepherding the lepers and families who came to live at the colony.

Lessons from Muang's service: Character and family matters

Like Chai Ma, the danger of sending a missionary alone to the field is undoubtedly reinforced by Muang's sinful err at Muang Baw. Still, reviewing Kru Muang's overall life and service, one is struck on how he stands out as an excellent example of what characteristics a successful missionary might have within Buddhist communities. Muang's exceedingly strong attributes differentiate him from many of his other contemporaneous workers who remained in the field for shorter periods and were seemingly less effective.

The necessity for churches today to seek and send out missionaries who are brave, faithful, and humble is as greatly needed now as it was then. All too often churches may be unwilling to send out their best workers into mission fields, as some believe this will weaken the churches at home. Herbert Swanson made this case when he reviewed the missionary work by the northern Thai Church in his book *Khrischak Muang Nua* and found it to be detrimental (Swanson 1984).

However, biblical witness contradicts this worldly view. Churches who send out their very best into the mission field often benefit from the work. Muang was known as a courageous man, whether it was his hunting and fighting off tigers or praying before a firing squad. Second, when Muang had obtained worldwide fame after the success of his movie career, he easily could have rested on his laurels. Instead, Muang and his wife were attentive to God and heard the similar Macedonian call that the Apostle Paul had received (Acts 16:9,10). They remained faithful to their call, even when the temptation of an easier life was before them. Both Muang and his wife could not be dissuaded or tempted from the task which God had given them. Finally, Kru Muang's sin of drinking alcohol in Muang Baw led him not to run away from the accusation but rather to confess when he was confronted by it. His humility in remaining on the mission field, accepting new parameters in his mission work by having more accountability systems around him, resulted in the growth of new mission work. His work among the lepers was particularly successful; in later years this became the backbone for the Chieng Rung church.

"Muang's humility in remaining on the mission field, accepting new parameters in his mission work by having more accountability systems around him, resulted in the growth of new mission work."

A second component learned from Muang's service is the focus evangelism work on family units. Just as Lin worked among the accused witch villagers in Shan State, so Kru Muang reached out among leper families in Yunnan. Often missionaries to Buddhists in their rush to see fruit from their efforts, seek out individual conversions, and perhaps do so to a strategic detriment. Alex Smith addresses this in *Family and Faith in Asia* when he writes:

> It takes discipline to keep the group in mind. Normally, time for diffusion of the gospel and its permeation to all members of the family network is required. Clear understanding and acceptance of the gospel may take even up to two and sometimes more years. The consistent change of life and the faithful witness of relatives, as well as their indigenous sensitivity to Buddhist cultural issues, have a marked effect on the acceleration of the process for the conversion of the whole family, extended network, tribe or village. By not withdrawing from normal relationships, interaction and customary events of the family and the local community, Christians' witness can portray genuine faith and commendable ethical living to the society at large (Smith 2010:30).

The church should be attuned in her cross-cultural missions work to be willing to witness and love the outcasts that Christ calls the church to love. She also needs to keep in mind a more strategic evangelistic vision of reaching families and villages together and having them come to Christ collectively rather than individually. As Cornelius' entire household was baptized by the Holy Spirit, so can God act among Buddhist communities today (Acts 10).

Conclusion

There are valuable lessons to be learned from each of these stalwarts of the northern Thai church. From Chai Ma, a lesson learned is how the sending of teams which have mutual hierarchy allows for greater accountability and the use of all gifts. From Lin and other northern Thai Christians, evangelistic methods using both apologetics and power encounter among Buddhists in Shan state are informative and were shown to bring about a number of conversions. Finally, the work of Muang, who showed bravery and humility in his work towards the disadvantaged and among family units is enlightening. Chai Mai, Lin, and Muang possessed outstanding missionary characteristics which brought them success in the different Buddhist fields in which they toiled. However, like the disciples of Jesus Christ, they were not sinless, and when these men did err, the northern Thai church had or later gained the capacity to forgive. This brought about repentance and renewal which gave great witness to the mercy given by God within the church and the surrounding Buddhist communities. Although these men are now long forgotten, churches planted by these northern Thai missionaries in Laos, Burma (Myanmar) and China continue to exist and worship today. These lessons learned from the past may be able to encourage churches today in their work among Buddhist communities.

References

Callender, Charles R. 1907. "Letter to the Friends of Kengtung Station." Chiang Mai: Board of Foreign Missions Collection, Payap University Archives. Vol. 276. April 15.

Dodd, William C. 1906. "Letter to Friends of the Keng Tung Station." Chiang Mai: Board of Foreign Missions Collection, Payap University Archives. Vol. 275. Nov 22.

Dukeman, Jeffrey A. 2017. "Mutual Hierarchys: A Framework for Ecclesiology." *Lutheran Mission Matters*. 25 (2) 317–29.

Ellis, Jordan. 2005. "Let's Get Real About Missionary Team Chemistry." Evangelical Missions Quarterly. 41 (4) 440–5.

Hibbert, Evelyn, and Richard Hibbert. 2014. *Leading Multicultural Teams*. Pasadena, William Carey Library.

House, Austin. 2017. *An Ethnohistorical Study of Thai Christians and Their Participation in Cross-Cultural Missions from 1870–1940*. Portland, OR: Western Seminary. Unpublished dissertation.

McGilvary, Daniel. 2002. *A Half Century Among the Siamese and the Lao: An Autobiography.* Bangkok: White Lotus.

Muang, Kru. 1933. "Facing of a Firing Squad," *Siam Outlook.* Chiang Mai: Payap University Archives. 110–3.

Peoples, Samuel Craig. 1915. "Letter to Charles R. Callender." Chiang Mai: Samuel Craig Peoples Collection, Payap University Archives. Folder 15, RG 008/90 (1) April 7.

Smith, Alex. 2010. "Evangelizing Whole Families: The Value of Family in the 21st Century." *Family and Faith in Asia.* Paul De Neui, ed. 1–30. Pasadena, William Carey Library.

Swanson, Herbert. 1984. *Khrischak Muang Nua.* Bangkok: Chuan.

________. 1982. "The Kengtung Question: Presbyterian Mission and Comity in Eastern Burma." *Journal of Presbyterian History.* 60 (1) 59–80.

Taylor, Hugh. 1942. "Kru Muang of Thailand." *Unforgettable Disciples.* New York: The Board of Foreign Missions of the Presbyterian Church in the United States of America.

Zehner, Damaris. 2005. "Building Teams, Building Walls." Evangelical Missions Quarterly. 41 (3) 362–9.

PART 2

Lessons of Emerging Faith from Key *Places* in Asian Mission History

CHAPTER 9

Christianity in Theravada Buddhist SE Asia

Stephen Bailey

This chapter reflects on the failure of Christian missions in South East Asia (SEA) to effectively engage the Theravada Buddhist majority groups. The majority Buddhist groups that are in focus here are the Burmese, Khmer, Lao, and Thai. This reflection is prompted by the reality that after more than 450 years of Catholic and Protestant missions the number of Christians among the majority Buddhist groups is less than one percent.

> "If Christianity is to seriously engage the majority SEA Buddhist ethnic groups it must be integrated into these societies in ways that are conversant with the social and religious realities that shape Buddhist family, village, and national identity."

Christian engagement with these Buddhist groups has been deeply influenced by the historic political, social, and economic exchanges between European Catholic and

Protestant nations and Buddhist SEA peoples. In what follows I will briefly outline this history and reflect on its impact on Christian-Buddhist engagement in terms of four overlapping eras. First, the classic era of SEA Buddhist Empires from the founding of the Angkor Empire (802 CE) to the end of the kingdom of Ayutthaya (1767). Second, the early Catholic missionary engagement from the arrival of Portuguese missionaries in Myanmar (1554) until the end of the eighteenth century. Third, the era of Protestant missionary engagement during colonial rule from the capture of Yangon in Myanmar (1824) until Laos and Cambodia gained their independence from France (1954). Fourth, the era of political independence beginning in 1955 to the present (2019). This last era has been marked by the end of Christendom (and the consequent acceleration of secularization of Protestantism) and globalization. The thesis of this chapter is that if Christianity is to seriously engage the majority SEA Buddhist ethnic groups it must be integrated into these societies in ways that are conversant with the social and religious realities that shape Buddhist family, village, and national identity.

The Classic Era of SEA Buddhist Empires: 802—1767 CE

Leonard Andaya argues that the early classic period of Southeast Asia (802 to 1430 CE) is important because it: 1) established the patterns of state leadership; 2) it has shaped the social memory of SE Asians as "the golden age" before the colonial denigration of state power and local culture; and 3) it grounded the identity of the majority ethnic groups in the cosmology and ethos of Theravada Buddhism (Andaya). This era began with the rise of the Khmer Angkor Empire (802–1430) and the Burmese Empire at Pagan (1044–1287). When these empires began to fade the Kingdom of Siam (1279–1438 in Sukhothai and 1351–1767 in Ayutthaya) and the Lao Kingdom of Lan Xang (1354–1707) came into their own classic era zeniths.

Osborn teaches us that these empires shared several characteristics (1997:252). First, a crucial key to their rise to power was rice cultivation along excellent water sources that provided a natural means of irrigation. The Pagan Empire's rice cultivation in the Irrawaddy River delta region, the Angkor Empire's cultivation of rice along the seasonally flooded Tonle Sap Lake and the Siamese Kingdom's use of the Chao Phraya River basin provided a crucial surplus of food and commodity for export. In fact, Angkor farms were sometimes able to grow three rice crops a year. This ability to cultivate rice surpluses was the key to wealth, the consequent increase in populations, and the construction of hundreds of magnificent temples and palaces. In Pagan and Angkor, the labor of slaves captured in war also contributed to the construction of these monuments to empire.

The mountainous geography of Laos, however, left the Kingdom of Lan Xang with less suitable land for rice cultivation along the Mekong River. Because it had limited paddy fields and a much smaller population to draw on, Lan Xang was not nearly as wealthy. Another factor that limited the prosperity of Lan Xang was the lack of a seaport that would have enabled international trade. Consequently, while Angkor, Pagan, and Sukhothai/Ayutthaya all left impressive ancient temple and palace ruins there are none to be seen in Laos.

A second shared characteristic was the adoption of a Brahmin-Buddhist religious cosmology as a foundation for statecraft. Prior to the arrival of these influences SEA peoples actively propitiated nature and ancestor spirits believed to inhabit homes, temples, objects, and territories. The belief that spirits play a significant role in local affairs and the ritual practices done to manage spirit activity continues to play a significant role in the religion of SEA. The adoption of Brahmanism and later Buddhism, however, provided an orderly way to situate these traditional beliefs within a wider global understanding of the world (Osborne 1997:22).

SEA Buddhism did not import the Indian Hindu caste system and by comparison is decidedly open to all social classes. The writing systems of the region are based on the Hindu Sanskrit system and the Hindu cosmology is assumed by Buddhists. While Brahmanism's influence takes a backseat today to Theravada Buddhism, some Brahmin rituals connected to the royal courts continue. Brahmin priests for example still play a role in the annual royal plowing rituals done by the kings of Thailand (formerly Siam) and Cambodia. Even in communist Laos Brahmin priests were recently part of the dedication ceremony of a statue memorializing King Fa Ngum, who founded the Lan Xang Empire (South China Morning Post, January 6, 2003).

An early form of Mahayana Buddhism gave way to Theravada Buddhism before the thirteenth century CE. The influence of early Mahayana Buddhism can be seen more clearly on Burmese Buddhism than in Cambodia, Laos, and Thailand. In these latter three nations, Mahayana Buddhism is only practiced today by the Chinese and Vietnamese immigrant communities.

Third, each of these empires developed similar understandings of leadership and power. One of the key characteristics of leadership was the personal nature of power. A second was a form of authority that scholars have referred to with the term *mandala* which refers to "the ways in which a ruler's power flowed outward from the center of his kingdom towards an often-distant periphery" (Rickelfs, et.al. 2010:38). Not only did a ruler's authority wax and wane based on geography but also from one era of time to the next. The *mandala* system required a king "to provide economic benefits for chiefs and other subordinate ruler" (39). In return subordinates paid tribute in material resources and with obedience and deference to the king. These exchanges took place in sizable bureaucracies that are more significant in terms of the ritual of deference they offer to leaders than for their efficiency in function. While this version of hierarchy can be used to exploit those in the position of client, at its best those in authority reciprocate the loyalty and deference they receive with protection, opportunity and a proportional share of resources.

SEA authority has "a strong religious and ritual character" (Ibid). Authority was traditionally perceived to rest as much upon the approval of spirits, deities, and karma as it did upon wisdom and military might. A king's success was ultimately explained as the result of his karmic merit and ritual power. Kings were thus seen as sacred lords with unique connections to the divine but were not worshipped as gods as they were at times in Indonesia (41–42). In time, kings became the sponsors and protectors of the Theravada Buddhist Dharma and the Sangha (the community of monks).

This classic era of SEA wealth and power, made legitimate through religious rituals of Buddhism, encouraged confident national identities rooted in Theravada Buddhism. Burmese, Khmer, Lao, and Thai peoples have long since been formidable interlocutors to European Catholics and Protestants. It is sadly ironic that the Christian story of God's victory over sin and death through the weakness of Christ's death on a cross should arrive in these Buddhist Kingdoms by means of European ships seeking wealth, power, and control.

The Arrival of Catholic Missionaries: 1554–18th Century

Though there is some evidence that Nestorian Christians arrived in Myanmar in the tenth century (Htoigintawng), the arrival of Roman Catholic Christianity into SEA occurred on the coat tails of two main European events. First, Portuguese and Spanish navigational dominance had launched them into a global competition to explore and control foreign lands for economic profit. Second, the Catholic Church in Portugal and Spain was eager to reestablish their religious influence and prestige in the wake of the Protestant Reformation of the sixteenth century (*French Indochina* 2018:93). Nearly all these exploring Europeans believed in the superiority of their ethnic group, civilization and religion over the peoples and religions they encountered. European merchant ships were distinct from Indian and Muslim merchant ships already in the region in that they came armed with weapons of war. Needless to say, well-armed merchant ships created a powerful leverage for negotiating trade agreements.

In Cambodia, Laos, and Myanmar the arrival of European merchants and Catholic missionaries came in the twilight of their empires. Myanmar's Pegu Empire had been severely weakened by the invasion of the Mongels in the thirteenth century and had split into smaller, weaker kingdoms even if the Taugoo Dynasty (1510–1752) had reunified the empire to some extent by the time the Europeans arrived. A letter written in 1644 by Jesuits in India shows that already there were 1,600 Catholic Europeans spread out in eight cities of Myanmar (Popeinmyanmar 2017).

Likewise, the power of the Angkor Empire (802–1430 CE) had begun to fade in the fifteenth century. Its remnants had suffered a series of invasions from Vietnam and Thailand by the time French Catholic missionaries arrived in the seventeenth century. The Lao Kingdom of Lan Xang (1254–1707) had dissolved into several small regional kingdoms by the time Catholic missionaries began any substantial work in the eighteenth century. The Lao had also been weakened by invasions from China, Vietnam, and Siam. In contrast, the Siamese Kingdom of Ayutthaya (1351–1767) was on the rise when the Spanish and Portuguese priests began their work. The Siamese alternated between accepting and persecuting the Catholics as they negotiated with foreign powers on trade. By 1662 the Catholics numbered 2,000 people in Ayutthaya and were served by one Spanish and ten Portuguese priests.

In each country, pioneering Catholic missionaries suffered from illness and lack of support from their sending nations. Initially they served only the local European Catholic populations. Later as European influence was consolidated through trade and the threat of military power, missionaries began to actively evangelize among the local populations. This caused several violent backlashes from local Buddhist populations. In 1576 a Portuguese Dominican priest who had been in favor with the Cambodian royal court was later put to death by the same king. In 1743 three Barnabite priests were killed by local people in Pegu. In northeastern Laos twelve priests were martyred in 1884 and five more in 1889 by locals unhappy with their influence.

When King Narai opened Ayutthaya to foreigners Catholics were free to minister to the local population. Later, under King Phra Phetracha, Catholic missionaries were opposed and a severe persecution began in 1688 that continued into the eighteenth century. At times the missionaries were forbidden to leave the capital or to use the Siamese language to teach. The situation became worse when King Taksin (1768–1782) expelled the Catholic missionaries altogether. But the missionaries' fortunes improved when Phra Phutthayotfa Chulalok, King Rama I (1782–1809), who wanted to make new trade deals with the Europeans, invited them to return.

Today the number of Catholics from the majority Buddhist ethnic groups in SE Asia is even smaller than the number of Protestants. But Catholic missionaries have made significant social contributions to these societies. They produced Latin, French, and Thai dictionaries, Bible translations, started schools, opened orphanages and hospitals, and advised kings when they were in favor. Their arrival however was under the shadow and in the wake of heavily armed Spanish, Portuguese, and later, French merchant—military ships. Traditional

Catholic hierarchy might seem to fit more easily into the hierarchies of SE Asian societies than the more egalitarian Protestant tradition. It was, however, never integrated into the local *mandalas* and has generally been seen as a European religious rival and challenge to Buddhist identity.

Protestant Missionaries and Colonialism: 1824—1954

Protestant missionaries arrived in Myanmar (1812) and Siam (1828) more than 100 years earlier than they did in Cambodia (1923) and Laos (1902). They operated under British and French colonial rule which at first restricted but finally facilitated missionary efforts, even if this assistance associated Protestant faith with colonial power.

American Baptist missionaries arrived in Myanmar (1812) before British colonial rule. Their work was severely restricted among the Burmese by the king until the British colonized southern Myanmar in 1824. Until 1831, the missionaries focused on reaching the Buddhist Burmese majority but when there was so little response, they shifted their attention to the tribal minorities who came into Christian faith in large numbers (Lim and Dengthuama 2016:5).

While the first Protestants in Thailand came from the Netherlands and Britain they were quickly joined by a steady stream of American Baptist and Presbyterian missionaries who worked in the capital and northern Siam. They did their work with relative freedom as long as they cultivated favor with the monarchy and local governors. As in Myanmar, the missionaries found the Buddhist Siamese very unresponsive to the Christian message. Many of their converts were Chinese or Siamese Chinese. Nearly a hundred years later American Christian and Missionary Alliance missionaries (CMA) would enter northeastern Siam (1929) and met the same lack of interest in Christianity among the local ethnic Lao.

In Cambodia, American CMA missionaries entered from Vietnam (1929) under the protection of French colonial authorities. They found the tribal minorities along the borders with Vietnam and Laos far more responsive to Christianity than the Buddhist Khmer. Likewise, in French colonial Laos, Swiss Brethren missionaries took up residence in southern Laos (1902) and CMA missionaries took up residence in the north (1929). There were only a small handful of Buddhist-background Lao Christians until tribal minorities accepted Christian faith in large numbers in the early 1960s (Andrianoff 2012:126).

The American Baptist and Presbyterian missionaries who worked in Myanmar and Siam were typically well-educated college, seminary and medical school graduates. They had been influenced by the theology of the Second Great Awakening (1790—1820) in the United States. Many came from a group of New England churches that rejected the emotionalism of the revivals while embracing its emphasis on spiritual renewal. These Americans fused Calvin's emphasis on the sovereignty of God with a belief in humanity's free will to accept or reject God. The result of surrender to God was holiness and holiness led to social activism and international missions. They were motivated by what they called "disinterested benevolence;" a pious willingness to suffer that led many of their missionaries into danger, illness, and death. The Christianity they preached was characterized by "'conversionism,' 'activism,' 'Biblicism,'" and the expectation that suffering was part of the Christian life (Eitel 2012:132). But the Christianity of nineteenth century American revivalism often struggled to find a place to connect with people who did not share their monotheistic concept of one eternal, independent God who sought to save the world from sin. Yet, Protestant activism produced translations of the scriptures, evangelism, schools, and hospitals. The missionaries established the first printing presses and published Christian literature as well as newspapers in local and foreign languages.

The Protestant missionaries who entered Cambodia and Laos in the early twentieth century (nearly a hundred years after the missionaries who had entered Myanmar and Siam) were evangelical Christians. For the most part, they had not graduated from the elite schools of the Baptists and Presbyterians. The Swiss missionaries in southern Laos were Brethren known for their piety rather than their academic degrees. They were primarily concerned with winning souls and establishing churches and less with building a civilized society. While they did some medical work, and started Bible schools, they did not invest in general educational schools and hospitals. The same was true of the CMA missionaries in northeast Siam and Laos. The impact they made on society at large was much smaller than that made by the Baptists and Presbyterians in Myanmar and Siam.

All of the early Protestants used a strategy of regularly "touring" new areas to establish relations with local leaders, preach the gospel, hand out literature and establish small Christian groups. These small, struggling Churches, were often made up of people from the same family. In Cambodia, Laos, and Siam, early Protestantism was associated with being a social outcast because many of the converts were lepers, people accused of sorcery, and anyone who sought refuge for one reason or another.

It is important to observe that American Protestant missionaries brought a form of Christianity that valued personal experience with God, individual piety, and the expectation of suffering. Being a Christian often meant standing alone against the demands of one's social group; a standard that is more reasonable in nations that protect individual rights than in SEA. It is not surprising that this Christianity found few footholds in SEA Buddhist societies whichare organized around patron-client relationships and obligations to community life. Far more difficult to believe than the resurrection of Jesus is the Protestant claim that a single individual can defy the elders and forsake obligations to the community; let alone strike out on a spiritual path unknown to the ancestors. Protestantism has always considered hierarchy suspiciously and this set its social implications of Protestantism into a head-on collision course with SEA identity embedded in hierarchy and *mandala* power.

Globalization and Entrepreneurial Missionaries: 1955—Present

The end of World War II led to the independence of Myanmar from Britain (1948), and Cambodia and Laos from France (1954). Siamese diplomatic agility made it the only SEA nation not colonized and thus motived the change of name in 1939 to "Thailand," Land of the Free. Protestant missionaries had been speaking about the need for self-governing, self-supporting and self-propagation churches since Henry Venn and Rufus Anderson articulated these values in the nineteenth century (Venn 2018). As colonialism began to be dismantled, the global climate favored a serious effort to empower local leadership and ownership of SEA churches.

At the same time dozens of newly formed missionary organizations sent missionaries into SEA. Each decade since has seen more and more Protestant denominations born (Barrett 2012:29). At the same time, hundreds more independent churches and mission organizations have also been established and have sent missionaries into SEA. These missionaries have not only come from the traditional Western sending nations but increasingly from Asia; especially from South Korea, Singapore, and the Philippines.

Three important trends have shaped this era of missionary effort. First, the lay movement into missions has filled the ranks of missionaries with short-term entrepreneurially-minded missionaries. Second, the global Pentecostal movement has mobilized thousands who carry an experiential and power-oriented form of Christianity into missions. Third, the Western Protestant belief in the separation of church and state which birthed secularism opened the way for free market principles and the culture of consumerism to deeply influence mission methodologies. The resulting form of Protestant Christianity disdains hierarchy and community obligation as it promotes entrepreneurial individualism as the means of mission and consumerism as its most common form of spirituality. The contrast with the hierarchy of Buddhist SEA and its spirituality of renunciation could not be more pronounced.

The journey into this situation can be historically traced from the pious New Divinity missionaries of New England, through the Evangelical mission movement, and into the recent Pentecostal/entrepreneurial lay missionary movement. The trend is in sync with the culture of globalization that promotes neo-liberal free market values, seeks short-term profits, social networking, cultural fusion, English, and the remaking of identity through social media. While SEA is by no means immune to the effects of globalization, its primary institutions continue to be guided by the tradition of hierarchy, deference, and reciprocity. Meanwhile most missionary efforts and local SEA churches communicate the gospel in decidedly egalitarian, entrepreneurial, and individualistic ways. Charles Kraft laments the gap between our contemporary knowledge of how to contextual the gospel and our failure to implement contextualization in mission (Kraft 2005:58–61). The immovable object of Buddhist SEA *mandalas* seems to have met the unstoppable force of entrepreneurial individualistic Protestant missions. So far, Protestantism's challenge to the *mandalas* appears to be tolerated as just another aspect of globalization.

“While many SEA Buddhist peoples admire foreign ideas and often refer to the Christian world as developed, they generally fail to see what it has to do with them.”

Today, we find most churches existing as a small sub-culture with little relevance to the larger SEA social scene. They are largely the product of the nineteenth and early twentieth century missionaries. Other churches, in urban contexts, imitate the socially flat, consumer based, contemporary global Pentecostalism churches. What both forms of church life seem to share is a common failure to effectively engage Buddhist majority peoples with a Christianity that speaks to their identity.

Some Implications

The history of Christianity in SEA appears to show that the Buddhist majority has generally seen missionary organizations and churches as often well-meaning but ultimately rival *mandalas.* Christianity is generally understood as another type of foreign power not unlike the power manifested in early trade agreements, colonialism, and the narrative that foreigners are more modern or developed. Ironically, while many SEA Buddhist peoples admire foreign ideas and often refer to the Christian world as developed, they generally fail to see what it has to do with them. It would seem that Christianity has operated within the geographical space of SEA without ever being integrated into its social space. SEA Christians operate within a Christian *mandala* that is outside of and independent from the existing social system that is narratively and ritually legitimized by the Buddhist *sangha.* A nineteenth century story from the life of Dr. Daniel McGilvary helps illustrate this reality.

While Presbyterian missionary, Dr. McGilvary was working in northern Siam in the late nineteenth century, among his first two converts were Mr. Noi Sunya, a traditional doctor who served the Prince of Chiang Mai, and his friend, Nan Chai. When these two friends became Christians they no longer felt the need to consult with the Prince over every important decision as they had in the past. They saw themselves as free from the orbit of the king and part of a new, powerful Christian *mandala.* After all, McGilvary had successfully predicted a solar eclipse, healed the sick, lived without fear of spirits and accepted into his care anyone that society had rejected. All of this suggested that McGilvary had a power that allowed him to defy the king, the cosmos, and the spirits. Furious by their lack of respect, the king had the two new Christians taken into the jungle and beaten to death. Many similar, contemporary stories (albeit with less violent endings) could be told (Wells 1958:55–56).

Here are three suggestions that might help Christianity more effectively engage Buddhist SEA. First, nothing is more important than integrating the church in ways that demonstrate respect and deference to existing *mandalas* at the level of the household, village, and nation. Respect and deference must be communicated regularly and ritually. Second, integration can only happen if it is guided by Buddhist people themselves through honest and open dialogue with Christians. It is time for open, respectful, and honest inter-religious conversations between Buddhists and Christians. Christians must learn to respect Buddhism through deep listening; a listening that seeks to understand rather than refute. They should humbly explain their mandate for Christian witness and seek the advice of Buddhists as to how witness should be done in appropriate ways. Many Buddhists are eager to help because they are compassionate people who want positive relationships with their neighbors. But Buddhists also want to be treated with respect and compassion in return. Such a dialogue will also require drawing on both Buddhist philosophical and Christianity theological resources and a willingness to receive and change as well as to contribute and share. Given the frequent triumphalism of the missionaries and churches in SEA it is uncertain whether they have the humility for such a path.

Underlying these suggestions is a conviction that peace between Buddhist and Christian communities is a pre-requisite to Christian witness. But peace can only be pursued successfully when both sides are ready to be changed in the process. I suspect Christians will find the prospect of change more frightening than Buddhists because a basic Buddhist doctrine says that we must accept that everything changes (*annica*). But the best missionaries know the truth of what Andrew Walls called the "indigenizing and pilgrim principles" (Walls 1996:7–8). These principles instruct one to observe that faith is changed every time it puts down roots in a new society. At the same time the faith is somehow able to maintain its authentic identity as it travels.

Inter-religious dialogue as a mission method does not require or expect agreement on every issue; even over time. While Christians are likely to be surprised by how much they have in common with Buddhists, there are clearly fundamental differences. But interfaith dialogue should not be entered for the purpose of convincing others of the superiority of one's own faith. It should be entered with the hope of deeper mutual understanding and community. Differences need not force us into separate communities. SEA Buddhists do not assume that disagreements are the end of the road in relationships. They see a long road ahead and one never knows what will be found if we walk together far enough. I believe that Christians must walk this road with Buddhists if they hope to effectively engage Buddhists in SEA.

References

Andaya, Leonard. 2018. "*Southeast Asian Histories: A Thematic Overview from Early Times to the Present.*" www.eastwestcenter.org/sites/default/files. Unpublished Power Point File.

Andrianoff, David, and Stephen Bailey. 2012. "Laos." *The Ecumenical Review.* 64 (2) 125–130.

Barrett, David B. 2012. "Status of Global Mission in the Context of AD 1800–2025." *International Bulletin of Missionary Research.* 36 (1):29.

England, Vaudine. 2003. "The Recognition of a 14th-Century King is Seen as a Government Bid for Legitimacy: Laotians Seize a Rare Opportunity to Celebrate an Ancient Monarch." *China Morning Post.* Hong Kong. January 6.

Rivers, Charles, ed. 2018. *French Indochina: The History and Legacy of the French Empire's Colonialism in Southeast Asia.* CreateSpace Independent Publishing Platform.

Htoigintwang. 2010. "The Growth of Christianity in Myanmar." Posted May 22, 2010.

Kraft, Charles. 2005. *Appropriate Christianity.* Pasadena, CA: William Carey Library.

Lim, Theodore, and Dengthuama. 2016. "An Overview of Christian Mission in Myanmar." www.globalmissiology.org. 3 (13) 2016.

Osborne, Milton. 1997. *Southeast Asia: An Introductory History.* (7th Edition). Chiang Mai, Thailand. Silkworm.

Popeinmyanmar 2017. "A Brief History of Catholic Church in Myanmar." October 11, 2017. www.popeinmyanmar2017.com.

Ricklefs, M. C., Bruce Lockhart, Albert Lau, Portia Reyes, and Maitrii Aung-Thwin. 2010. *A New History of Southeast Asia.* Palgrace: McMillan.

2018. "Venn, Henry (1796–1873): Anglican Missions Administrator and Theorist." Boston University, History of Missiology. http://www.bu.edu/missiology/missionary-biography/t-u-v/venn-henry-1796–1873/.

Walls, Andrew. 1996. *The Missionary Movement in Christian History: Studies in the Transmission of Faith.* Maryknoll, NY: Orbis Books.

Wells, Kenneth. 1958. *History of Protestant Work in Thailand: 1828–1958.* Bangkok: Church of Christ in Thailand.

CHAPTER 10

Historic Highlights from Protestant Missions to Asian Buddhists

Alex G. Smith

Analyses of over five centuries of past missions to Buddhists reveal lessons for advance, both in encouragements and warnings. These affect future church planting productivities. The twenty-first century demands applying efficient methods and effective strategies to reach majority folk Buddhists, including most Chinese. This chapter will illustrate confirmations and spotlight cautions from past mission in Asia. God's workers used diverse strategies and tactics to reach Buddhists. My wide angled panorama observes a broad terrain of intercultural encounters. Analyzing history reveals valuable insights.

Mission Lessons from the Reformation Era 1500–1800

The sixteenth century Reformation dealt with a nominal, formalized, Christianized state church throughout Europe. Decadent pseudo-Christianity required renewed, personal commitments to Christ, a timely message for that era. Unfortunately, as re-evangelizing Europe took priority, reformers sadly neglected mission to the nations through strategic errors.

First, by rejecting monasteries, seen as corrupted, reformers did away with a key missionary structure from centuries past (Winter 1999:226). Eliminating the monastic system thereby ignored launching significant missions to unreached nations for about three centuries (Pierson 1999:263). Reformers failed to develop alternate structures for missions. Instead, their energies, resources and attention were engrossed in repelling the Catholic Counter Reformation (Neill 1964:220). At the same time Catholics increased mission endeavors, entering the new world alongside colonialism. Lesson: maintain mission sodalities.

“Eliminating the monastic system thereby ignored launching significant missions to unreached nations for about three centuries.”

A remarkable major Protestant exception was the Moravians. In 1732 Count Zinzendorf sparked a vigorous missionary vision, stimulating Moravians to reach unchurched peoples. This powerful movement sent members, often with their families to serve where Christ's message was absent. Within the first thirty years Moravians sent 226 missionaries to ten nations. Small missionary bands lived with the people, mostly evangelizing individuals. They started small churches in dozens of nations. Moravians set the model for future missions, strongly influencing William Carey and Hudson Taylor, pioneers to the coastlands and inlands respectively.

Second, as reformers restarted mission in the early nineteenth century, they changed earlier historical modes of evangelizing whole groups. Instead of biblical family ingatherings, reformers' primarily called individuals to salvation (Beaver 1999:244, 249). They garnered converts, one by one. Edwin Bliss affirmed that the method of early Christian mission “has been individual rather than general, personal rather than national” (1908:206). Consequently, isolated believers faced significant social problems in their communities. They stood out as loners before unbelieving families, relatives, and associates. This strategy produced gathered, disjointed churches of mostly unconnected individuals, which unbelievers viewed as “foreign” misfits.

God sometimes overruled the reformers' flawed strategy, ushering whole tribes and family-kinship groups into God's kingdom. Early Catholic missionaries like John Montecorvino served Buddhists and Mongols in Peking, China (1294–1328). Several thousand came to faith. In 1549 Francis Xavier entered Japan. A large movement occurred but was severely persecuted later (Beaver 1999:243). Other religious group movements also occurred. In 68 A.D. animistic Siamese converted en masse to Buddhism (Smith 2009:7) and in 1956 Hindu Dalit untouchables turned similarly to Buddhism (Sangharakshita 1986:127f).

Evaluating Modern Mission Era 1800-present

The Colonial Period accompanied the era of exploration. Christianized West occupied land after land. Missions followed under the ruling colonialists' protection and power. A mission mentality evolved declaring "to civilize is to Christianize." Mabie affirmed, "The legitimacy of foreign missions as the profoundest agency in the ongoing civilization of the world, is beyond question" (1908:86). Bliss wrote, "not even among the South Sea Islanders was 'the gospel of the clean shirt' more needed. With most, the very conception of orderly, and what to Americans seems decent, living had almost to be created by special instruction" (1908:206–207). Thus, colonial imperialistic approaches infected Christian mission. Contextualization rarely appeared on the church-planting horizon. Westernization and civilization did. Church services, ceremonies, and buildings were modeled after Western Christianity. National peoples viewed churches and local disciples as Western and thereby foreign.

Slowly Protestant missions emerged from the Reformation. In 1792 William Carey became the Father of Modern Missions. Influenced by diaries of navigator James Cook and impacted by colonial exploration, Carey went to India's Bengali area. Against great odds, including British commercial opposition and through much personal pain, the Serampore Trio (Carey, Ward, and Marsh) established a church. Proclaiming Christ's saving gospel was Carey's priority. In 1809 near Lal Bazaar, Calcutta they built their first church structure. Today, after 210 years it survives and still functions.

God sometimes overruled the reformers' flawed strategy, ushering whole tribes and family-kinship groups into God's kingdom.

Carey's 1792 landmark *Enquiry* argued, "Would not the spread of the gospel be the most effectual means of their civilization? Would that not make them useful members of society?" (1988:54). Poignantly Carey prioritized the gospel as agent to civilization. He also desired to improve economic, health, and living conditions in his adopted land. He established experimental gardens and introduced the best seeds and roots from England. Robert Speer wrote about Carey,

> The missionary methods which he advocates include agriculture, the introduction of good cattle, and promotion of the conscious interests of the people.... He engaged in the manufacture of indigo. He made the best type of paper in India. He devised new methods of paper-manufacture. He introduced the first steam engine erected in India. He began the first Indian newspaper (1933a:149–150).

Early missionaries like Judson and his wife exhibited incredible dedication despite tensions between Civilization and Christianity. In 1812, because of the British American War, they were forced to locate in Buddhist Burma. They faced horrendous trials under most difficult circumstances, including imprisonment (Smith 1999:7–8). Many fellow pioneers persevered, depending on God and faith. Under extreme situations they evangelized nations and initiated churches. Critics called it foolish folly. Despite all, the sacrificial lives of the pioneers sprouted sustainable, indigenous churches. Lessons call current missionaries in times of affluence and ease to exhibit equal perseverance.

Critics charged that missionaries destroyed cultures, de-cultured peoples, and dominated power structures. In some case, this was sadly true; unprincipled European traders and colonial authorities were the worst culprits devastating cultures and denigrating native peoples. They decimated the resources and disenfranchised peoples. For example, in mid-1500s Spanish explorers looted and enslaved Amerindian tribes and the British waged the infamous Opium Wars with China in the 1840s.

Headquarters' control of missions then centered in cities like New York or London. In 1865 Hudson Taylor reversed that, moving China Inland Mission's administrative decisions to the field of China. Today's Third World Mission Movement should beware lest they return to former patterns of similar control from centers like Singapore, Seoul, Sao Paulo, or Nairobi.

Weaknesses of early mission stations

The early dominant practice became gathering individual, isolated, and unconnected converts into protective compounds. This Mission Station approach provided safety and survival for missionaries and places of refuge and work for converts. Socially rejected believers often facing death threats found haven in mission compounds. The missionaries accepted, protected, healed, educated, and employed them so they could thrive. Hired as cooks, builders, teachers, printers, evangelists, catechists, and colporteurs, these lone believers formed the church (McGavran 1981:46–8).

Those quick to criticize Mission Station approaches, seldom recognize it was the only practical method for those adverse pioneer conditions, where survival was urgently paramount (Smith 1999:35–40). The problem was missionaries did not adapt better methods when conditions changed. Thus, small dependent ingrown churches developed. Usually significant group movements failed to emerge. McGavran reacted to weaknesses of "one by one against the tide," advocating rather catalyzing people movements in different strata of society and ethne (1981:39f). That lesson still needs reinforced implementation.

Conflicts about indigenous emphases

Possibly the most significant values for missions are indigenous church principles. On occasion, from Carey to today, indigenous methods were emphasized. Unfortunately, vested interests in Western and majority world agencies, funders, and administrative controllers sometimes keep indigenous methods on the sidelines, rather than at center stage.

Certainly, Carey desired to develop indigenous work. He encouraged local believers to take charge of ministry and multiply their witness widely. He established Serampore College to raise educational levels of aspiring native Christians and to influence Indian Hindus and Buddhists towards the gospel.

In the 1800s Rufus Anderson, Henry Venn, and John Nevius advocated indigenous principles. Thus, fresh methods of doing mission arose. This Three Self emphasis became a major thrust through the early 1900s (Brown 1950:33f, 291f). Roland Allen served in China after Nevius. Espousing Three Self methods, Allen also

> wanted the forms of the church to be adapted to local cultural conditions and not be imitations of Western Christianity. To accomplish this, missionaries would have to hand over responsibility to the local leaders in the community, who would not be professional clergy either in their training or in their compensation (Anderson 1998:12).

Ideally, churches were to be self-supporting from the beginning (Allen 1962:154–6). They should also be self-propagating and self-determining. Alan Tippett taught additional characteristics of indigenous churches, but Three Selfs were foundational (1973:148–163). Tippett emphasized the church's important self-image in its community, seeing "itself as *the* Church of Jesus Christ in its own local situation, mediating the work, the mind, the word and the ministry of Christ in its own environment" (ibid. 155). From early days Karen believers in Buddhist Burma modeled indigenous principles (Bliss 1908:262–3). Using indigeneity normally precluded inherent problems of "rice Christian" dependency that plagued Mission Station approaches (ibid. 291).

Nevius recognized that serious weakness in the context of Buddhist-influenced China. He advocated leaving believers in their settings to serve local communities rather than isolating or extracting them from their normal locations. Do not send them to some distant centers or institutions to be discipled or trained. Nevius maintained, "Christianity should not disturb the social relations of its adherents" (1958:19). Believers should "illustrate the Gospel in the spheres of life in which they were called" (ibid). From 1 Corinthians 7, Nevius suggested believers be self-supporting, remaining in professions they occupied when first accepting Christ. If farmers, then remain farmers. Also let them manage their own church fellowships as unpaid leaders and determine their Christian work. Indigenous believers were the best local witnesses, sharing Jesus with their extended families and friends. In the late 1880s, while some missionaries rejected this, many adopted Nevius' approach, particularly in China and Korea. Significantly, through applying Three Self methods, Korea and North Thailand produced significant growth, unusual in Buddhist nations.

"Indigenous believers were the best local witnesses, sharing Jesus with their extended families and friends."

However, Nevius' methods brought reactions. Some agencies, both Western and Asian, felt threatened, fearing loss of control. Indigeneity countered the status quo, especially relinquishing control in both raising and distributing funding. Indigenous principles also seemed to make institutional training establishments less relevant. Often the missionary establishment endorsed indigeneity but released little control. Unfortunately, these tensions still exist today.

Contention in three-fold foci for mission and evangelism

Christ's Great Commission led reformers into three major mission activities: proclaiming, teaching, and healing (Matt 9:35). Applying these they planted churches, established schools, and built hospitals, obeying the biblical mandate to evangelize, educate and heal (Smith 1999:36–40).

In time three-fold approaches led to tensions in priorities. What method was best? Some said, "Evangelize first, then educate Christians as agents of future nation transformation." Others advocated, "Educate non-believers so they may later become Christians and thereby influence nations for God" (1999:94–6). In Thailand during the late 1800s dissension and rifts divided workers, especially concerning prioritizing education of Buddhists. Pressure to choose evangelization or social betterment caused division and confusion. In time social, educating influences dominated (ibid).

Under Daniel McGilvary's "evangelize first" approach, the northern Thai church grew from 40 members in 1879 to 4,000 in 1911, and to 6,934 by 1914. All expected continuing increase (ibid). But after 1915 something prompted dramatic decreases in growth rate. The movement began to plateau through 1940. Sadly, after McGilvary died the education emphasis took priority over evangelistic church work. Missions built more schools and hospitals. To staff them with qualified teachers, many educated Thai pastors and Western missionaries were reassigned from church work to educational institutions. This caused neglect of nurturing new converts, paralyzing Thai church escalation. As insufficient nurture precipitated its plunge, annual average church growth rate plummeted to a mere 0.7 percent per annum (ibid. 158). At the same time, institutions grew steadily in number, name and fame (ibid. 161).

Sadly, that quarter century's membership stagnation was not due to a lack of receptivity. In fact, reaping remained strong, equal to previous decades. My research between 1913 and 1940 identified 16,132 new Thai converts plus another 8,627 school children were baptized. In 1913 Presbyterians had 6,921 members (ibid. 158). In 1940 it was 9,399, barely 2,500 net gain, despite 16,132 new adult baptisms. Sadly, the loss of 13,000 magnified reality that 82.7 percent of adult baptisms were not retained (ibid. 93f, 157–169). Had the majority of 25,000 new baptisms been preserved, the church would have potentially skyrocketed to 30,000 members. But lack of nurturing, pastoring, and discipleship caused grave loss and plateauing. Hundreds of new families came in the church's front door, only to leave out the back. Globally, early twentieth century missions experienced similar deceleration as the social gospel and education took precedence.

> "With prominence given to human services, proclaiming saving faith was often neglected or relegated a lower priority. The preference became works not words, deeds not beliefs, and action not faith."

With prominence given to human services, proclaiming saving faith was often neglected or relegated a lower priority. The preference became works not words, deeds not beliefs, and action not faith. Balancing both was needed. Changes in mission strategy can devastate church expansion. Clearly, sound discipling and nurture must accompany evangelistic receptivity. The lesson is never stop evangelizing in order to consolidate. Like double rails of train lines, both must be maintained in parallel tracks simultaneously alongside each other.

Changes in Post War Mission Organizational Structures

Using various methods and theologies, agencies and denominations working in the same field produced competitive confusion. One solution was "comity," a system for delegating spheres of influence (Bliss 1908:137–8). Prior to World War II comity carefully divided and distributed regions within countries to different mission organizations for exclusive development. However, after the war many newer agencies, independents and Pentecostal denominations entered mission fields. This stirred renewed vision and stimulated mission activity. But since newcomers had no assigned places in comity, they freely went anywhere they liked. Therefore, comity lost validity.

Throughout the Colonial Era National Missionary Councils were launched. The International Missionary Council of 1921 expressly declared that the "only bodies entitled to determine missionary policy are the missionary societies and boards, or the churches which they represent, and the churches in the mission field" (Rouse 1967:367). Thus, National Christian Councils represented both missionary agencies and church denominations. However, after World War II, new movements to gain independence among the younger churches in colonial countries brought structural changes for church and mission. The World Council of Churches was launced in 1948. Soon after, National Council of Churches replaced National Christian Councils. Thereafter, National Council of Churches (denominations only) eliminated missionary societies and muted their voices at national levels. This organizational change affected missions' future, particularly in conciliar denominations, not unlike reformers doing away with monasteries.

By the mid-1930s disgruntled attitudes towards mission increased, particularly after releasing Laymen's Foreign Missions Inquiry 1930–1932 (Rouse 1967:376). It leveled criticism at several areas of mission and strongly questioned methods. In January 1933 Robert Speer responded to these criticisms in *"Rethinking Missions" Examined.* Some of the Inquiry's critical influencers held that all religions were equal and arose from human seeking (Speer 1933b:27–35). The Inquiry advocated increased social service, a call to "fulfill the religious life of the Orient" (ibid. 28). Consequently, this reduced emphasis on the uniqueness of Christ because all non-Christian religions are "brothers in a common quest" (ibid). Negative criticisms in the Inquiry called for basic changes in age-long theology and demanded changes in methods. Many liberal missions and some evangelicals implemented these faulty recommendations. Christians should respect followers of other religions, but still maintain Christ's uniqueness.

In the mid-1900s, younger churches called for a moratorium on mission, coining the motto "Missionary go home." This coincided with Western nations calling for missionaries to return home to help their troubled churches. Many Western congregations experienced declining memberships, reduced resources, and burgeoning social problems. This precipitated new changes in missions. The national denominations wanted more control, but when asked if they desired workers or finances, they generally chose the latter. Had indigenous methods been solidly in place, this would not have been a question. Thus, through foreign funding many younger churches virtually became "indigenized" front churches for Western denominations. Consequently, boards gave funds to national churches and withdrew many expatriate missionaries. Those remaining became fraternal workers under control of denominations or NCC. This put deadly dampeners on apostolic mission. Churches became inward-looking, not outward focused.

Dynamics on world mission changed. National pastors claimed they alone should be evangelists to their own peoples. Fraternal workers should only fit into specific roles national churches assigned. Deciding such policies replaced Sovereign God, disparaging God's calling workers from all nations to be part of his global outreach to all barely reached peoples. Rouse wrote that new younger churches as "minorities in their respective peoples, were now strong enough to assume much of the burden not only of their own support and direction, but also of the evangelization of their respective lands" (Rouse 1967:370). This was flawed methodology, particularly for peoples with tiny percentages of Christians. Decades passed before these churches accepted significant responsibility for world mission.

Ethne or People Movements and Third World Missionaries

At the 1974 Lausanne II Congress on Evangelism, Ralph Winter emphasized six Unreached Blocs as major challenges for mission. Donald McGavran promoted working toward people movements to harvest unevangelized groups. Both stimulated a new vision and era for mission. Now it was no longer sufficient to see a Christian presence in each political nation only, but also vital to plant the church in every tribe, tongue, and people—*panta ta ethne*. This initiated new missions using modern methods such as mass media (literature, radio, film), hi-tech Bible translations, literacy projects, and also faith healing campaigns—often over television. It also gave rise to considerable canned methods of evangelism and discipling initiated in the West, and frequently exported as globally valid. Not all methods were culturally sensitive to the ethne.

Twentieth century concerns for more contextual approaches increased. Strangely, as Latourette indicated, this had roots in rising nationalistic mission churches with their response "of resentment of non-white peoples at white domination" (Latourette 1970:49). Largely, contextualization was

> initiated and promoted by missionaries and to that extent was artificial. Some of the nationals opposed adopting indigenous forms of architecture on the grounds that even when modified, these were associated with non-Christian traditions and so would compromise the Christian faith (1970:50).

Recent decades proliferated writings on contextualization like the C1–C6 continuum, insider movements, and others.

Past indigenous movements under Prophet Harris (Africa), Ko-Tha-Byu (Burma), and Cargo Cult leaders (Pacific Islands) exemplified insider models. They expected the gospel to permeate whole societies through indigenous agents, transforming communities into God's kingdom on earth.

Another exciting phenomenon of the last quarter century is rising majority world missions. China's Back to Jerusalem Movement for 100,000 missionaries is remarkable, though currently about 20,000. Like early Korean and Singaporean missions, initial efforts may take ethnocentric approaches. Time and experience will usually remedy that. Today's global church involves taking Christ to the whole world, often by independent individuals, inexperienced agencies, or ill-prepared churches. Applying lessons from history is urgently required.

Conclusion

The greatest mission challenge of this century is to apply adequate methods and effective strategies to reach majority folk Buddhists, including Chinese. Unfortunately, eighty-six percent of Buddhists do not personally know a single Christian (Johnson 2009:14–6). That should motivate believers to sacrifice comforts and live among them with perseverance, become genuine friends, be credible to them, pray for them, be sensitive to cultural contexts, and find gospel openness. God's best methods are still live human witnesses who exhibit God's transforming power.

To accomplish this requires revamping thinking and curriculum of seminaries and missionary training institutions. It requires changing Western academic models to more practical intercultural models and indigenous oriented communication. Furthermore, reducing academia's standards for laity and decentralizing their training will multiply resources for mission. Training to reach diaspora in homelands and ethne overseas includes non-traditional professional service. The Philippines is progressing in this, although academies still lag behind in adapting.

Adjustments revising curriculum in the 1970s Theological Education by Extension were not always applied adequately for indigenous churches or their intercultural missions. A revolution of practical training and appropriate courses will remedy that. Constricting regulations, standards, and accreditations are based on Western mentality. Make these more flexible and dynamic to meet practices for mission churches and indigenous agencies. A new generation of training methodology and revised practical curriculum for laity provide giant leaps forward for future missions to Buddhist frontiers.

Finally, careful reviews of warnings and encouragements from history's strategies already discussed provide lessons for future mission. Hopefully global majority world missions will not repeat past errors. Creative experimentation is encouraged, following biblical principles, testing, and evaluation before general adoption.

Set mission goals to plant reproducible indigenous churches and train members of functional congregations to serve and impact communities. Mobilizing mission thrusts can complete the urgent task of evangelizing all unreached Buddhist peoples in our generation.

References

Allen, Roland. 1962. *Missionary Methods: St Paul's or Ours?* Grand Rapids: Eerdmans.

Anderson, Gerald H. 1998. *Biographical Dictionary of Christian Mission.* Grand Rapids: Eerdmans.

Beaver, R. Pierce. 1999. "The History of Mission Strategy." In *Perspectives on the World Christian Movement: A Reader,* Third Edition. Ralph Winter and Steven Hawthorne, ed. Pasadena CA: William Carey Library.

Bliss, Edwin Munsell. 1908. *The Missionary Enterprise: A Concise History of its Objects, Methods and Extension.* New York: Fleming H Revell.

Brown, Arthur Judson. 1950. *The Foreign Missionary.* New York: Fleming H. Revell Company.

Carey, William. 1988. *An Enquiry into the Obligations of Christians to Use Means for the Conversion of the Heathens.* Dallas TX: Criswell Publications.

De Neui, Paul. 2009. *Communicating Christ in Asian Cities.* Pasadena: William Carey Library.

Hocking, William Earnest. 1932. "By the Commission of Appraisal." In *Rethinking Missions. A Laymen's Inquiry after One Hundred Years.* New York: Harper & Brothers.

Johnson, Todd M., and Kenneth R. Ross. 2009. *Atlas of Global Christianity 1910–2010.* Edinburgh: Edinburgh University

Latourette, Kenneth Scott. 1970. *A History of the Expansion of Christianity Vol. 7 Advance through Storm.* Grand Rapids: Zondervan.

Mabie, Henry C. 1908. *The Divine Right of Missions.* Philadelphia: American Baptist Publication Society.

McGavran, Donald A. 1981. *Bridges of God: A Study in the Strategy of Missions.* New York: Friendship.

Minutes of the International Missionary Council. 1921. Lake Mohonk, New York. Oct. 1–6.

Neill, Stephen. 1964. *A History of Christin Missions.* Harmondsworth, Middlesex, England: Penguin.

Nevius, John L. 1958. *The Planting and Development of Missionary Churches.* Philadelphia: The Reformed and Presbyterian Publishing.

Pierson, Paul. 1999. "A History of Transformation." In *Perspectives on the World Christian Movement: A Reader,* Third Edition. Ralph Winter and Steven Hawthorne, ed. Pasadena CA: William Carey Library.

Rouse, Ruth, and Stephen Charles Neill. 1967. *A History of the Ecumenical Movement 1517–1948.* Philadelphia: Westminster.

Sangharakshita. (Dennis P. E. Lingwood).1986. *Ambedkar and Buddhism.* Glasgow: Windhorse.

Smith, Alex G. 1999. *Siamese Gold: A History of Church Growth in Thailand: An Interpretive Analysis 1816–1982.* Bangkok: Kanok Bannasarn.

________. 2009. "Some Historical Views on Asian Urban Extension: Complexities of Urban and Rural Relationships." In *Communicating Christ in Asian Cities: Urban Issues in Buddhist Contexts.* Paul De Neui, ed. 1–39. Pasadena: William Carey Library.

Speer, Robert E. 1933a. *The Finality of Christ.* New York: Fleming H Revell.

________1933b. *"Re-thinking Missions" Examined.* New York: Fleming H. Revell Company.

Tippett, Alan R. 1973. *Verdict Theology in Missionary Theory.* Pasadena: William Carey Library.

Winter, Ralph D. 1999. "The Two Structures of God's Redemptive Mission." In *Perspectives on the World Christian Movement: A Reader,* Third Edition. Ralph Winter and Steven Hawthorne, ed. Pasadena CA: William Carey Library.

CHAPTER 11

Is Japan a Mud Swamp? Exploring Causes of *Kirishitan* Persecution in Japan's Edo Period

Eiko Takamizawa

In 1587 the "Ordinance of the Deportation of Christian Missionaries" entered into effect. Japan closed the country for almost three centuries against Christian mission until 1873 when the "Edict of Banning Christianity" was removed. During this period Roman Catholic believers, called *Kirishitan,* faced cruel persecution by national rulers throughout the country. By the end of Edo period (1603–1868) 700,000 converts were finally eliminated from Japan either by apostasy, exile, or martyrdom. The ways of persecuting *Kirishitans* were more atrocious than simple execution because the purpose of the persecution was not to eliminate the believers, but to demonstrate the consequences of becoming Christian. How could such brutal persecution happen on a national scale?

Shusaku Endo, author of the historical novel, *The Silence*, had his apostatized missionary confess, "This country is a more terrible swamp than you can imagine. Whenever you plant a sapling in the swamp the roots begin to rot; the leaves grow yellow and wither. And we have planted the sapling of Christianity in this swamp" (1999:147). Was it Japanese cultural soil that caused such cruel and atrocious persecution for three centuries? Japanese culture is known for its resistance against foreign beliefs and practice as well as a strong loyalty to the Japanese worldview. But are there other factors in the Christian mission approached that triggered such long and atrocious persecution in Japan? This chapter revisits the interaction between the Japanese rulers and the Roman Catholic missionaries to explore the causes that led to the severe persecution of the *Kirishitan* and the closure of Christian mission in the Shoku-Ho and Edo period.

Historical Setting

In Europe, the fifteenth and sixteenth centuries were the age of "Imperio Portogues." The improvement of navigation technology gave birth to the onset of the Great Seaway for European nations. Portugal first colonized Africa and accumulated wealth through slave trade. She expanded her territory to Latin America and Asia by dominating the sea. This was paralleled with the expansion of Roman Catholic territory as a Counter Reformation movement. Within Roman Catholic nations, Spain competed with Portugal and eventually divided the whole world by the Papal Line of Demarcation in 1493. (Parry 1982:194). Later, King Phillip II annexed Portugal and continued to colonize Asian nations with the aid of Roman Catholic missionaries. In the seventeenth century however, England and the Netherlands took over the Portuguese colonies. This rivalry among European nations lies as the backdrop of the Japanese encounter with the Christian mission.

"Japan encountered Christianity in a period of continuous battles and intrigue."

Roman Catholic Missionaries arrived in Japan in 1549 during an era of civil war. The warlords, called *Daimyo*, fought against one another to achieve rule over the nation. Among them were Nobunaga Oda (1534–1582), Hideyoshi Toyotomi (1537–1615), and Ieyasu Tokugawa (1543–1616). Political alliances and betrayals ran rampant among the daimyos, throughout the imperial court, and even amidst some religious groups. It was Nobunaga who firstly achieved victory in these wars and contributed to the unification of the nation in the sixteenth and seventeenth centuries. Japan encountered Christianity in a period of continuous battles and intrigue. In such political milieu the introduction of the matchlock gun by Portuguese merchants six years prior to the arrival of Jesuit missionaries opened the door for missionaries to easily enter Japan. For the daimyos, who craved stronger weapons to win over their rivals, the high-quality European arms and artifacts were of immense attraction to Japanese leaders. Missionaries often found themselves acting as mediators between the daimyos and the European traders. For the Japanese daimyos, missionaries were not only the evangelists of the new religion for spiritual salvation, but also the ones who brought great opportunity to obtain the advanced artifacts and weaponry of Europe (Nakamura 2009).

The Initial Success of Jesuits Mission and Nobunaga Oda

Francisco Xavier and his team came to Japan from India in 1549. Xavier employed the adaptation method in his mission toward the Japanese, unlike the colonization method used in Latin America. With this humble attitude, Xavier approached the local rulers in Yamaguchi district to obtain permission for propagation. He preached the simple Christian doctrine and some ethical teaching against immoral practices among Japanese men. He continued the teaching in the street twice a day, and within two months, 500 Japanese were baptized and a church was founded in this district. During his term of two years and three months, approximately 1000 were baptized, and the number increased further within a short period of time following (Kurokawa 2014). Xavier emphasized cultural sensitivity in his mission approach to the Japanese. His follower, Cosme de Torres, adapted Japanese silk clothing and a diet of fish and vegetables without meat. Luis de Almeida together with Gasper Torres followed Xavier's adaptation approach and began social services for the poor including a general hospital and orphanages. This respectful attitude of missionaries attracted more Japanese to the new religion (ibid). Xavier's letter to Ignatius Loyola lists his view on the qualifications for the Japanese missionaries: refined character and knowledge that produces endurance, patience, humility, sacrificial spirit, and perseverance to endure persecution, philosophy and apologetics as well as astrological knowledge (Higashibaba 2006:10). Xavier's positive opinion about the Japanese and his humble approach to them opened more opportunities for Jesuits for propagation of the Christian faith in Japan.

Nobunaga Oda was the first daimyo who conquered the rivals and became the national ruler, the "Tenka bito," [The One Who Rules the Whole World] in that period. Religious groups also held great power in those days and the monks at Hieizan Enryakuji Temple had formed a quasi-kingdom with its own territory overseen by its own military. Nobunaga abhorred this movement of corrupt Buddhist monks with their secular ambitions. In 1571 Nobunaga attacked Hieizan Enryakuji Temple and killed a few thousand Buddhist monks and followers including women and children. He also persecuted a cult called, "Nagashima Ikko Shu" by burning more than twenty thousand followers. Nobunaga's criticism against Buddhists was recorded in the diary of his subject. "(Monks) were shamelessly and fearlessly indulging in lusts and gluttony and controlling the local rulers" (Shincho Koki, n.d.).

It was in this context that Nobunaga first met Christian missionaries. He appreciated the sincere commitment of the priests and the Christians expressed through the serious propagation of their faith even at the risk of their lives (Nakamura 2009). Nobunaga invited missionaries many times into his court to learn about the situation in Europe and to learn about Christian beliefs as well. Among them were Cosme de Torres, Gnecchi-soldo Organtino, Alessandoro Valignano, Luis Frois, and other Jesuit missionaries. Andrew Ross records the positive impression the missionaries left with Nobunaga, "each proved to be good speakers of Japanese and extremely scrupulous with regard to matters of Japanese etiquette, they were able to gain permanent access to the dictator" (1994:52). Nobunaga became a fan of European culture and wore a European coat on public occasions. He used Western artifacts such as clocks and the globe, not to mention Western armor, helmets, guns, canons, and other military materials and employed an African man arranged by the missionaries as his own guard (Russell 2008:24).

Jesuit missionaries after Xavier also employed the adaptation policy and tried to enculturate into Japanese life and society: learning Japanese religious customs, wearing silk priestly clothes, and keeping the Japanese diet without meat in their lifestyle. However, the Superior in Japan, Francisco Cabral, arrived in Japan and instead took the colonial approach—prioritizing European style over that of the Japanese. Cabral did not allow missionaries to learn the Japanese language nor Japanese to learn Portuguese. He discriminated against Japanese believers by depriving them of opportunities for education and would not admit Japanese to leadership. Cabral's negative attitude created so much internal conflict between missionaries and Japanese believers that Valignano, the itinerary Supervisor over Asia, needed to come and remove Cabral from his position. His successors Gasper Coelho and Valignano tried to recover from the chaos Cabral had created, but the damage was done. Nobunaga met these Jesuit missionaries including Cabral more than twenty-seven times, but never became a Christian (Higashibaba 2001:126). It is possible that Nobunaga held some suspicion of European colonialism behind the missionaries' activities, which he could see in their colonization of the nations in Southeast Asia: Portugal colonized Goa in 1510 and Malacca in 1511; Spain colonized Manila in 1565. Nobunaga learned about Christian doctrine and appreciated their teaching and religious life to the point that he allowed missionaries to build a *Seminario* in his territory. However, in the last years of his life he started deifying himself and claimed to be the only deity in the universe. He made his birthday a Holy Day and made his subjects worship a stone that represented him on the Holy Day (Nosco 1997:40–41). It was only a few weeks right after these acts that Nobunaga's life ended in a famous betrayal incident by his closest subject, Mitsuhide Akechi in 1582.

Change of Attitude Toward Christians under Hideyoshi

Hideyoshi Toyotomi, a subject of Nobunaga, became "Kampaku Dajo Daijin," the minister of the nation in 1586. His encounters with Christianity were mainly of four kinds: direct encounter with the missionaries, confrontation by missionaries and a European navigator, the report by the Tensho European Envoy, and contextualized Christian teaching in the Tea Ceremony instructed by his Tea master, Senno Rikyu.

His first reaction toward Christian mission was the same as that of Nobunaga's. Hideyoshi appreciated the Christian teachings. However, his interests were more in the material and military benefits given through the missionaries than in spiritual matters. Hideyoshi had a great ambition to take control over the entire nation not just some territories that Nobunaga had ruled. Hideyoshi made political strategies such as, "Katana Gari [sword hunting],"which deprived people of their right to carry weapons, "Taiko Kenchi [Hideyoshi's Land Survey]," which examined each daimyo's land for systematizing taxation, and "Hitobarai Rei [National Census for Military Organization]" which controlled social status of people and enhanced his military power. He also had ambitions of expanding his control to the continent. In order to achieve his ambition, stronger weapons and gunpowder were crucial. Hideyoshi, therefore, showed great interests in maintaining good relationship with missionaries as mediators for trade and as possible military allies.

Regarding Christian belief, Hideyoshi also showed interest in Christian teachings. He once said to a missionary, "If Christianity does not condemn those who have mistresses, I may become one" (Boxer 1967:135). He was known for his loose morality regarding women. He enjoyed the European artifacts brought by missionaries. Like Nobunaga, he used European style armor. Upon meeting missionary Coelho, Hideyoshi offered the generous permission of free propagation of Christianity and building of churches in his territory with the condition that missionary would arrange two Portuguese battleships for Hideyoshi. This was for the expedition to Kyushu area and eventually to Korea and China. Coelho consented to arrange the ships and received a verbal permission to propagate Christianity throughout the nation. However, Coelho failed to get agreement from the Portuguese side and could not arrange the two ships as he promised. In spite of this disappointment, Hideyoshi made an expedition in 1586 to Kyushu in order to subdue rival daimyos in the area. Upon arrival in Kyushu, he discovered that a significant number of daimyos had converted to Christianity and some were aggressive in making his subjects Kirishitans. The first Kirishitan Daimyo in Japan, Sumitada Omura, who was baptized by Cabral, persecuted Buddhists monks and Shinto priests, and destroyed Buddhist temples and Shinto shrines. Sumitada even dedicated the Nagasaki port to the Jesuits as a church property. Ukon Takayama, another Kirishitan daimyo who was Hideyoshi's close subject, was also found to have persuaded his samurais to convert to Christianity. Observing this impact of Christianity in his kingdom, Hideyoshi sent an open letter to all Jesuits with four questions. 1. Why are the "Padres" so desirous to make converts, and why do they use force on such occasions? 2. Why do they destroy Shinto shrines and Buddhist temples and persecute bonzes instead of accommodating them? 3. Why do they eat useful and valuable animals like horses and cows? 4. Why do the Portuguese buy many Japanese and export them from their native lands as slaves? The following year, Hideyoshi installed an edict to expel all "Padres" from Japan, and the next day he issued his edict to ban Christianity. This was the turning point of Hideyoshi confirming his suspicions against missionaries and their activities (Kanda 2011:100).

After changing his attitude toward Christianity, Hideyoshi punished his two prominent individuals: Ukon Takayama and Tea Master, Sen no Rikyu. Ukon had converted to Christianity and had begun spreading his influence among his subjects as mentioned above. Hideyoshi commanded Ukon and other Kirishitan daimyos to abandon the Christian faith, but Ukon chose Christianity over Hideyoshi's order at the cost of his position, property, and life. Hideyoshi expelled Ukon from his position and territory. Rikyu was a tea master and a close friend for Hideyoshi in his tea circle. Rikyu's wife became Kirishitan and his five core disciples out of seven also became Kirishitan. Rikyu was the most popular tea master of the day and developed a new form of tea ceremony called "Wabi Cha." Toshio Takahashi observes the Christian influence in Rikyu's tea philosophy (2007:42–60). George Van Driem also writes that Jesuit missionaries try to adapt Japanese culture, especially the tea ceremony as a good way to contextualize the Holy Communion service. He explains, "Because of the solemnity of Japanese ritual, the tea ceremony presented to Jesuits with what they assessed to be the most fitting native cultural vector that would be conductive to the dissemination of Christian teaching and liturgy" (2019:277).

Many historians including contemporary Tea Masters who are the successor of Sen no Rikyu recognize similarities between the Japanese Tea Ceremony and the Christian Mass, although the view on the degree of the Rikyu's involvement in Christian faith differs (Yamato 2009). After expelling Ukon, Hideyoshi suddenly ordered Rikyu to commit "hara-kiri." No concrete reason was found for this severe punishment. However, there is a possibility that Hideyoshi became furious and took severe acts toward Rikyu, if Hideyoshi discovered that Rikyu implemented Christian teachings in the tea ceremony as a hidden message (Henmi 2018).

Another significant influence that might have changed Hideyoshi's attitude toward Christianity was a report from the Tensho European envoys organized by Valignano in 1582. In this trip, Valignano took four Japanese young boys, the sons of Kirishitan daimyos, Mansho Ito, Martino Hara, Julian Nakaura, and Miguel Chijiwa to Europe. The purpose of this trip was two-fold: to introduce Japan and Jesuit's activities in Japan to the European world in order to raise financial support for the Jesuit mission work in Japan. The other purpose was to show the prosperity of Christian civilization in Europe to future Japanese leaders. The trip took eight years. On the way to Europe, the boys were trained in language, Western manners, music, and knowledge about Europe. They met King Phillip II and Pope Gregory XIII and were welcomed with parades by governors from different regions from all over Europe (E-Kokuho 2019). King Phillip II was impressed with the quality of the Japanese swords the boys carried and recognized the huge potential in Japan. He welcomed them to the European community by granting Roman citizenship to one of them. However, Valignano's wish to raise funds to expand mission activities in Japan was not fully achieved. This led the missionaries in Japan to engage more in trading. The envoy returned to Japan after eight years when Hideyoshi took rule. The boys were invited by Hideyoshi and played Western chamber music before him and reported on their experiences in Europe. One of the topics was about the Japanese slaves sold in slave markets in Europe. In those days the price of one barrel of gun power was fifty slaves (Onizuka 2006). Hideyoshi's attitude toward Christian mission changed after he heard these boys' report the bad treatment of Japanese slaves all over Europe. Hideyoshi included the topic of slave trade in the public questions to Jesuits. In the same year, Hideyoshi issued the decree of banning missionaries and interdiction of the slave trade.

In 1596, a Spanish galleon headed for Mexico, the San Phillippe, was shipwrecked near Japan and asked for help from the local authorities. Hideyoshi, who previously had assisted wrecked ships, changed his attitude and confiscated all the freight. He sent a letter to inform the crew that he has heard from Portuguese Jesuit missionaries that the Spanish are pirates and had colonized Peru, Mexico and Philippines and that they were trying to do the same to Japan (Yoshida 1708:1632). Believing this word against the Spanish, Hideyoshi took a firm attitude against the Spanish ship that had Franciscans, Dominicans, and Augustinians on board. Being aware of Hideyoshi's attitude, the navigator of the San Philippe challenged Japanese authority by showing in his world atlas vast Spanish territories spread all over the world in contrast to the tiny nation of Japan.

The following year, 1587, Hideyoshi martyred twenty-six Kirishitans and missionaries, including children in Nagasaki, as the first Kirishitan martyrdom in Japanese history. Hideyoshi, who ruled as the supreme authority over Japan, died of an unknown sickness in 1598. Some suspect poisoning by European arsenic, others believe he died of venereal disease according to the record of his death by the Jesuit scribe of Japanese history, Luis Frois.

Severe Persecution under Tokugawa and His Successors

Ieyasu Tokugawa was the most capable and powerful warrior after Hideyoshi died. Daimyos formed the East Army under Ieyasu and the West Army under Mitsunari Ishida and fought over the position of supreme power at the battle of Sekigahara in 1600. The East Army had 75,000 soldiers against the West one with 85,000, and the former won within a half day. One of the reasons for the victory of the East Army was due to a series of complex alliances and internal betrayals among local daimyos who eventually joined the East Army. However, there were Western powers behind both armies: Spain and Portugal supported the West Army, and England supported the East Army.

England appeared in Japanese history from the time of Ieyasu. William Adams, the navigator for a Dutch Ship, the Liefde, arrived in Japan at this time. Hearing this news, the Jesuits strongly suggested the authority to execute Williams and his crew. However, Ieyasu met with Williams and learned about the conflict between Roman Catholic nations against Protestant nations in Europe. Ieyasu was impressed with William's honest sharing about the European situation and appointed him as his personal translator and negotiator. Ieyasu gave him a Japanese name, "Anjin Miura" (Suzuki 2019). This was the moment that Protestant nations in Europe joined Japanese trading. Ieyasu preferred English and Dutch Protestant groups who did not emphasize religious propaganda as much as the Spanish and Portuguese whose main members were the Jesuits and other Roman Catholic orders. Ieyasu was well aware of the political situation among the European nations by this time. As the number of Kirishitan daimyos and samurai was increasing continuously, he ordered a census of all Kirishitans in his dynasty. He found that at least fourteen of his major subjects were believers. Knowing the dedication of Kirishitan daimyos under Nobunaga and Hideyoshi, Ieyasu became very cautious of the connections of these daimyos with European powers.

Although Ieyasu and the Japanese leaders were well aware of the political intentions and the threat of European powers, the trading benefits from the interaction with European merchants and missionaries still remained strong. In 1608, the crew of a Japanese trading ship had a conflict in Macao. The Portuguese captain, Mor Andrea Pessoa, subdued the conflict at the cost of the lives of many Japanese crew members. The following year, Captain Mor visited Japan to give an apology and to negotiate treaties. Unintentionally, he became the target of revenge by Ieyasu. Those days, the Portuguese merchants controlled the trading of raw silk between Macao and Japan which Ieyasu did not want to lose. However, Spanish merchants promised a raw silk trade with Japan, and Ieyasu decided to attack the Deus, a Portuguese trading ship. Pessoa died in the explosion of the ship. These incidents between European traders and missionaries made the Tokugawa authority more suspicious of the European attempt to colonize Japan.

"The banning of Christianity was issued in 1612, followed by the expelling of the "Padres" from Japan."

The banning of Christianity was issued in 1612, followed by the expelling of the "Padres" from Japan. There was a rumor that Kirishitan daimyos and samurais would attack the Tokugawa Shogunates around that time. In 1614, foreign trading was limited to only Dejima and Hirato in Kyushu. The persecution became harsh when Ieyasu, the influential ruler died in 1616. Hidetada Tokugawa, the second Shogun, further promoted the persecution of Christianity by prohibiting all daimyos to have Kirishitan subjects or believers in their territories. Those who had relationships with Padres and Kirishitans had their property confiscated and members were tortured and sometimes burned to death. With this harsh attitude of the Shogun Hidetada, many daimyos who once were sympathizers of Christianity turned into persecutors (Pagges 1940:7). In 1619, his "Banning of Christianity" was issued and fifty-two Kirishitans were martyred in Kyoto, which was followed by fifty-five martyrs in Nagasaki, the Kirishitan district. In the next four years, Kirishitans in Edo and Tohoku areas were also martyred. Even in Hirato, where European trading was allowed, thirty-eight believers were martyred (Ross 1994:52).

Fumie was the tool used to find Kirishitans. A fumie was made of either stone, wood, or paper with an icon image on it of Jesus Christ crucified. The Tokugawa dynasty commanded local rulers to interrogate all village members by asking them to trample on the Fumie image with their feet. Those who hesitated to do so were identified as Kirishitan and punished with persecution.

During such harsh oppression, a riot occurred in Shimabara area in Kyusu. It was a farmers' riot against the atrocious rulers who had imposed high taxes and oppression against the farmers. The inhabitants under this local ruler who were severely oppressed were mostly Kirishitans. The leader of the riot was Shiro Amakusa, one believed to be appointed by God. He led the resistant movement as a young Japanese boy of seventeen. In his profiles, he is always shown wearing a neck covering, an adopted Western custom. This shows his connection to European power. In this riot, Shiro called the Kirishitans all over Japan to stand against the Shogunate, communicating the promise of the Portugal military ships to support this Kirishitan resistance. Approximately 40,000 villagers were besieged in Hara castle waiting for the Portuguese ships to rescue them. However, Portuguese ships did not arrive. Instead, the Shogun Iemitsu sent 120,000 troops to subdue this riot in a rural village in Kyushu and used Dutch ships to threaten the resistant to assure no possibility of a Portuguese rescue. About 40,000 Kirishitans were massacred in the castle and only one escaped by apostasy. After this incident, Kirishitans tried to hide themselves by escaping into remote islands or areas, or by disguising their faith as Buddhists or Shintoists using modified icons such as Maria Kannon, Mary Buddha. These believers were called *Kakure Kirishitan*, Hidden Christians. They survived in hiding during the period of persecution and the closure of the nation called, "Sakoku," (Chaining Nation period), until the country was forced to re-open by the American Black Ship led by Mathew Perry in 1858.

Summary and Conclusion

This brief overview of the Christian encounter with three national rulers in the premodern period of Japan reveals the Christian contribution to the atrocious persecution toward Kirishitans. Firstly, missionaries presented a version of the gospel that was intertwined with political and economic intentions. Although the missionaries came to Japan with genuine dedication to God, even at the risk of their lives, their dedication was not free from the political and economic agenda of the Roman Catholic Church in Europe of the day. The fact was that missionaries' arrival was followed by merchants and trading, and it eventually led to military occupation as seen throughout Asian and other parts of the world. Japanese rulers were cautious of the development of international relationships through missionaries.

Secondly, the integrity of Christians was questioned when Japanese rulers found out that missionaries and Kirishitan daimyos were aggressively forcing the Japanese to convert to Christianity. Temples and shrines were destroyed and monks and priests were persecuted by Kirishitan daimyos. Even many of them were involved in slave trading for the sake of gunpowder and other merchandise from the continent. Missionaries who built hospitals and orphanages in Japanese societies were at the same time mediators for slave trading. Several edicts banning Christianity referred to the slave trade, especially the Tensho Envoy that reported seeing Japanese female slaves sold like animals in Europe. Hearing of this, Japanese rulers further enforced the persecution of Christian missionaries and their followers.

The discrepancy of the life of missionaries and Kirishitans might have contributed to the suspicion of the Japanese rulers about Christianity. The impact of Christianity was evidenced by a rapid expansion, the conversion of numerous local rulers and samurai especially in the west area of Japan. Some of the converts forced conversion upon their subjects. Villagers were forced to become converts and persecuted those who do not obey including other religious groups. This aggressive attitude challenged the Japanese identity.

Japanese who value harmony could have sensed the hypocrisy and ungodliness among Christians.

Thirdly, any level of internal conflict among believers damages the Christian testimony. The conflicts between Roman Catholic orders: Jesuits, Franciscan, Dominican, and Augustinian, Portugal and Spain, and the bigger conflict between Roman Catholic and Protestant Church, shadowed the heart of Christian mission under political aspirations. Japanese who value harmony could have sensed the hypocrisy and ungodliness among Christians. Internal conflicts among Christian orders halted Christian expansion. That the mission orders were in conflict with one another was symptomatic of the political conflicts from the nations and denominations from which they came: Spain versus Portugal, England versus Netherlands, Roman Catholic versus Protestant, and the list goes on. All this raised serious questions and suspicion among Japanese rulers.

Fourthly, this internal conflict demonstrated another aspect despised by the Japanese. These conflicts were actually expressions of the superiority complex of European ambition and Western colonialist intentions over Japan. The condescending attitude by Europeans toward the Japanese damaged the trust built by humble and sincere missionaries. Cabral's colonial policy once practiced in Japan left a very negative image of Christianity to the Japanese. Others who approached Japan with arrogance and a prideful attitude that did not accommodate to Japanese religious life and customs were seen as a threat to Japanese peace.

Japanese rulers were interested in Christianity and its teachings and appreciated the commitment the missionaries and believers demonstrated and lifestyle dedicated to God. However, when the rulers sensed political and economic attempts expressed in condescending attitudes, this reinforced suspicions that the dangers of colonization were inextricably intertwined with the Christian faith, and therefore they reacted harshly. The Japanese rulers were observing other Asian nations where Christianity was introduced and eventually were overruled by European nations.

Fifthly, as we observed in Senno Rikyu's tea ceremony having similarity with Christian communion service, such a strategy of contextualization could be regarded as a deception of Christians. This could create hostility in non-believers, especially if the main message imbedded in the ceremony was primarily Christian belief. Lee Hung-Koo addresses the concern for this danger of the Insider Movement strategy (2011:258).

Lastly, the dedication of the Kirishitans became a threat to the authorities. When the persecutions accelerated, many believers did not give up their commitment to God in spite of the suffering and martyrdom they might go through. The Japanese rulers felt threatened by the dedication and the commitment of the Kirishitans to God over Japanese rulers. Japanese religions basically function to bless the nation and the rulers as well as the people. Religions serve human beings. The Christian faith, however, demands total commitment and dedication of the believers to God.

The dedication of Nagasaki to the church by the first converts might have caused a great fear of losing the nation. This was neither comprehensible nor acceptable to the ordinary Japanese.

"Are the denominations and mission agencies free from any rivalry or competition with other Christian denominations and groups? Do Christian missions and missionaries today keep Christian integrity in our ministries and life as God's agents in our words, deeds, and lifestyle?"

The long and severe persecution against Christians in the Premodern Era in Japan was not necessarily because of the resistance by Japanese indigenous cultural soil, but also because of the un-Christian approach by the Christian mission and the Kirishitan daimyos. This chapter explains that Japanese rulers rejected Christianity and persecuted Christians atrociously because Christianity was already smeared by the mud of human greed and the filth of pride in their mission to Japan.

The sad history of Roman Catholic mission in Japan throws questions to today's Protestant mission, too. Are Protestant missions free from political and economic agendas intertwined or hidden in their propagation? Are the denominations and mission agencies free from any rivalry or competition with other Christian denominations and groups? Do Christian missions and missionaries today keep Christian integrity in our ministries and life as God's agents in our words, deeds, and lifestyle? One hope that a review of this history will inspire is that the blood of these martyrs will be the seed for revival of the church. We hope that this seed will blossom into full bloom in Japan in the future.

References

Boxer, C. R. 1967. *The Christian Century in Japan 1549–1650.* Berkley: University of California.

E-Kokuho. 2019. "Tensho Kenou Shisetsu Ki." National Museum. http://www.emuseum.jp/detail/100816/000/000.

Endo, Junko. 1999. "Reflections on Shusaku Endo and Silence." *Christianity and Literature.* 48 (2) 145–48.

Gonoi, Takashi. 1990. *Nihon Kirisuto Kyoshi.* Tokyo: Yoshikawa Kobunkan.

________. 2002. *Nihon Kirishitanshi no Kenkyu.* Tokyo: Yoshikawa Kobunkan.

Henmi, Munekuni. 2018. "The Influence of Christianity in Tea Ceremony." Miyagi: Tomitani Church, unpublished speech given September 22.

Higashibaba, Ikuo. 2001. *Christianity in Early Modern Japan: Kirishitan Belief and Practice.* Leiden: Brill.

________. 2006a. *Kirishitan Daimyoshi Saikou: Shinko Juyo no Shukyogaku.* Tenri: Tenri Daigaku Oyasato Kenkyujo.

________. 2006b. *Kirishitan Shi Saikou: Shinko Juyo no Shukyogaku.* Osaka: Oyasato Kenkyujo.

Hun-tae, Chang. "A Biblical Model for Missionary Ethics." *Gospel and Mission.* 14 (1) 291.

Kanda, Chisato. 2011. "Bateren Tsuiho ni Kansuru Ichikousatsu: Luis Frois no Bunsho wo Chushinni. [A Study of Bateren Deportation Order: Exploring the Documents by Luis Frois]." *Bungakubu Journal, Shigakuka Hen.* 37 (1) 65–110.

Kurokawa, Tomobumi. 2014. *Christian Mission in Japanese History: Mission Activities and Figures.* Tokyo: Kyobunkan.

Lee, Hoon-Koo. 2011. "A Study on God's Mission in the Book of Daniel." *Gospel and Mission.* 14 (1) 233–60.

Nakamura, Bin. 2009. *Nihon Kirisutokyo Senkyo Shi: Xavier kara Konnichi made.* Tokyo: Inochino Kotoba Sha.

Nosco, Peter. 1997. *Confucianism and Tokugawa Culture.* Honolulu, HI: University Hawaii.

Onizuka, Hideaki. 2006. *Tenno no Rozario: Nihon Kirisutokyo Koku Ka no Sakuryaku.* Tokyo: Seiko Shobo.

Pagges, Leon. 1938. *Nihon Kirishitan Daimyo Shumonshi,* Trans. by Kogoro Yoshida. Tokyo: Iwanami Bunko.

Parry, John Horace. 1982. *The Age of Reconnaissance: Discovery, Exploration and Settlement.* Oakland, CA: University of California.

Ross, Andrew C. 1994. *A Vision Betrayed: The Jesuits in Japan and China, 1542–1742.* Maryknoll, NY: Orbis.

Russell, John G. 2008. "Excluded Presence: Shoguns, Minstrels, Bodyguards, and Japan's Encounter with Black Others." *Zinbun.* 40 (March) 15–51.

Suzuki Kahoru. N.d. "Supein Gaiko to Uraga Minato." https://www.klnet.pref.kanagawa. jp/digital_archives/kyoudo_kanagawa/kyoudo_kanagawa052_suzuki.pdf.

Takahashi, Toshio. 2007. *Busho Takayama Ukon no Shinko to Cha no Yu.* Tokyo: Inochi no Kotobasha, Forest.

Van Driem, George. 2019. *The Tale of Tea: A Comprehensive History of Tea from Prehistoric Times to the Present Day.* Leiden: Brill.

Yamato Shohei. 2009. "Chano Yu no Michi ha Seisho ni Tsuzuku: Senno Rikyu ha Kurisuchandatta [Tea Ceremony leads to the Bible]: Senno Rikyu was a Christian." VIP Kansai International. Unpublished lecture given March 8.

Yoshida Kosei. 1708. *Tosa Monogatari.* Chosokabe: Motochika Ki.

CHAPTER 12

The Lasting Impact of Christianity upon China from the Taiping Uprising

Cristian Dumitrescu

The relationship between Chinese history and missionary Christianity is complex. Some political and economic rebellions in China's history have been associated with the way the Christian message influenced certain individuals to become revolutionaries. For example, the Taiping Rebellion's leaders were influenced by Christian missionaries, and the ideology of the revolt was clearly based on biblical teachings. The rebellion, although aiming to upset the Qing dynasty, is not remembered today as a political one. Most historians refer to the Taiping movement as a religious movement influenced by a foreign religion. Such an attempt to abandon the Confucian and Buddhist teachings at the time was seen as blasphemy to both the Chinese Empire and to its traditional religions. However, the Taiping movement attempted to contextualize Christianity for the Chinese. This chapter presents some of the successful contextualization attempts, as well as some lessons contemporary workers in China need to learn in order to avoid the mistakes of Hong Xiuquan and his "Heavenly Kingdom."

The Beginnings

The Taiping Uprising was indissolubly linked to Hong Huoxiu, later known as Hong Xiuquan. Hong came from what we would call today a dysfunctional family in Hua county of rural China, thirty miles north of Canton. The Hongs were from the Hakka group, a minority considered "guest people." What mainly differentiated Hakkas from the other Chinese was that their women did not practice foot binding, and they married strictly within their own tribe (Spence 1994:25). Hakkas came from the plains of central China and considered their language to be "in direct descent from the purest language of ancient Chinese civilization" (26). They followed the teaching of Confucius, but the popular practices were a mixture of folk Buddhism and animism.

After Hong Xiuquan's mother died his father remarried; there were no siblings from the second marriage. Hong lived with his two older brothers, their wives, and an older sister. Hong Xiuquan himself went through the pain of losing his first wife from an arranged marriage. He was a passionate student and researcher and became a teacher at the local village school.

Following the tradition of many of his ancestors, Hong Xiuquan diligently prepared to take the rigorous state examinations in order to become a magistrate. The exam was comprised of the sixteen Confucian principles considered essential for the education of the people. In 1836, at age twenty-two, Hong joined the many other contestants in Canton for the ceremonies and the examinations. However, on the way to the examination, Hong passed by a couple of men that were going to change his destiny. One of them was a Protestant missionary, Edwin Stevens, the other man was a Chinese Christian convert, Stevens' translator. They distributed Christian tracts written in Chinese by their first convert, Liang Afa. Hong took some of the materials but was too busy to carefully study them, his mind being focused on the exams ahead. However, something struck Hong in that brief glance: the Chinese character for his name was part of the table of contents, both in the story of Noah and in that of Lot. He returned home not passing the second phase of the examinations.

The Heavenly Vision

The following year, Hong tried again to pass the state examinations, only to fail once more. On his way home he felt exhausted, a complete failure. He called on his family to see them for what he believed would be his last time. While he was there saying his parting words, he feared that because of his failure he would end up in hell. He had a dream expecting to meet all the mythical creatures described in the *Jade Records,* a popular nineteenth century Chinese religious tract that describes the tortures and torments of the underworld. In his dream he was welcomed by a woman who called herself his heavenly mother who, after purifying him, sent him to meet one who was called his heavenly father who gave him a golden seal and a sword to fight evil spirits. In an ensuing cosmic battle, he was joined by an elderly brother. Although apparently victorious, he was sent by his heavenly father to continue the fight on earth, where evil spirits brought havoc and confused people. When waking up, Hong Xiuquan announced that he was the heavenly king, terrifying his entire earthly family. Finally, Hong calmed down, but the dream and vision remained alive in his memory.

In the meantime, the Opium War took place between 1839 and 1842 around Canton. The scenes of massacre and pure evil on both the British and the Chinese sides left Hong Xiuquan with many questions unanswered. It was not until 1843, when a friend and distant relative, Li Jingfang, visited Hong and discovered the tracts he had received in 1836 written by Liang Afa, that Hong himself read the tracts and discovered literal parallels between some passages from Isaiah and the cruelty and destruction witnessed during the Opium Wars. In those tracts, Hong also read a description of the story of creation and the Fall and identified the same cosmic conflict he had seen in his dream years before. Hong not only identified the characters involved in the war, but read that the heavenly father, Ye-Huo-Hua, sent his son, Jesus, on earth to fight and win the war. For Hong, since Jesus was his older brother, there was no doubt that he himself was God's Chinese son, according to the titles he had received in his vision.

The literal interpretation of the dream led Hong to convert Li Jingfang and they baptized each other. They each ordered a double-edged sword with the inscription, "Sword for Exterminating Demons" (Spence 1994:67). Hong Xiuquan made two new converts from among his cousins, Hong Rengan and Feng Yunshan, who, after being baptized, became his closest allies in the fight against evil. They poured over the text of Liang Afa's brochures trying to identify every possible character or element in the real world. In the meantime, the three friends made converts from their own families and other friends and carried Hong Xiuquan's message further.

The first step in their fight against evil was to remove the tablets in honor of Confucius from the schools where they were teaching. The result was that parents no longer sent their children to the schools, and finally Hong and his friends lost their jobs. The local communities slowly turned against them. Hong Xiuquan and Feng Yunshan decided to travel all the way to Guangxi where the Hakka tribe had migrated over the past decades. On the way, they were welcomed by hosts, entertained, and several accepted their message of repentance and were baptized. Hong and Feng spent about six months in Guangxi area, teaching, and baptizing about one hundred people.

Doctrinal Clarification

Hong realized that he needed to write and pass on his message to people in print in order for them to study and remember it, as Liang Afa had done. His own conversion experience convinced him of the effectiveness of this strategy. Being a scholar, Hong was able to write in verses no longer than seven characters, and in couplets and rhymes that were easy to remember for oral transmission. He wrote "Exhortations to Worship the One True God" (Spence 1994:72). Hong settled on six commandments necessary for one to be on the way to righteousness: never follow the path of lust; always obey your parents; never kill people; never steal; stay away from all magic and witchcraft; and never gamble.

After some time, Hong decided to return to his family, but Feng, by mistake, remained in the area. While Hong resumed his school teaching, Feng continued to spread Hong's message with unexpected success. One of the reasons for such success was the previous missionary work in the region of the Moravian German missionary, Karl Gutzlaff, who had distributed tracts in 1836 with Edwin Stevens along the Chinese coast. Gutzlaff served as translator for British officials and had learned the local Cantonese culture very well. He concluded that before the message was to be passed on to people, missionaries needed to listen and watch in order to contextualize their presentation. "In style we ought to conform entirely to the Chinese taste" (quoted in Spence 1994:88). The genius of Gutzlaff resided not only in contextualizing the message, but also in creating more than converts, making them missionaries. In 1844 he created the "Chinese Union" with the purpose of turning newly established congregations into missionary societies. He reported great success in the Guangxi area.

"The genius of Gutzlaff resided not only in contextualizing the message, but also in creating more than converts, making them missionaries."

Gutzlaff did not seem to worry much that the new Chinese converts were not yet trained or that they still practiced a syncretistic type of Christianity. He published more than fifty tracts on basic Christian topics, such as repentance, forgiveness, prayer, everlasting life, the Beatitudes, Creation, and the Fall. He also chose passages from the opening of Paul's letters that emphasized the missionary nature of Christianity. Working with Gutzlaff was Issachar Roberts, a Baptist from Tennessee. Roberts returned to Canton immediately after the end of the Opium War in 1842. He lived like a Chinese, dressed like a Chinese, learned the Hakka language, and built a chapel where he gathered the Chinese converts, emphasizing the need for baptism by immersion.

In the meantime, Hong Xiuquan wrote new tracts, this time connecting with teachings found in the classic Chinese books *Rituals* and *Changes.* He developed the idea that in the past the Chinese had shared good values and hospitality with the rest of the world. Hong argued that the present lack of harmony was due to the limited nature of clans and tribes (in fact, selfishness), and that harmony should be sought with everyone, in every culture and country. He also contended that the current superstitious beliefs had developed over generations, and that the original Chinese ethos should be recovered by going back to the origins. He showed how different dynasties had gradually changed the name of God and had added associated traditions and rituals with them. He insisted that it was not the Dragon of the Eastern Sea that brought rain after receiving sacrifices, but it was the Great God of the foreigners that brought the flood for forty days. He wrote against the divinity of evil forces and claimed that Yan Luo [ruler of the underworld] could not be divine and at the same time turn against God.

It is necessary to remember that Catholic Jesuits had worked in China and attempted the first translations of the Bible in Chinese two centuries before the Protestants. As Thomas Reilly contends, the translation of the name of God "was the most controversial question in the translation process" (2004:22). *Shangdi* was the name for God most frequently used by the Chinese people and indicated the Supreme Being and divine authority. *Shangdi* was also the God worshipped by the ancient Chinese in their classical writings. Although Matteo Ricci had used the term *Shangdi* [Sovereign on High] with great success especially among educated Confucianists, Pope Clement XI, however, had insisted upon use of the term *Tianzhu* [Lord of Heaven] as part of the Rites Controversy. Hong Xiuquan challenged the Chinese emperor's title of *Huangdi* as an attempt to usurp God's authority and position. Both titles contained the particle indicating divinity "di."

In 1846, one of Roberts' converts visited Hua and urged Hong to visit Canton to connect with Gutzlaff and Roberts. A year later, following an official invitation letter from Roberts, Hong Xiuquan and his cousin Hong Rengan finally met Roberts and for the first time the two Hongs read the Bible in Gutzlaff's Chinese translation. Hong Xiuquan asked Roberts to baptize him who was eager to do so. However, being ill-advised, Hong also asked Roberts to guarantee his financial support after baptism. This raised Roberts' suspicion that Hong was interested in baptism only for material advantage. As a result, Hong left Canton without being baptized. However, he did not return to Hua but headed west in order to search for Feng. After being robbed on the road, then borrowing money to travel, Hong reached Guangxi and was directed by the Chinese Union members to Thistle

Mountain where Hong finally found Feng. This was the time when Hong started introducing himself as "I the king" (Spence 1994:95).

His direct reading of the Bible enabled Hong to find even more parallels between the biblical text and his vision. He found that the Ten Commandments explicitly forbade the making of any images of things in heaven or on earth. As a result, Hong became more convinced that his mission was to fight against idols and evil. He was convinced that the Old and the New Testament were pure and without error, and he rewrote some of his earlier tracts containing his vision, this time turning against Confucianism that he found faulty and misleading. He inserted some scenes where Confucius was judged by God directly, and Hong's mission became to prove Confucianism wrong, besides desecrating material idols and images.

This iconoclasm led Hong and his friends to challenge the first local deity, King Gan, whose statue on Thistle Mountain they toppled and destroyed. As a result, Confucian people arrested Feng and his hosts and handed them over to the Guiping township to be tried. The accusation presented them as a large group of troublemakers fighting against the traditional religion and against the rules of the Qing dynasty. Feng defended the group by reminding the magistrate of the recently signed agreements that allowed foreigners to worship and to introduce the One True God. However, the ongoing imprisonment and bad treatment of converts and leaders leading to death had become regular, and that triggered Hong's ill sentiments against the Qing courts and government. Common people responded to Hong's message, but the gentry were not happy with it.

In the meantime, some worshippers of what became known as the One True God had experienced visions and fallen into trances, often confirming the details of Hong Xiuquan's dream. Others, however, spoke against the sacred text and the leaders had to listen to them and assess whose message came from above and whose message did not. The confirmation often came with miracles attached. Over time, two men stood out and were recognized as speaking messages with divine authority: Xiao Chaogui, speaking with voice of Jesus, and Yang Xiuqing, speaking with the voice of God.

Due to repeated attacks by robbers when the True One God-fearers travelled between the now four main zones they occupied in the area, Hong became convinced that they needed an army, supplied and ready to clear the area of banditry. Often, the bandits were called "demons," a handy justification for attacking places in the name of the heavenly King. In fact, since the army was assembled, Hong Xiuquan called himself very often the "Taiping King," and his residence "the court." By 1850, inside the house where he lived, Hong began to wear a yellow robe that was particularly assigned only for the emperor.

Another major development was the doctrine of purity and purification needed before the Taiping Kingdom could be established. Purity required separation between males and females, husbands and wives. One lady and one young fellow were chosen as models to follow. Families were promised to be reunited after the goal of establishing the Kingdom was realized. The natural outcome was no biological growth for the God worshippers. However, this doctrine was in stark conflict with the filial piety of the Confucians who emphasized the crucial need to have at least a baby boy to pay respect to the father. At the same time, since men and women lived now in separate quarters, women could also form military units.

Hong also developed an apocalyptic view of the end of the world. He called his family from Hua to join him at Thistle Mountain, both out of fear of abduction and ransom practiced by bandits but also out of concern for his new apocalyptic beliefs and visions. He concluded that the Taiping Kingdom could not be realized without his earthly family being around him.

With hostile gentry against them, non-Hakas reporting their every move to the government, and the increasing level of violence with bandits, the tension between Hong and his now multiplied followers and the Qing government escalated. Hong and his counselors decided to stockpile quantities of guns and gunpowder, well aware that this would raise suspicion. Hong began to wear the imperial yellow robe publicly, and imperial and army banners were designed. Military units began to train regularly, and plans were drawn up for both defense and attack.

> Taiping soldiers were expected to memorize the Ten Commandments, to attend worship services where they prayed to Shangdi as the Heavenly Father and sang their version of the traditional Christian doxology, and to attack and destroy religious statuary regarded as idolatrous (Reilly 2004:11).

The ritual reciting of the Ten Commandments and Hong's commentaries attached to them, was considered a probing of loyalty toward the heavenly King. Sarcasm and ignorance regarding the Ten Commandments were punished drastically. As Spence notes, "the Ten Commandments themselves become the basis both for daily life and for future hope" (1994:128).

Paradise Found

During their first encounter with government troops in December 1850, Hong's armies killed one high-ranking official, a deputy police magistrate who was labeled as a "demon," and representative of the evil Qing government. The Jintian village, where Hong was based, became the center of conflict. Many bandit forces joined the God worshippers in their fight against the government forces, but they had a hard time following the discipline in the Taiping ranks. During 1851 more clashes took place between Hong's forces and governmental troops around Jiangkou.

In March 1851, Hong Xiuquan finally announced the establishment of the Taiping Heavenly Kingdom. A new public ritual was established combining "celestial advice on the kingdom, rewards for the virtuous, and stern punishments for the backsliders" (Spence 1994:134). Disobeying military orders was declared equal to disobeying God or one of his earthly representatives. Reciting the policy became part of the daily ritual, together with the Ten Commandments. In September 1851, Hong and the Taiping armies conquered the walled city of Yongan.

While in Yongan, Hong introduced a new calendar of Taiping time developed by Feng Yunshan a few years previously. The calendar was based on the Chinese classical texts and some Western time structure to provide 366 days during a twelve-month year with seven days week. Each seventh day, the Sabbath, was declared a day for prayer and rest. The calendar was supposed to be purified from all demonic delusions and confusions and promised a happy and peaceful time directly determined by the Heavenly Father.

The time of respite in Yongan was also used to clarify their ideology and doctrine of war. The justification for fighting and killing was sharpened and the current Manchu emperor, Xianfeng, a non-Hakka and as such a barbarian, and his government were identified as the primary evil forces and demons to be eradicated. Since they attacked and tried to destroy the Heavenly Kingdom, they became the primary targets of the Taiping army.

Hong and the Taiping army moved swiftly through the country to Wuchang and Nanjing, and finally Nanjing was declared the Heavenly Capital. The promise of an earthly paradise had always seemed attractive, but during their marches the location had never been identified. Now they had a visible place to call home in Nanjing. An egalitarian social system was developed and implemented, with strong supervision under the military structure. Equal division of land was practiced, as well as distribution of money or gifts. However, leadership enjoyed more and more luxury and the puritanical rules separating women from men did not apply to them.

In Nanjing the Taiping leaders imposed their religion and destroyed all Taoist and Buddhist temples. They burned and smashed images and cult objects. Exception was made for Muslims, and partly for Catholics. They seized printing presses from the Confucian scholars, employed 400 skilled workers, and started printing Bibles and the new materials written by Hong Xiuquan. The translation available to them was Gutzlaff's initial translation into Chinese at Hong Kong. Interestingly, Genesis was published only up to chapter 28, ending with Jacob's dream of the heavenly beings coming down the ladder, and with his words that in that place heaven was on earth, and the Lord's presence was revealed. They also excluded Gen 19:31–38, the story of Lot's daughters' incest. In the books of Exodus, Leviticus, and Numbers, Hong and his entourage found justification for their own social organization along military lines.

Beside printing religious books, scholars were also invited to write in praise of the new emperor and the Heavenly Capital and the Heavenly Kingdom. At the same time, Peking was dubbed "the Demons' Den" and its surrounding region "the Criminal Province" (Spence 1994:181). The names of cities and provinces were changed according to the estimation of Hong Xiuquan if they were loyal to his rulership or not. All other literature, including Taoist, Buddhist, or Confucianist books were to be burned. The names for sun and moon were reserved for Hong and his wife and banned for public use. The same rule applied to the names of Jesus and Christ. A cultural revolution based on religious lines was well under way.

Representatives of foreign nations present on the coast of China became interested in visiting and assessing the potential of the rebellion. British, French, and Americans sailed to Nanjing and had contact with the leaders of the movement. They all noticed the mixture of a religious reform with cultural and political undertones. In the words of French minister M. de Bourboulon in his note sent back to the French government, after visiting the city,

> What stands out most for me from all that I have seen is the strength of this revolutionary movement, which promises nothing less than to accomplish a complete transformation, at once religious, social and political in this immense Empire, by tradition a land of custom and immobility. Whatever doubts may exist about its ultimate success, whatever obstacles the indifference of the masses and the resources of the Tartar dynasty may yet oppose to the rebellion's triumph, it is clear to me that this revolt is one of formidable character and proportions; that it is led by men who, be they fanatical or ambitious, have faith in the success of their venture, and who, besides their audacity, have in their favour ideas, a strength of organization, tactics, in short a moral force which gives them great superiority over their adversaries (quoted in Spence 1994:203).

McLane, the American envoy, on the other hand, suggested that the US should request official access to the interior of China, "to give a truly Christian direction to that movement, which though now shrouded in heathen darkness, is yet founded on the text of the Bible" (209).

The Downfall

Unfortunately, the future military campaigns to conquer Peking and destroy the Manchu "demons" failed utterly. The Qing army was much better prepared than the Taiping forces and wiped them out ruthlessly. By now Xiao Chaogui, speaking with voice of Jesus was dead. There was a void that would be soon filled by Yang Xiuqing who claimed to speak with the voice of God. However, Yang started to gradually and subtly confront Hong Xiuquan and his doctrine and policies. He ventured to even rebuke Hong publicly and humiliate Hong's officers, removing their influence. Besides growing his own influence around Hong Xiuquan, Yang realized that he could not radically change the doctrine and philosophy of the movement unless he removed the authority of the Bible. He announced himself not only as the "Fourth Brother" but also as the "Comforter," a direct allusion to the third person of the Godhead, the Holy Spirit.

With his new authority as a person of the heavenly council, Yang launched a direct attack on the Old and the New Testament, announcing that they contained some falsehood. In addition, realizing the unhappiness of some people that Confucian sources were completely denied and destroyed, he claimed that some of the Confucian books "advocate Heavenly feelings and truth" and should be removed from the list of demonic items (quoted in Spence 1994:225). By doing this, Yang actually replaced Hong Xiuquan as the scholar and authority in religious matters. Yang clearly sought to establish himself as the preserver of Heavenly Kingdom's values, at the same time tried to reassert traditional Chinese values. In Spence's words,

> The challenge to Hong Xiuquan, and to his followers, is unmistakable: the biblical word of God, which has carried them all so far, is now to be altered by the hands and minds of men. But the words of God as revealed through Yang are correct in every detail, and none shall presume to alter them (233).

As a result, Bible printing stopped.

Yang was not satisfied to simply be part of the Taiping leadership. He wanted full power. One day, after sending Hong's officers on far away missions, he approached Hong requesting that he would be given the same status and respect as Hong. Sensing the danger, Hong secretly called back all his officers to Nanjing and approved the killing of Yang. However, this led to power fighting among the rest of Hong's officers to the point that they killed each other except for one. But even this one left in disgust when he saw Hong Xiuquan appointing his own relatives as officers and kings, including Hong's own four-year old son.

Since Yang was no longer alive, Hong felt compelled to check if indeed the Bible contained any falsehood. He started from Genesis and changed or removed some of the chapters and passages that did not fall in line with the Taiping doctrine. Every passage that spoke of sexual immorality was removed or changed. Noah did not get drunk but fell and became naked, Tamar did not sleep with Judah but Judah got a second wife who got pregnant with teens, and so on. In order to justify his own filiation to God, Hong removed from John 3:16 the word "only." The last step was to change the name of his empire from Taiping Heavenly Kingdom to God's Heavenly Kingdom in 1862. Everything was now divine; his kingdom, his army, even himself. His empire extended over thirty million people, and several regions extending to the north, south, and west of Nanjing.

Unfortunately, foreign troops abandoned their announced neutrality and started to fight alongside the Qing forces against the Taiping movement. Further attempts by the Taiping troops to seize Shanghai failed, either due to the strength of the government army or inclement weather. By the time Nanjing was surrounded by the "demonic" forces, Hong Xiuquan fell ill, and died shortly. Without any vision and direction, and with the people in the city starving to death, the generals took the eldest son of Hong and, dressed in Qing uniforms, left the city during the night and headed south. The epilogue: one by one the generals and the Taiping heir were caught and executed.

Lessons

After the Fall of Nanjing, the Qing emperor ordered an erasing not only of the Taiping doctrine and its effects, but also of everyone who embraced it. It is believed that millions of people died because of their choice to worship *Shangdi.* Although the memory of most aspects of the Taiping Rebellion was effaced, one relationship is alive even today: the relationship with missionary Christianity. The resulting cultic religion of the Taiping Uprising had very little to do with Christian or biblical beliefs, but it is still perceived as the outcome of Christian missionary activity. This impact would be seen half a century later, during the Boxer uprising, when Christian missionaries were attacked first. In summary, four lessons are worth noting.

Christianity and politics

Commenting about the Taiping religious movement, Thomas Reilly notes,

> When the Taiping religion left Hong Xiuquan's hands, it was no longer a Western religion, a foreign creed. The Taiping faith, albeit kindled by Anglo-American Protestantism, developed into a dynamic new Chinese religion, one whose conception of the title and position of the sovereign deity challenged the legitimacy of the imperial order (2004:4).

For Hong Xiuquan, the Taiping Christianity was rather a restoration of the old traditional faith in *Shangdi.* The Taiping revived religion directly challenged the Qin emperor whose title, *Huangdi,* had both the meaning of emperor and God. The Taiping believers denied sacredness to the imperial system and wanted to worship only *Shangdi,* not the corrupt human emperor. It would be useful to look at the current trends in Chinese religious law from the Taiping history. Today, Christianity seems to be perceived not simply as a foreign religion, but as an attempt to detract Chinese people from worshipping their political leader.

Reformation or restoration?

However, Taiping believers did not ask for just a reform of the imperial system; they called for the complete change of it, based on religious authority. They saw themselves as restorers of the ancient Chinese religion, and only by implication, of the political order. "They related their faith more to the native Chinese classical religious tradition than to popular forms of sectarianism.... Religion was at the heart of the Taiping movement, and Taiping culture was the physical expression of these religious beliefs" (Reilly 2004:5). In this context, it would be necessary to check how much of Chinese Christianity is still biblical, and what aspects are more cultural adaptations or influences. There is no indication that either Catholic or Protestant missionaries changed the way they taught Christianity after the Taiping history was over.

Reilly claims that "the Taiping movement was from start to finish a religious movement" (2004:5). However, these religious beliefs led Hong Xiuquan to attempt a redesign of the Chinese culture according to his vision. Such a cultural revolution was expected to be the outcome of a religious restoration of the worship of *Shangdi.* It is worth noting that Chinese communists in the twentieth century tried to use the Taiping Uprising as a prototype for their own cultural revolution that reached its climax under comrade chairman Mao.

Orthodoxy or heterodoxy?

The third major lesson comes from the relationship between Christian missionaries and the Taiping religion. Issachar Roberts finally visited Nanjing, hoping to become the first missionary to cleanse the Taiping doctrines of their pagan Chinese influence and of Hong's claims based on his vision. He even wrote to fellow missionaries about the great opening for reaching the inland China with the orthodox message. However, Roberts, Gutzlaff, and the other well intended missionaries distanced themselves from the Taiping leadership. The opportunity to guide and support was lost, although for the Chinese this relationship was, and still is, surviving. The question, again, is how much of Christianity has been contextualized, and how much was rejected because of the native elements introduced by Chinese Christians during the time of isolation from the rest of the world? Do we, as Western Christians, consider Chinese Christians true Christians, or do we label them as a heterodox branch unqualified to be called Christian? As the church in the West declines and the church in the majority world expands, are Westerners in any position to make those judgements today? Historical records indicate, Taiping leaders could not understand the reaction of Christian missionaries who let them down at their greatest moment of need.

Exclusivity or complementarity?

The final lesson derives from the inability of Christian missionaries to find anything good in the local traditional religion. While Catholic and Protestant missionaries rejected Confucian philosophy and Buddhist religion altogether, the Taiping leaders gradually acknowledged that Christianity could complement and complete Confucianism. The question remains: how much of Confucius' writings are known to modern missionaries to China, and what attempts are there (if any) to bridge from biblical teaching to Confucian philosophy and way of life could we learn from it?

Conclusion

The Taiping Uprising, although a historical event that created a movement influenced by biblical teachings, did not leave behind a community of believers. However, the Taiping history teaches Christian workers in China several valuable lessons for the current political and religious context: mainly, to carefully consider past experiences with Christianity existent in the collective memory of those in the context where God is sending them.

References

Boardman, Eugene Powers. 1952. *Christian Influence upon the Ideology of the Taiping Rebellion 1851–1864.* Ann Arbor, MI: Cushing-Malloy.

Clarke, Prescott, and J. S. Gregory. 1982. *Western Reports on the Taiping: A Selection of Documents.* Canberra: Australian.

Cohen, Paul A. 1977. *History in the Three Keys. The Boxers as Event, Experience and Myth.* New York: Columbia University.

Michael, Franz. 1966. *The Taiping Rebellion: History and Documents.* Seattle, WA: University of Washington.

Platt, Stephen R. 2012. *Autumn in the Heavenly Kingdom: China, the West, and the Epic Story of the Taiping Civil War.* New York: Random House.

Reilly, Thomas H. 2004. *The Taiping Heavenly Kingdom: Rebellion and the Blasphemy of Empire.* Seattle, WA: University of Washington.

Spence, Jonathan D. 1996. *God's Chinese Son: The Taiping Heavenly Kingdom of Hong Xiuquan.* New York: Norton & Company.

Christianization Lessons from Mission History in China

David S. Lim

Based on mission history in China, what lessons can we learn to help us fulfill Christ's mandate to disciple all peoples (Matt 28:19–20) in our time? The Center for the Study of Global Christianity estimates that in 2020 there will be 150 million Christians in China, approximately 10.5% of the population. This is a dramatic increase from 1970 when less than 2% were considered Christian. At the same time, the persecution of Christians in China has intensified, especially since President Xi Jinping took power in 2012. In a national conference in 2016, President Xi called on leaders to reassert Chinese Communist Party's (CCP) control over religion. According to him, uniting all Christian believers under CCP leadership is necessary to preserve internal harmony and ward off foreign forces that use religion to destabilize the regime.

With the return of a strict anti-religious regime, could the Chinese church return to her earlier revival movement implementing insights learned from her past? There were at least nine instances in history when Christward movements (XM) almost evangelized China to become a Christian-majority country. We are now living in the tenth opportunity for that to occur. This chapter concludes with suggestions from these instances that can be applied for more effective missions in China and elsewhere.

Nestorians

The first instance was when a delegation of Nestorian Christians led by Alopen arrived in Chang'an the capital of the Tang dynasty in 635. By 638 the first cathedral was built and twenty-one Persian monks ministered from there. The Nestorians enjoyed much freedom to evangelize, and soon Christian communities were established from northwest Xinjiang to southeast China. Emperor Taizong welcomed them since they adopted much of Daoism and Buddhism. Good relations continued after his death in 649 (Palmer 2001). He was succeeded by his son Gaozu, who built monasteries for the Nestorians in many cities.

But when Gaozu died in 683, his successor soon adopted Buddhism as the state religion. Persecution began, mobs destroyed churches. The Nestorians struggled until 845 when an imperial edict ordered all religious clergy to leave monasteries and do secular work. Although Buddhism suffered the most, more than 2,000 Christian monks and nuns were forced to abandon their vocation. The fledgling church was weakened further.

The Nestorians recovered briefly in large and powerful communities during the Mongol Dynasty (1268–1372). But they suffered severely during the anti-foreign nationalist upsurge led by Zhu Yuanzhang, the first Ming emperor. Zhu had previously been part of a revolt against Mongol rule organized by a religious group called the "Red Turbans." Many of the rebels believed that the change of dynasty would bring in the Maitreya Buddha, a messianic figure, to rule China and the world (Aikman 2003:29). Yet most historians believe that it was the religious freedom the Nestorians enjoyed that tragically destroyed their spiritual life and caused their final demise (Moffett 1998:420).

Franciscans

The second opportunity came through a lay adventurer named Marco Polo who visited Kublai Khan, grandson of Genghis Khan in 1266. Polo returned to Europe with an amazing request: the Khan would like Europe to send one hundred "wise men of learning in the Christian religion." He wanted experts in Western science and learning, qualified "to show plainly to [Kublai] and to the idolaters and to the other classes of people... that the Christian faith and religion is better than theirs and more true than all the other religions." If the pope could send such missionaries, "he and all his potentates would become men of the church" (Moffett 1998:445–6).

Yet instead of the one hundred missionaries requested, only one, Franciscan John (Giovanni) of Montecorvino (1246–1329), arrived in Beijing in 1294, after

Kublai's death. John was welcomed by Kublai's successor, grandson Timur Oljeitu (ruled 1294–1307). Despite great opposition from jealous Nestorians, John built a big cathedral in the capital in 1299, and six years later claimed that 6,000 Chinese and Mongols had been baptized. John tried to establish a native clergy by training orphans, but without success. With clerical reinforcements sent from Rome, the Catholics established a thriving community in the port of Quanzhou, Fujian Province.

But the tide was turning again against Christians in China. The *Pax Mongolica* that had enabled relatively safe travel across Eurasia, was being changed from within by the growing conversion of Mongols to Islam. However, the main reason may be that to most Chinese, Christians belonged to a foreign religion, since their initial and continuing support came from foreigners. By the time the rebel armies swept into Beijing in 1368, China was in the throes of one of its periods of anti-foreignism and hostile to Christianity. By the end of the fourteenth century, Christianity had disappeared from China.

Jesuits

The third instance was when Matteo Ricci landed in Macau in 1582. Ricci worked his way towards Beijing slowly before receiving permission from the initially suspicious authorities to live in China's capital in 1601. His approach was to enter the world of China's ruling intelligentsia. He first dressed as a Buddhist priest, but when he discovered that clergy from Buddhism and Islam were less respected than members of the scholar-gentry class, he adopted the robes of a Confucian scholar. He devoted himself to intense language proficiency and wrote many literary works in Chinese explaining Christian concepts to the educated. But it was his skill as a clockmaker that provided him access to the emperor himself.

Ricci and other Jesuits who followed him acquired influence in the imperial court through their mechanical, mathematical, cartographical, astronomical, and diplomatic skills. By 1605, 1,000 had been baptized. Five years after his death, that number had risen to more than 5,000, including a significant number of court eunuchs and women. Ricci sought to impart Christianity as being in accord with Confucian thought. In 1632, one of Ricci's first converts, Xu Guangqi was appointed grand secretary to the emperor, one of the highest positions in the Confucian bureaucracy.

As evidence of their diplomatic skill, the Jesuits were not removed from their influential positions even when the Ming Dynasty was overthrown by the Manchus in 1644. Two of Ricci's successors, Adam Schall von Bell and Ferdinand Verbiest, were given imperial appointments in astronomy. Verbiest established close relations with Emperor Kangxi and tried to persuade him to adopt the Catholic faith by being baptized. Kangxi politely declined; he was conscious of his unique role as a religious linchpin in Chinese culture. A respected historian of China's relations with the West made this analogy: "The conversion of the Chinese emperor to a foreign religion would have seemed almost as monstrous [to the ruling Chinese gentry class] as if the Pope had become a Mohammedan and still remained head of the Catholic church" (Franke 1967:55). Yet it seems Kangxi did convert to Christian belief, with or without baptism. Many Chinese Christians point to two classical Chinese poems attributed to him: "The Cross" and "Poem on Truth;" these poems strongly suggest his conviction of the Christian faith (Aikman 2003:33).

Yet the Jesuits were followed by the Franciscan, Dominican, and Augustinian orders, which eschewed the cultivation of the ruling class in favor of outreach to China's lower classes. As the fame of the Jesuit achievement became known in Europe, organizational jealousies and theological disputes arose. Most controversial was the "rites controversy" over ancestral veneration. Jesuits argued it was purely cultural and unrelated to issues of faith. Other Catholics argued it was idolatry. The debate intensified until the early eighteenth century, when the Jesuits appealed to Kangxi for his ruling. Well informed about Christian doctrine (perhaps even a believer), he ruled that the rites were cultural, not religious. But in 1715, the pope criticized the Jesuits in a papal bull for compromising gospel truth in their acquiescence to Chinese traditions.

Kangxi was infuriated by this decree and began to speak of banning foreign Christianity in China. He died in 1723, but the following year his successor, Yongzheng, issued an "Edict of Expulsion and Confiscation." Church buildings were wrecked or turned into granaries, schools, or public halls. All Catholic missionaries were expelled, except for a few Jesuits who served as court astronomers. There may have been about 300,000 Christians in China then. Through sporadic persecution that number dwindled in the next century. Until 1860, Catholics were pressured to recant, and evangelizers were executed by strangulation.

Protestants

Protestant missions to China started in the nineteenth century with Western colonial expansion. In 1807 Robert Morrison of the London Missionary Society (LMS) came to Macau. He strived for fluency in Chinese to become a Bible translator and scholar of Chinese culture. By the time he died in 1834, he had produced a Chinese dictionary and a translation of the full Bible.

It was Western colonial pressure that forced China to open her doors to the West and to the gospel. Between 1839–42, the British fought against China when the latter refused to allow the import of opium. In 1842 China was forced to sign the Treaty of Nanjing by which Hong Kong was ceded to Britain, and China opened five ports to foreign trade, as well as to foreign residence, whereby more Western missionaries entered China. When China lost the Second Opium War, she was forced to sign the Treaty of Tianjin in 1860, which had a "toleration clause" granting foreign missionaries the right to evangelize and freedom for the Chinese to believe in Christianity.

On the whole the Protestant approach was to establish "mission stations" ministering mainly to the needs of the few baptized converts disowned by their communities for becoming "running dogs of imperialists." By 1905 the anti-Manchu and anti-foreign Boxer Rebellion resulted in the deaths of nearly 200 missionaries and over 2,000 Chinese Christians. Yet there were at least five more instances when the opportunity for China's Christianization occurred between this period and 1949.

Taiping Rebellion

The fourth instance was a short-lived misguided attempt of a quasi-Christian uprising called the "Taiping Rebellion" which brought China almost to the verge of being ruled by a Christian cult. In 1834 Hong Xiuquan, a candidate for the official exam for entry into the scholar-gentry class, received a Chinese gospel tract in Guangdong. He did not read it carefully until nine years later when yet another failure in the exam enraged him against the Manchu rulers. Strange visions led him to believe that he was called by God to cleanse China of its corruption by overthrowing the empire.

At first Hong's "Society of God-Worshippers" practiced an austere lifestyle that segregated men and women with a pious approach to *Shangdi,* or God. He announced his rule as the Taiping ("universal peace") Kingdom. Initial Protestant Christian support for the new movement was enormous but died down after Hong announced that God had told him that he was the younger brother of Jesus. Yet, some foreign Christians still saw hope in the movement. Griffith John of LMS wrote in 1860, "I fully believe that God is uprooting idolatry in this land through the insurgents, and that he will by means of them, in connection with the foreign missionary, plant Christianity in its stead" (Neill 1986:244).

From 1850 until its final suppression in 1864, which was achieved with the help of Western military advisors eager to uphold the Qing dynasty, the insurrection devastated central and southern China, leading to the deaths of about 20 million Chinese. Henceforth, Chinese officialdom will remember that Christianity could trigger a revolt against a government just as easily as the religious Red Turban revolt at the end of Mongol rule. For a more detailed account of the life and work of Hong Xiuquan refer to chapter 12, "The Lasting Impact of Christianity Upon China from the Taiping Uprising" by Cristian Dumitrescu in this volume.

China Inland Mission (CIM)

The fifth opportunity came with Protestant faith missions. Hudson Taylor founded CIM in 1865 and came to China in 1866 pioneering the use of the "three self" indigenous church principles (self-governing, self-propagating, self-supporting). Implementation was radical. The movement would be interdenominational, without requirement of formal education, Chinese dress would be worn, and mission authority would be in China, not London. Rejecting the prevailing "Mission Station" approach, the CIM missionaries went from village to village appointing local elders from among their first few converts, entrusting them to evangelize their neighbors.

Yet CIM's biggest hindrance was her inability to recognize ancestral rites as civil veneration of elders rather than idolatry. This has reinforced the perception of Christianity as a "foreign religion" up to this day. Moreover, CIM and other Western missionaries underwent extreme suffering and martyrdom due to anti-foreign resentment stirred up Christianity's association with Western "gunboat diplomacy" that humiliated China. This exploded several times into anti-Christian demonstrations. One historian commented on the departure of foreign missionaries in 1949–52, "The Christian missionaries had to pay a particular heavy price for the mistakes of their predecessors, and reaped the hatred that had been sown in the past" (Franke 1967:138).

Karl Ludwig Reichelt

Yet there was a sixth potential for a Christward movement, this time among Chinese monks: *Tao Fong Shan* ("The Hill of the Christ Wind") in Hong Kong. It was founded by a Norwegian Lutheran missionary, Reichelt (1877–1952) who arrived in China in 1903 and was troubled to see the poor relationship between Christians, especially Western missionaries, and the general population. He made a sustained study of the life and practices of Confucianism, Buddhism, and Taoism.

He built a Christian monastery in Hong Kong in 1930, which introduced "the universal, cosmic, all-embracing Savior Jesus Christ" to all who visited his institution. Using Chinese temple architecture, this Christian community sought to demonstrate contextual integration of the Christian faith with Chinese culture, including ancestral veneration. Converts were baptized, but instead of letting them join existing churches, he encouraged these "Friends of the *Dao*" to disperse and evangelize in their temples and monasteries. He wrote, "Although not joining the external church, such enter the yearly increasing number of unknown and unregistered Christ-followers" (Kung 1993:122). This model had a centralized and expensive structure, difficult to replicate. For more on this strategy refer to chapter 6, "Reaching Out to Karmic Monastic Communities" by Rory Mackenzie in this volume.

Sun Yatsen and Chiang Kaishek

The seventh instance began in 1911 when the Qing dynasty was toppled by a democratic revolution led by two Methodist Chinese: physician Sun Yatsen and his military chief Chiang Kaishek. A republic was officially founded the next year, bringing an end to two millennia of imperial rule. But the new republic was not strong enough to deal with the anarchy in the country. Warlords competed for power from 1916–28. Sadly, Sun lacked the political savvy to govern and died in 1924, while Chiang was unable to overcome the rise of the Chinese Communist Party (CCP) and to check the corruption that crept into his Kuomintang (Nationalist) Party.

Further, neither one could check the rising tide against Christianity. On May 4, 1919, Chinese students staged a huge anti-Japanese demonstration in Beijing against the international injustice meted out to China in the Treaty of Versailles in France. This "May Fourth Movement" launched the intellectual revolution in modern China, and soon turned from a patriotic movement into a New Culture Movement during 1920–1922. In their acclaim of science, the intellectuals denounced traditional Chinese culture and beliefs, rejecting also all religions, including Christianity, as superstitious. An anti-Christian movement spread throughout China with great intensity during the years of collaboration between Chiang's Kuomintang and Mao's CCP (1924–1927). Christianity was attacked as the cultural arm of Western imperialism. In response, many churches separated themselves from foreign missions and began to establish themselves independently.

In June 1928 Chiang imposed a military peace on the country, establishing his capital in Nanjing, and for ten years tried to reconstruct the economy. During this decade the church enjoyed a breathing space as the government adopted a friendly attitude towards Christianity. The National Christian Council launched a Five-Year Movement (1929–1934) to stimulate evangelism and revival. The 1930s also saw the rise of indigenous evangelists such as Wang Mingdao, John Sung and Watchman Nee who all contributed to revival.

But when the Japanese invaded China in 1937, the life of the nation and the church was devastated again. Missionaries had to evacuate, Christian institutions had to relocate, and believers suffered. Yet the church grew from 560,000 in 1936 to nearly 700,000 in 1945. Soon after the Japanese surrender, the Kuomintang and the Communists broke out into full-scale war, which ended when Chiang fled to Taiwan, and Mao Zedong established the People's Republic on October 1, 1949.

James Yen's Rural Education and Reconstruction Movements

The eighth instance was led by a social movement organizer named Y. C. James Yen (1893–1990). When he was ten, he studied at a CIM school and became a Christian there. He graduated from the Christian secondary school in Chengdu, and from the University of Hong Kong. In 1916, after finishing another bachelor's degree at Yale, he left with forty other Chinese students to voluntarily serve the 30,000 Chinese working in France. While there, he developed insights into the education of common people, and formed a course to teach written Chinese to more than 3,000 preliterate laborers.

After returning to China in 1921, Yen established a ministry for the education of commoners in Shanghai and served as the head of YMCA's Education Committee. Soon his work to raise literacy moved from the urban to the rural areas. He organized the National Association of Mass Education Movements (MEM) in Hebei and recruited many experts to turn the county into the science research center of China. He then set up education programs for rural reconstruction in many sites throughout China, benefiting more than five million people. Mao Zedong was one of its volunteer teachers! His "Ten Year Plan" included the reduction of illiteracy; agricultural, health, and other basic infrastructure developments; self-government in villages, and civic duty.

Yen inspired several intellectuals and professionals to serve sacrificially in villages, promoting many reforms and social services. His work helped transform rural China and spread to many other countries in Asia and Africa. He had to flee China in 1950, but in 1985, five years before his death, the Chinese government welcomed him back acknowledging his immense contribution to mass education and rural reconstruction.

Yen later recalled that since the mid-1920s, he no longer regarded himself as a "Christian" ("church member"), but as a "follower of Christ," implying a direct relationship with Jesus. He criticized most missionaries for not being in touch with the realities of China but welcomed the support of all Chinese and foreign Christian organizations which addressed the problems of village life. What if he had combined his community development programs with evangelistic outreach?

House Church Movement/Networks (HCM)

The ninth instance of an interrupted XM extended from 1970 to 2000. In 1949, on the eve of the establishment of the People's Republic (population 450 million), the country had 840,000 Protestant believers in 20,000 churches. They were served by 5,600 missionaries, 8,500 Chinese evangelists, 3,500 Bible women, and about 2,100 ordained Chinese pastors. Catholics had 3,274,000 baptized believers, served by 3,090 foreign priests and 2,698 Chinese priests. This was a time of massive transition in China when the Communists seized power, ending free religious expression. The Communist government required all foreign missionaries to leave and by 1953 this was accomplished.

Government policy and control

In the 1950s the government's Religious Affairs Bureau created the Three Self Patriotic Movement (TSPM), which formed the official state church, China Christian Council controlled by the government. All existing churches and religious groups were pressured to join. Non-conforming churches were closed, properties seized, printed materials burnt, and all leaders sent to re-education camps. Those who refused to join were judged counter-revolutionaries and imprisoned. Under such pressure the majority of Protestant church leaders submitted to TSPM's demands.

By 1958 practically all churches had been brought under state control. As shepherds were attacked, flocks scattered. Rural churches were closed. Even pastors who declared their support for the TSPM were required six months of political studies. The 200 plus churches in Shanghai were reduced to eight, and the sixty-six in Beijing to four.

This meant that those churches refusing to register with the government now found themselves leaderless. This began a house church movement (HCM) with leaders such as Wang Ming-Dao, Watchman Nee, and David Yang. These, and others, would lead the church through the persecution following the fall of the "Bamboo Curtain" in 1950, and prepared the ground for the ninth opportunity for China's Christianization from 1970–2000.

Incidental multiplication through persecution

Persecution in the 1950s brought two positive effects: the Chinese church now became truly Chinese, and it became more united. But above all, it simplified the practices of church and mission, so that multiplication happened spontaneously. The house church was forced to go back to the Bible, simplify her ecclesiology, and streamline her operation. She affirmed "the priesthood of all believers," where all the "extraneous" things were put aside living the words of Jesus. What emerged was a XM, which grew from modest beginnings to over 100 million believers in China today.

House churches were illegal and violators were prosecuted with years of imprisonment or back-breaking hard labor. Forbidden visitors, deprived of Bible reading, and isolated from all, these saints suffered years of internment. Meanwhile they became witnesses for Christ to their fellow prisoners, resulting in many secret prison fellowships.

The worst persecution was during the Cultural Revolution (1966–69). Young radical Red Guards went on a rampage all over China. Armed with Mao's "little red book," they set out to destroy old ideologies, customs, morals, and habits. They stormed city halls, broke into police headquarters, took over university buildings, and publicly humiliated and beat up Party officials, intellectuals, and anyone whom they considered not "proletarian."

For religion, they destroyed temples, monasteries, and stormed the few churches that remained. They searched believers' homes, looking for Bibles and Christian literature to confiscate or burn. In those days practically all Christians, including TSPM leaders, were attacked, and forced to parade the streets. Some of the believers were literally beaten to death. Others suffered permanent paralysis. Several house church leaders were arrested and sent to labor camps. For a while even clandestine house church activities were suspended.

But out of this "death," a great spiritual army began to rise up after the initial attacks of 1966–69. A few lamented the spiritual desolation and began to pray for a revival. They went around villages in search of believers urging them to arise from their fears and to meet secretly in small groups to encourage each other. Gradually these small groups grew into house churches of 50–200. Deprived of pastoral leadership, lay leaders rose up to lead prayer meetings and to minister. Steadily house churches sprang up in countless villages and cities, as many witnessed signs and miracles.

"Miracles were reported from nearly every part of China: the sick were healed, demons were exorcised, and even a few dead were raised."

Persecution differed according to location but came mainly from central government policy. In March 1979 the CCP began to restore its policy of limited religious toleration in order to enlist support for the Four Modernizations program. This was followed by the restoration of the TSPM in August 1979 and the reopening of churches in cities. During 1979–80 the HCM enjoyed a short period of unprecedented freedom, especially in the countryside. Miracles were reported from nearly every part of China: the sick were healed, demons were exorcised, and even a few dead were raised. Witnessing the saving power of Christ, even atheistic Communist Party and Youth League members believed. It was a time of unprecedented revival.

But on March 31, 1982 the Central Committee of the Chinese Communist Party issued Document No. 19, the "Three Designates" policy stating: (1) Christians may worship only in churches designated by the TSPM; (2) only designated pastors are allowed to preach; and (3) they can do so only within their own designated districts. Under this new policy house church leaders were forbidden to do itinerant preaching, and churches not approved by the TSPM must close down.

Intentional multiplication through youth mobilization

This renewed restriction came at a time when house churches were enjoying a great revival at the grassroots. Itinerant evangelism was developing in many parts of China, especially in Zhejiang and Henan. Preachers became bolder than ever, preaching even in their neighboring provinces. As a result, many turned to Christ, and the number of Christians in China grew from less than one million in 1949 to over thirty-five, if not fifty million in 1982. Desiring to see the whole nation turn to Christ, many house churches organized evangelistic teams to do cross-county and cross-provincial missions. These evangelistic outreaches ran into direct conflict with the government's religious policy of containing Christian activities within the four walls of TSPM churches. As a result, many incidents of conflict developed between the TSPM officials and house churches. Many itinerant preachers were arrested by the local Public Security Bureau. Others became fugitives.

Implementing the Three Designates became more vigorous in 1983 when the government launched an "anti-crime campaign." House church meetings were disbanded, many itinerant preachers were imprisoned, some detained without trial, others sentenced for years as "counter-revolutionaries."

The renewed persecution forced many house churches to go underground again. Itinerant evangelists fled to neighboring provinces and to Inner Mongolia. In their flight they developed new horizons of mission. Meanwhile, in 1985 HCMs in central China started to establish three-month seminaries undercover to train itinerant evangelists. Between 1986–87 they established eleven "seminaries of the field," each sending graduates out to do pioneer mission work.

Over the years, house churches developed effective network structures. As more were established, they were grouped into new pastoral districts. When the number of pastoral districts reached ten, a Regional Council was organized, and served as the basic unit for regional inter-church unity and cooperation.

HCMs in China have mainly been lay movements. Leaders are usually lay leaders who hold regular jobs as farmers or workers and who use their spare time in the evenings and weekends to conduct meetings and exercise pastoral care. This was a key factor in their explosive growth from 1970–2000. The slow growth since 2000 may be attributed mainly to the clericalization that began in the 1990s when many foreign churches and ministries persuaded many churches to adopt their "denominational" training, materials, and structures again.

Mission China: Back to Jerusalem (BTJ) Movement

One of the most amazing developments at this time has been the creation of the "Back to Jerusalem" Movement (BTJ) (Hattaway 2003:23), a movement in which HCM leaders were inspired by the Holy Spirit to take the gospel where it had never been before. Their logic ran like this: "Since the gospel came to us (Chinese) from Jerusalem, we are obligated to take the gospel to every nation between here and Jerusalem. We are obligated to take the gospel back to Jerusalem."

The HCMs have a vast supply of potential missionaries indeed. Furthermore, the increasing surplus of Chinese farm workers, perhaps the largest bloc of unemployed or under-employed laborers in the world (numbering 200 million in 2015), may facilitate recruitment of missionaries among rural Christians. The idealism of the original main leaders like Brother Yun, Peter Xu Yongze, and Enoch Wang, to send 100,000 by 2010, as "ants, worms and termites" among the unreached, particularly Muslims (cf. Hattaway 2003) has proven to be spiritually mature and strategically astute, but historically premature and practically ineffective so far. For instance, church leaders in the Middle East have stressed that future missionaries to that part of the world should acquire some sort of professional status and have in-depth understanding of Islamic culture. There are few Chinese Christians who meet these two criteria, especially with regard to quality training in cross-cultural issues (Chan 2013:182–91).

Recommendations and Conclusions

Will China's Christianity thrive in this new wave of persecution? China's church has been severely persecuted several times before. Mission history in China shows a series of events that enhanced or impeded attempts at her becoming a Christian-majority nation. Our challenge is to learn humbly from these attempts and apply the lessons appropriately. In summary, here are three I suggest for China and elsewhere.

Christianization through Christward movements

Christianization can be achieved through building relationships especially with community leaders. Leaders of XMs come through holistic community development that empowers "people of peace/shalom" (Luke 10:5–7) to lead others to Christ. These women and men can lead only if they remain in their social status. Multiplication occurs when each Christ-follower (especially leaders) obeys the command to "love God and love others" adapting to the context without being extracted from their community (1 Cor 7:17–20).

Christward movements through multiplying small groups

Movements of people to Christ are based on disciple-making from the bottom-up, in small meetings not large gatherings. People can be evangelized and discipled to mature spirituality through participation in "house churches" like in New Testament times. Direct and constant communion with God and with a small community of fellow disciples is enough for spiritual vitality. This "small group discipleship" approach is not only pastorally effective, but also missionally strategic restraining institutionalization which results in nominal Christianity.

Christward movements in and from China to Asia and the world

China remains less than ten percent evangelized and Asia the least evangelized continent (less than eight percent) with vast populations who have little access to the gospel. With the BTJ vision, a faithful remnant can be discipled to do effective evangelization of Asia and the world, with all the advantages and disadvantages of representing a new superpower/empire.

We have shown that historically, by God's grace, biblical Christianity can prevail in China through XMs and can perpetuate continuous spiritual vitality through revival movements. Let us learn from the various Christward and revival movements throughout church history. By following recommendations here, Christianity will change China over the next decade, and in doing so, also change the world.

References

Aikman, David. 2003. *Jesus in Beijing: How Christianity is Transforming China and Changing the Global Balance of Power.* Washington, D.C.: Regency Publishing Inc.

Bays, Daniel, ed. 1996. *Christianity in China: From the Eighteenth Century to the Present.* Stanford: Stanford University.

________. 1993. "Christian Revival in China, 1900–1937." In *Modern Christian Revivals.* E. L. Blumhofer and R. Balmer, ed. Urbana: University of Illinois.

Broomhall, A. J. 1981. *Hudson Taylor and China's Open Century: Barbarians at the Gate.* London: Hodder & Stoughton.

Brother Yun, and Paul Hattaway. 2002. *The Heavenly Man.* London: Monarch.

Chan, Kim-kwong. 2013. "The Back to Jerusalem Movement: Mission Movement of the Christian Community in Mainland China." In *Mission Spirituality and Authentic Discipleship.* 172–92. Wonsuk Ma and Kenneth Ross, ed. Oxford: Regnum.

Chao, Jonathan, ed. 1989. *The China Mission Handbook: A Portrait of China and its Church.* Hongkong: Chinese Church Research Centre.

Covell, Ralph. 1995. *The Liberating Gospel in China: The Christian Faith among China's Minority Peoples.* Grand Rapids: Baker.

Dawson, Christopher, ed. 1996. *Mission in Asia: Narratives and Letters of the Franciscan Missionaries in Mongolia and China in the Thirteenth and Fourteenth Centuries.* New York: Harper & Row.

Dilley, Andrea P. 2014. "The Surprising Discovery of Those Colonialist, Proselytizing Missionaries." *Christianity Today.* January 8. https://www.christianitytoday.com/ct/2014/january-february/world-missionaries-made.html.

Franke, Wolfgang. 1967. *China and the West: The Cultural Encounter, 13th to 20th Centuries.* New York: Harper Torchbook.

Fulton, Brent. 2015. *China's Urban Christians: A Light that Cannot be Hidden.* Eugene, OR: Pickwick.

Gerlach, L. P., and V. H. Vine. 1970. *People, Power, Change: Movements of Social Transformation.* New York: Bobbs-Merrill.

Hamrin, Carol Lee, and Stacey Bieler, ed. 2009. *Salt and Light.* Beijing: Zhongguo Dangan Chuban She.

Hattaway, Paul. 2003. *Back to Jerusalem: Called to Complete the Great Commission.* Carlisle: Piquant.

Hunter, Alan, and Chan, Kim-kwong. 1993. *Protestantism in Contemporary China.* Cambridge: Cambridge University.

Kung, Timothy. 1993. "Evangelizing Buddhists." *International Journal of Frontier Mission.* 10 (3) 118–23.

Lambert, Tony. 1991. *The Resurrection of the Chinese Church.* London: Hodder & Stoughton.

________. 1999. *China's Christian Millions: The Costly Revival.* London: Monarch.

Latourette, Kenneth Scott. 1929. *A History of Christian Missions in China.* London: SPCK.

Lee, Thomas. 2011. "A Mission China: An Analysis of Its Ten Affecting Factors." In *Mission History of Asian Churches.* 21–43. Timothy Park, ed. Pasadena, CA: William Carey Library.

Lim, David. 2010. "Ancestor Veneration and Family Conversion Revisited." In *Family and Faith in Asia: The Missional Impact of Extended Networks.* Pp. 183–215. Paul de Neui, ed. Pasadena, CA: William Carey Library.

Ma, Li, and Jin Li. 2018. "Divergent Paths of Protestantism and Asian Nationalism: A Comparison of Two Social Movements in Korea and China in 1919." *International Bulletin of Mission Research.* 42 (4) 316–25.

Moffett, Samuel Hugh. 1998. *A History of Christianity in Asia, Vol. 1: Beginnings to 1500.* New York: Orbis.

Neill, Stephen. 1986. *A History of Christian Missions.* London: Penguin.

Palmer, Martin. 2001. *The Jesus Sutras: Rediscovering the Lost Scrolls of Taoist Christianity.* New York: Ballantine Wellspring.

Patterson, Ross. 1999. *The Continuing Heartcry for China.* Tonbridge: Sovereign World Ltd.

Ross, Andrew. 1994. *Vision Betrayed: The Jesuits in Japan and China, 1542–1742.* Edinburgh: Edinburgh University.

Shih, Vincent Y. C. 1967. *The Taiping Ideology: Its Sources, Interpretations and Influences.* Seattle: University of Washington.

Sunquist, Scott. 2017. *Explorations in Asian Christianity.* Downers Grove, IL: IVP Academic.

Talman, Harley, and John Jay Travis, ed. 2015. *Understanding Insider Movements.* Pasadena, CA: William Carey Library.

Wang, C. Y. 1966. *Chinese Intellectuals and the West, 1872–1942.* Chapel Hill, SC: Univ. of South Carolina.

Wang, Wenzong. 2015. "Timothy Richard: A Missionary who Impacted the Late Qing Dynasty." In *Builders of the Chinese Church: Pioneer Protestant Missionaries and Chinese Church Leaders.* G. Wright Doyle, ed. Eugene, OR: Pickwick.

Woods, Paul. 2018. *Shaping Christianity in Greater China: Indigenous Christians in Focus.* Eugene, OR: Wipf & Stock.

Xin, Yalin. 2016. "The Role of the Host Families in the Missional Structure of a House Church Movement." In *Evangelism and Diakonia in Context.* 315–24. Rose Dowsett, et al, ed. Oxford: Regnum.

CHAPTER 14

Christianity's Journey to The Roof of the World

James E. Morrison

The land of Tibet seems to have a certain aura about it, the proverbial Shangrila, a remote and exotic destination, a prized conquest for both the intrepid explorer and missionary alike. Part of the mystique may be that Tibet has been closed for many centuries in a self-imposed exile aimed to keep foreign influences at bay. Missionary engagement has been sparse and intermittent, and the expansion of Christianity there, due to a range of factors, is still in its infancy. This chapter will attempt to tell some of the story of Christianity's journey to Tibet and draw some missiological conclusions. However, contributions to missiological theory and practice may more be about why it has not expanded rather than why it has or is still to do so.

In this chapter "Tibet" refers to the Central Tibetan Plateau (often called The Roof of the World), with the capital city of Lhasa, the area which today is a province of China. Mention will be made of work among Tibetans on the fringes, but the central focus will be on Tibet proper.

Theoretical Framework

Nehrbass has identified six broad categories or "lenses" through which the history of missions is typically written and suggests historians of missions would do well to identify the lenses through which they are writing and analyzing history. His six categories are:

> 1) Viewing God's guidance of the process; 2) Following the lives of "great missionaries;" 3) Celebrating legacies, mission boards, and churches, 4) Highlighting the role marginalized actors played in the missionary effort; 5) Emphasizing specific mission strategies; and 6) Building missiological theory... Furthermore quality histories of mission make clear which theoretical lens is being employed (Nehrbass 2018:4, 24).

The Major Players

Following that framework, I will be focusing on the main players involved (who are typically known to us through biographies), the minority or overlooked voices, the underlying mission strategies, some general themes, as well as commenting on the relative success and failure of these missionary endeavors. The underlying premise of this study is that God is actively at work in the world. Neill stresses the sovereignty of God in the expansion of Christianity by calling it "the great miracle of history" (1990:478). Nehrbass rightly points out:

> The history of mission, like any other sub-discipline of Christian thought, is the study of *Missio Dei:* of how God has moved dynamically over time, and how we fit into that bigger picture in our present context (2018:19).

The forgotten Nestorians

In his 2008 book, *The Lost History of Christianity: The Thousand-Year Golden Age,* noted historian Philip Jenkins has given voice to the oft-overlooked church of the East. Jenkins has traced the extent and influence of the Eastern church in a detailed account that clearly exposes the myth of Christianity being exclusively a European religion or that the expansion of Christianity was primarily a European phenomenon. The Nestorians are one group that may have been maligned as being "technically heretical" (Neill 1990:55) and as a result have often been neglected from the larger narrative. However, our journey very much begins with the Nestorians.

During a period of rapid Nestorian expansion Timothy I, the celebrated Patriarch of the Nestorian Church between 780–823, is alleged to have claimed that he "recently appointed a metropolitan bishop for the Turks and is about to do the same for the Tibetans" (Jenkins 2010 Campbell Lecture). Furthermore, on a list of places where the *Trisagon,* one of the oldest Christian prayers, is recited, Timothy records Tibet (known as Tangut in Syriac) on that list (Early Tibet 2007). It is unclear, however, whether Tangut refers to Tibet proper or a Tibetan area in the province of Gansu. Tsering (2006:322) suggests Tangut may have been in modern day Gansu province of China and not Tibet itself. Carus has even suggested

Nestorians were so active and successful "for a time it seemed that Nestorian Christianity would be the state religion of Tibet" (1909:173).

Further evidence of Nestorians can be seen by the distinctive Nestorian symbol of a cross joined to a lotus—a symbol of Buddhist enlightenment, which has been found inscribed on Tibetan manuscripts dating back to the ninth and tenth century (British Library). A cave painting dating to the ninth century Tang dynasty, shows a Nestorian cross on the crown and crosses adorning the necklace of a Tibetan saint or bodhisattva (British Museum). To have made in-roads into artwork in this way may suggest the Nestorians had considerable influence.

> "Though we do not know exactly what the Nestorians did in Tibet, or of their relative success, one could comfortably assume that they taught prayers, and catechisms, taught the Bible in some capacity, and were culturally sensitive enough to present the gospel with indigenous motifs."

Textual evidence further suggests Christian Nestorian activity. A divination text dating to the ninth and tenth centuries contains a surprising reference to "the god called 'Jesus Messiah'" (Early Tibet 2007). Kapstein, among others, has found numerous biblical references in ancient manuscripts, including the famous story of Solomon's dealing with a disputed maternity case (2000:30). Noted Tibetologist Geza Uray has found further textual evidence of Christian borrowings which he attributes to Nestorian influence (1983). The time of Timothy roughly coincided with Tibet's assimilation of Buddhism (Kapstein 2000:31), and perhaps there was a season of open curiosity towards Christianity before Tibetan Buddhism became widely entrenched. Or, at least there seemed to be a certain level of toleration that was not there when Catholics and Protestants would arrive on the scene much later. Jenkins claims "some historians believe that Nestorian missionaries influenced the religious practices of the Buddhist religion then developing in Tibet" (2008:92). Had not the Nestorian church essentially died out at the beginning of the fourteenth century, it is possible to imagine an alternate history of Tibet.

After the era of the Nestorian period, there is a gap of some five hundred years before the next round of missionaries appears on the scene. During that time, Tibetan Buddhism had extended its religious dominance. By the end of the seventeenth century, from far across the Tibetan Plateau and right up to Mongolia, Lhasa, the capital of Tibet had become the center of the Tibetan Buddhist world (Tsering 2005:111).

The Jesuit pioneers

Neill makes the bold statement that the single most important event in the missionary history of the Roman Catholic Church was "the foundation of the Jesuit Order" (1990:126). Portuguese Father Antonio de Andrade was the first Jesuit to make it into Tibet proper. Disguised as a Hindu pilgrim, Andrade set out from India in 1624. After ploughing his way up through the Himalayas, enduring altitude sickness and snow blindness, he finally arrived in Tsaparang, the capital of the Guge kingdom in western Tibet in 1625 (Tsering 2005:112; Houston 1991:18–20). The king of Guge welcomed the strange visitor, considering him to be a high lama. He allowed Andrade to teach his religion and on April 12, 1626, the foundation stone of "the first church was laid in Tibet with the name of Our Lady of Hope" (Aguilar 2010:62). In subsequent years, twelve Tibetans were baptized including the queen (ibid. 62).

The mission, however, was short-lived. In 1630, due to political turmoil and an uprising lead by monks who felt jealous and threatened by the mission, Andrade and others stationed there had to flee. The church was completely destroyed and a few years later the door to Tibet had closed. The first Jesuit attempts ended in failure (Aguilar 2010:62).

After another lengthy hiatus of no missionary engagement, on August 17, 1715, the Italian Jesuit Ippolito Desideri, who had long held ambitions of starting a mission in Tibet, began the long and hazard journey from Ladakh to Lhasa. During his journey, while fighting frost bite, lice and bandits, Desideri fortuitously met the caravan of a Mongol princess who took pity on him and allowed him to travel with her to Lhasa. Her band of soldiers protected him from thieves and her yaks kept him supplied with yak-butter tea. He finally arrived in Lhasa, after the six-month journey, on March 18, 1716 (Pomplun 2010:67–8). Desideri was welcomed by the Mongol governor who had recently deposed the sixth Dalai Lama, who gave him freedom to preach and even a room to stay in the prestigious Sera monastery (Tsering 2006:113–4).

Desideri, who was a great scholar trained in medieval philosophical debate, gave himself wholeheartedly to language study. He attained a very high degree of fluency in both written and spoken Tibetan. To use his words,

> I applied myself with an incredible ardor, with the whole of my strength, to the exercise of my work and a study of the language especially… for almost six years, studying from early morning until my nightly repast, sustained throughout the day … on a most useful and nourishing beverage called *cha* [tea] (Pomplun 2010:70).

Desideri's studies paid off and he wrote five major works on Christian theology in Tibetan (Gispert-Sauch 1990:32–3), attempting to prove the truth of Christianity and expose the flaws of Lamaism (Houston 1991:14). He primarily spent his energies debating with monks and used philosophical methods to justify the Christian faith (Tsering 2005:114) with a focus on the Trinity (Pomplun 2010:74–5, 87–9). Unfortunately, Desideri's superiors in Rome decided that the Capuchins were to take charge of the mission in Tibet and he very reluctantly left Lhasa in April 1721. As Tsering notes, "His withdrawal from the field for administrative reasons seems one of the less fortunate episodes in church history" (2005:114).

The Capuchins

Once the Capuchins were settled in Lhasa, they opened a small dispensary and worked on translating catechisms and prayers. They did not seem to have the facility of language that Desideri had, and rather than engage directly with monks, they distributed tracts among them. This did not prove to be a very wise move. Much of the literature was trampled into the ground and two monks who were caught reading them were publicly flogged (Tsering 2005:115). Despite the tension this caused, the Capuchins persisted and in 1726 they opened a small chapel. By 1742 there were twenty-seven baptized converts. However, when the new believers refused to bow down to the Dalai Lama, combined with growing political tensions, a revolt lead by monks insisted all missionaries and Christians be expelled from Lhasa. The Capuchins were lucky to escape with their lives. No sooner were they out of the city when their chapel was destroyed (Tsering 2005:115–6). The only thing that remains to this day is their church bell which they had lugged with them all the way from Rome. The bell is still housed in the famous Jokhang temple in Lhasa and the monks call it the "Jesus bell." Its Latin inscription reads TE DEUM LAUDAMUS TE DOMINUM (We praise you, O God, we acknowledge you as Lord).

The French Catholics

After the Capuchins departed, there was again a period of no engagement with Tibet for approximately one hundred years. This was largely due to political instability and growing Tibetan xenophobia. In 1846, the Vatican assigned the *Missions Etrangeres de Paris* (MEP) to be responsible for mission work in Tibet (Bray 1995:83). The MEP primarily worked on the fringes. They did make attempts to establish a mission in Lhasa, but the Lhasa government suspected they were politically motivated and refused them entry (ibid. 96). The MEP did, however, have some success on the eastern border. In 1863, the MEP were able to claim 700 converts (ibid. 88). In 1896 they published in Tibetan *A Summary of the Deeds of Jesus Christ and the Books of the Bible.* The Lhasa government reacted strongly to this large number of converts and issued an edict for all Tibetan converts to recant and return to Buddhism or be killed. Some fled, others were killed, including some of the missionaries (ibid. 88). The mission relocated further to the fringes yet remarkably a Catholic church still exists today in Markham. The parents of one of my neighbors attended the Catholic church there. He gave me a copy of this book, originally published in 1896, which is still used by the congregation today.

The Moravians

At about the same time the MEP were working on the fringes, the Moravians, in 1853, had commenced work in Ladakh. Though they never made it to Lhasa, their story is still significant. Robert has rightly observed that,

> Although cross-cultural missions were not a big priority for Protestants in the sixteenth century, the focus on Bible translation and distribution was the breakthrough that would define the outward movement of Christianity in later centuries (2009:36).

The first Moravians who set out to reach Tibetans were part of that wave of Bible translation. The brilliant linguist, Henrich Jaeschke, made an incredible contribution to the study of the Tibetan language and translation work. In 1881, Jaeschke published a Tibetan-English dictionary which is still in print today. Jaeschke also translated the New Testament. Translation work continued after his death most notably by August Francke and Joseb Gergan who, through an epic struggle, translated and published the entire Tibetan Bible in 1945 (Bray 1983:50). Allan Maberly has told this remarkable story in his 1977 book *God Spoke Tibetan.*

Today there is still a Moravian church in Leh, Ladakh, and it has been accepted as a very small minority in that culture (Bray 2011:114). One of the great grandsons of Joseph Gergan is preparing a New Testament in colloquial Ladakhi (ibid).

Mission stations on the fringes

From the 1800s onwards, the door to Tibet was firmly closed. Protestant missionaries set up mission stations on the fringes hoping to make it to Lhasa. None of them did. Their efforts on the borders were zealous, if not very successful. In 1888, the China Inland Mission (CIM) established a mission base on the north-east border of Tibet. In 1895, the Christian Missionary Alliance (CMA) also set up a base there (Tsering 2006:121). In 1897, CIM set up another base in the east of Tibet in Kanding. George Kraft, Victor Plymire, Geoffrey Bull, George Patterson, Robert Ekvall, and Annie Tyler are some of the notable missionaries of this era. Their biographies record accounts of lawlessness, resistance to the gospel, and "persistent political instability" (Bray 2011:111). The story of angry Tibetans revolting against the missionaries is a common theme (Tsering 2006:122). Ultimately political instability in these areas, combined with the rise of Communism in China, forced the missionaries to leave with little to show for their efforts. From the 1950s until mid-1980, no missionaries were allowed in these border areas (Bray 2011:113). In the mid-1990s, Tibet started to open up to foreign influences and a trickle of English teachers and business people have been able to reside there somewhat tenuously. The next chapter of missions to Tibet is yet to be written.

One name that cannot be overlooked in the history of missions to Tibet is the Indian evangelist, Sadhu Sundar Singh. Sundar was an itinerant preacher and not part of a mission organization. He made a number of forays into Tibet over a period of ten years. Though battling ill health, and against the advice of friends, in April 1929 Sundar made one last trip into Tibet and was never seen or heard of again. His disappearance and death were never solved, and the impact of his preaching is unknown (Thompson 1992).

Lessons to be Learned

What can be learned and what missiological conclusions can be drawn from this brief sketch of Christianity's somewhat unfinished journey to the Roof of the World? In order to do this systematically, the activities of the major players will be assessed in turn, followed by some concluding thoughts.

Lessons from the Nestorians

Though we do not know exactly what the Nestorians did in Tibet, or of their relative success, one could comfortably assume that they taught prayers, and catechisms, taught the Bible in some capacity, and were culturally sensitive enough to present the gospel with indigenous motifs. Though some may have considered their approach syncretistic, they appear to have been following the Pauline contextual model of Acts 17. The presence of the Nestorians was significant enough to influence sacred art and religious writings, no small feat. They also seemed adept at existing alongside the majority religion without the power brokers feeling threatened or undermined by their presence. This is in contrast to strategies used by all who followed after them.

Lessons from the Jesuits and Capuchins

Robert has suggested that,

> The significance of the Jesuits as missionaries, besides their ability to stay on course despite isolation and hardships, was their mission practice of "inculturation"—adapting themselves to the cultures they went to serve (2009:38).

While this is true to a certain extent in Tibet, and with their devotion and commitment unquestioned, the Jesuits may have focused too much on trying to "prove" the truth of Christianity through philosophical debate as well as expressing negative sentiment about the local religion. Desideri believed his apologetic writings "exposed Lamaism" (Houston 1991:20) which he openly said was "founded by the devil himself" (Gispert-Sauch 1990:37). He may have overestimated the quest for truth within the culture. The focus on apologetic material, while potentially stimulating to a small band within the educated elite, may have been misguided. Tibetan Buddhism is not essentially epistemologically focused. Tsering has noted,

> Most people in the Tibetan Buddhist world are unconcerned with gaining enlightenment, meditating, or practicing tantric rituals. Like their shamanist ancestors, they see religion as a means to solve problems of everyday life (2006:85).

As Neill has pointed out, early Catholic missionaries did not engage in Bible translation. The scriptures for them were still locked in Latin (1990:177). None of the Catholic missionaries to Tibet engaged in Bible translation. Rather, they translated prayers, catechisms, and apologetic materials. They also wrote in the register of the upper *chos skad* "religious language" and not in the vernacular. Had they engaged in Bible translation in a style that engaged the wider population, they may have had more impact.

The Capuchins also often took a dismissive approach to Buddhism. The Regent of Tibet accused them of "speaking evil of the Tibetan religion" and seeking to destroy it (Engelhardt 2005). Handing out literature did not prove to be a popular approach. The target audience was monks and lamas, who, once they realized the Capuchins were not just engaging in friendly interfaith dialogue, rioted and dispelled the missionaries. The Capuchins were eventually "seen as subversive not only of spiritual but also of political authority in a culture where there was no clear boundary between the two" (Bray 2011:113).

Lessons from the French Catholics

Like the Jesuits and Capuchins before them, the *Missions Etrangeres de Paris* (MEP) did not translate the Bible, rather, they too translated prayers, catechisms, and materials about the life of Christ. Curiously, they chose to use a different term for God than the term Desideri and earlier Catholics had used. They used a coined term that many Tibetans still find dissonant to this day (Morrison 2018). The small church planted by the MEP is still in existence and, based on personal communications with both foreigners and Tibetans who are familiar with it, the church is largely considered to be syncretistic. To continue to operate a church in that context for so many years, however, is still no small achievement.

The MEP was seen as a political threat to the Tibetans. It appears that the missionaries themselves were largely to blame for this as "the mission consistently claimed French government backing" (Bray 1995:93) and would often declare themselves official representatives of the French legation in Beijing. Rather than impressing the Tibetan government with an assumed authority, this led to Tibetan hostilities (ibid). Clearly the MEP would have done well to distance itself from any political entities.

Lessons from the Moravians

Robert has noted the importance of vernacular Bible translation in the spread of Christianity. Though the Moravians led the way in linguistic research and Bible translation, they did not follow the Protestant tradition of producing vernacular Bible translations. Jaeschke, though he did have good reason, went against the advice of his own Moravian mission and produced a translation written in the highest register of religious language (Bray 2011:107). This high register translation could only be read by those with a monastic education. The goal was to reach monks far and wide across Tibet, but because of profound dialect differences and a highly literal style of translation, the Bible was not nearly as widely understood as had been anticipated.

The legacy of the Moravians still lives on today. Though the Bible translation may not have been the "breakthrough" Robert has observed elsewhere, it laid a foundation for future translation work (2009:36). As Tsering notes, "The Moravian missionaries were marked by their great devotion, faithfulness in prayer and high standards of scholarship" (2006:119).

Lessons from missions on the fringes

Despite valiant efforts, the various mission stations had only a precarious foothold on the borders of Tibet and in the end produced little lasting results. Pioneer missionary, Victor Plymire (1881–1956), who labored long on the Tibetan border, made the distribution of tracts one of his main evangelistic strategies. The tracts were "simple expositions of Christian teaching written in Tibetan, but in a style that would have been recognisable at an American revivalist meeting" (Bray 2011:111). He was indicative of other mission station endeavors that focused on literature distribution. Bray has identified two main reasons for the lack of success of these missions. Firstly, it was "the continuing linguistic and conceptual challenge of communicating the Christian message in a manner that … truly "made sense" to the Tibetan mind" (ibid. 113). Secondly, it was the political environments they operated in. The missionaries needed the permission of local centers of power and these were typically corrupt and unstable (ibid). Had the mission stations had more emphasis on a holistic approach, relevant vernacular translation, culturally aware gospel presentations, and less emphasis on literature distribution, they may have had greater impact.

Conclusions

Nehrbass argues that a nuanced approach to theory-building, one that looks at a range of factors, is required in order to avoid generalisations and provide in-depth analysis of the historical record (2018:4). In the case of Christianity in Tibet, one could perhaps focus primarily on geography, the tyranny of distance, the harsh environment and how this has shaped the story. Or one could focus on the political machinations that have inflicted Tibet over the centuries, the various dynasties that have come and gone in China, and in more recent history the rise of Communism which both closed and more recently has opened up Tibet. Furthermore, one could focus on the political workings of various mission societies. Or that the early Catholics were at the mercy of their ecclesiastical orders and "quarrels about jurisdiction" (Gispert-Sauch 1990:38) where the best outcome for the gospel did not always result.

If, as Robert has suggested, vernacular translations were a main key to Christian expansion, one can see why the story of expansion is still to take place in Tibet—the lack of vernacular scriptures. Further, attempts to reach Tibetans were almost exclusively aimed at monks and lamas who became hostile when they felt their positions were being threatened by conversions. Little was done to engage ordinary Tibetans. This approach reflected the deliberate strategy that a turning to God would be a top-down rather than a grassroots movement. With perhaps the exception of the Nestorians, gospel presentations were largely done from a Western perspective. Contextualizing the gospel so that it made more sense to the Tibetan mind may have seen greater fruit.

Finally, in summarizing some of the main causes for the lack of penetration of the gospel in Tibet, one does not want to overlook the spiritual dimension. In 1892 Hudson Taylor stated, "To make converts in Tibet is similar to going into a cave and trying to rob a lioness of her cubs" (Hattaway 2013:316). Even if Taylor slightly over-stated things, clearly there is an element of spiritual warfare involved and this is another factor as to why Tibet has had little exposure to the gospel in both Word and deed. Geoffrey Bull, pioneer missionary on the fringes of Tibet, who had a lengthy incarceration for his faith, wrote in one of his accounts,

> If one examines the history of those who have sought to enter Tibet it is significant to notice that many, if not all of those who have presumed to go up against these gates of evil, have been mauled in one way or another by the very talons of the devil. In my own case I had no inkling at that time how severe that mauling was ultimately to be (1966:70).

Most Tibetans are still to hear the message and see it in action. However, as Tibet has opened up in the past two decades, and a small band of missionaries have been able to reside there, vernacular translations are emerging, and many Tibetans are now hearing and seeing the good news for the first time. Perhaps Robert's "breakthrough" is just around the corner.

References

Aguilar, Mario, I. 2010. "The Jesuits in Tibet at the Time of the VI and VII Dalai Lamas." *The Tibet Journal.* 35 (3) 61–77.

British Library: http://idp.bl.uk/database/oo_loader.a4d?pm=IOL%20Tib%20J%20766.

British Museum: http://idp.bl.uk/database/oo_loader.a4d?pm=1919,0101,0.48.

Bray, J. 1995. *French Catholic Mission and the Politics of China and Tibet 1846–1865.* Proceedings of the 7th Seminar of the International Association for Tibetan Studies. 7 (1) 83–96.

________. "Early Protestant Missionary Engagement with the Himalayan Region and Tibet." In *Ladakhi Histories, Local and Regional Perspectives.* Boston: Brill.

________. 2011. "Sacred Words and Earthly Powers: Christian Missionary Engagement with Tibet." The Transactions of the Asiatic Society of Japan. 3 (1) 93–118.

________. 2014. "Stumbling on the Threshold: Annie R. Taylor's Tibetan Pioneer Mission, 1893–1907." *Bulletin of Tibetology.* 50 (1–2) 91–116.

Bull, G.T. 1966. *Tibetan Tales.* Hodder and Stoughton, London.

Carus, P. 1909. "Nestorius and Nestorians." *The Open Court.* 1909 (3) 3.

Des Missions Etrangeres. 1896. *A Summary of the Deeds of Jesus Christ and the Books of the Bible* (*Ye shu kri sto'i spyod pa dang gsung rab rnams kyi mdo bsdud zhes bya ba bzhugs so*). Hong Kong: Imprimerie De La Societe.

Early Tibet. 2007. *Christianity in Early Tibet.* https://earlytibet.com/2007/12/02/christianity-in-early-tibet.

Engelhardt, G. 2005. "Between Tolerance and Dogmatism: Tibetan Reactions to the Capuchin Missionaries in Lhasa, 1707–1745." Zentralasiatische Studien. 34 (2005) 55–97.

Gispert-Sauch, G. 1990. "Desideri and Tibet." *The Tibet Journal.* 15 (2) 29–39.

Hattaway, P. 2013. *Peoples of the Buddhist World: A Christian Prayer Diary.* Pasadena, CA: William Carey Library.

Houston, G.W. 1991. "Jesus and His Missionaries in Tibet." *The Tibet Journal.* 16 (4) 8–27.

Jaeschke, H. 1881. *A Tibetan-English Dictionary.* Delhi: Motilal Banarsidass.

Jenkins, P. 2008. *The Lost History of Christianity: The Thousand-Year Golden Age.* New York: Harper Collins.

________. 2010. Campbell University, The 11th Annual Religion Lecture Series. https://vimeo.com/10783370 & https://vimeo.com/10785748.

Kapstein, M.T. 2000. *The Tibetan Assimilation of Buddhism: Conversion, Contestation and Memory.* Oxford: Oxford University.

Maberly, A. 1977. *God Spoke Tibetan.* Orange, CA: Evangel Bible Translators.

Morrison, J. 2018. *The Contextualization of the Term for "God" in Tibetan: The Case for Dkon Mchog.* La Mirada, CA: Biola University. Unpublished manuscript.

Nehrbass, K. 2018. *Missiological Historiography: How Historians of Mission Construct Practical Theories.* La Mirada, CA: Biola University. Unpublished manuscript.

Neill, S. 1990. *A History of Christian Missions.* London: Penguin.

Patterson, G. 1956. *God's Fool.* London: Faber and Faber.

Pomplun, T. 2010. *Jesuit on the Roof of the World: Ippolito Desideri's Mission to Eighteenth-century Tibet.* Oxford: Oxford University.

Plymire, D. V. 1983. *High Adventure in Tibet.* Springfield, MO: Gospel Publishing House.

Robert, D. 2009. *Christian Mission: How Christianity Became a World Religion.* Wiley-Blackwell.

Thompson, P. 1992. *Sadhu Sundar Singh.* Carlisle: OM Publishing.

Tsering, M. 2006. *Sharing Christ in the Tibetan Buddhist World.* Central Asia Publishing.

Uray, G. 1983. "Tibet's Connections with Nestorianism and Manichaeism in the 8th-10th Centuries." 399–429. In Steinkellner & Tauscher, eds. *Contributions on Tibetan Buddhist Religion and Philosophy.* Vienna: Arbeitskries für Tibetische und Buddhistische Studien Universität Wien.

Barriers and Bridges to Mission in Cambodia: An Historical Perspective

Paul Ka-Ming Au

> *Hardly had he arrived when he began to study the Khmer language, but very soon he realized that the Cambodians had no desire to change their religion. After a year passed at the court of Longvek, he left for China and then returned to his native land* (Ponchaud 1990:23–24).
>
> *It happened sometimes that while I was preaching, many round me hearing me very well, and being very satisfied with what I told them, that if there come along any of these priests and said, 'This is good, but ours is better,' they would depart and leave me alone* (Chandler 2008:98).

The quotes refer to Gaspar Da Cruz, a Portuguese Dominican, who was the first recorded missionary to Cambodia in 1555. He came, he saw, and he left. His missionary effort was the beginning of centuries of frustration and bafflement for many earnest Christians who tried to share the gospel in Cambodia. Despite all these difficulties a recent survey estimates there are 420,000 Christians in Cambodia, out of a population of fourteen million; nearly three percent of the population could be Christian (Hyde 2012:73). The thesis of this chapter is that there are important lessons to be learned from the past which should inform current church and mission strategy in Cambodia. This chapter has three main parts: part one gives a historical overview of the major phases of mission in Cambodia, part two summarizes historical bridges and barriers, and part three notes implications for today.

Major Phases of Mission Effort

Since 1555, the missionary endeavor has waxed and waned in Cambodia depending on world events, regional politics, and internal stability. But before Da Cruz stepped off his ship, Cambodia had already been birthed, grown to a great empire, shrunk, and by the sixteenth century was in steady decline. What was the historical context of the early Christian mission in Cambodia?

Before the birth of Christ there were fortified settlements and trade with India in the area now known as Cambodia. There was no single nation yet but there were various polities or kingdoms which vied with one another, Funan and Chenla, where Sivaism and Buddhism were already being practiced alongside animist beliefs. But in 802 A.D. King Jayavarman II moved his capital to the north of Tonle Sap, the Great Lake, and founded the "Angkor Empire" (Tully 2006:7). By then ancient Khmer was being used alongside Sanskrit to record the acts of kings and historic literature in stone stela (Coe 2003:97). This empire lasted 500 years, ending in 1327, more than 200 years before Da Cruz arrived. The first wave of missionary effort came in the "Post-Classic" or "Middle" period of Cambodian history, which lasted from 1327 to 1863. This was a period of constant national decline when the nation was racked by internal division and a succession of kings looked to external forces and modern weapons to stabilize the nation. Christian mission to Cambodia began when the country was open to the outside and looking for aid; but still overshadowed by memories of the Angkor Empire.

1555–1659: The first Christian missionaries

For a hundred years the first missionaries were Catholic priests from Portugal and Spain. The first recorded contact with Europeans was by King Ang Chan in 1515 when he purchased canons and crossbows from the Portuguese in Java (Ponchaud 1990:23). He used the weapons to defeat his rivals and the Siamese. After this initial commercial contact, Gaspar Da Cruz was sent from Malacca to Cambodia by the Vice-King of the Portuguese Indies because traders had intimated that, "Cambodians had a great desire to become Catholics" (Ibid).

The need for weapons and commerce kept the door open for Catholic priests and consequently they enjoyed permission to learn the language and teach people. It was during this period the first Christian literature was translated into Khmer. However, the period was racked by insecurity as Cambodia fought a series of wars with Siam. As the Siamese ascended, Cambodian kings looked for help. King Satha even promised to be baptized if the Spanish and Portuguese would destroy his enemies (26). Other Cambodian kings looked to Vietnam and one even became a Muslim as they sought various patrons; this internal factionalism only weakened the nation further. In response to requests for help, a series of expeditions were sent from Malacca, some military and some religious, but they all ended in disaster. Some never reached their destination and a whole series of missionaries died due to disease and general insecurity in Cambodia. Ponchaud remarks that by the beginning of seventeenth century the, "Evangelization of the Khmer people themselves had practically not begun" (1990:27). But events in Japan, Vietnam and other parts of Asia started to change the situation. Persecution of Catholics in those nations caused a mass migration to safe havens, one of which was Cambodia. These refugees were established by the Catholic Church in their own villages but there was no attempt at integration with the local Khmer communities.

1659–1863: 200 Years of insecurity and rivalry

In 1659, a new missionary charter was drawn up by the Catholic Church, partly as a result of the Council of Trent and investigations made after the mass persecutions across Asia. Some points are still very relevant for missions today: create a local clergy, avoid involvement in politics and adapt to local customs (1990:34–36). Instead of delegating the evangelization of the colonies to the kings of Spain and Portugal, the Apostolic See sought to directly fulfill its missionary mandate. New Apostolic vicars were appointed from Rome to certain geographical areas and commissioned to carry out the charter. Pierre Lambert de la Motte was appointed over a huge area, from Siam to Southern China which included Cambodia.

Unfortunately, this period was marked by rivalry between the new Apostolic vicars and the missionaries under the patronage of Spain and Portugal. This went as far as false accusations leading to imprisonment of some missionaries and even murder. A Portuguese Catholic family hired someone to attack a new priest and he bled to death. Despite the good intentions of the new charter Christianity made very little progress due to internal church factionalism, and the perpetual insecurity caused by the rise of Siam and Vietnam. By the end of the seventeenth century there was very little to show for all the effort and sacrifice.

Again, external events altered the situation in Cambodia. In 1750 Vietnam expelled all foreign missionaries and the Apostolic vicar, Bishop Lefevbre, relocated to Phnom Penh; until then the Apostolic vicar had always been based in Siam or Vietnam. Missionaries again made serious attempts to learn Khmer and began to focus their efforts on Cambodians as opposed to ministering to the mainly Vietnamese Catholic refugees in Cambodia.

In 1768, Gervais Levavasseur, a priest from France, arrived in Cambodia. He learned Khmer and translated important prayers and a catechism into Khmer. He was the first missionary to establish the structures necessary for a truly Khmer church, the notable feature being the use of the Khmer language and the push to ordain Cambodians. He became known as the "Apostle of the Khmers." However, the whole period was racked by war and the swings of power between Vietnam and Siam. For a brief period, from 1841 to 1846, Cambodia even ceased to exist having been effectively divided by its neighbors, Vietnam and Siam. Referring to this period, Ponchaud comments, "The church of Cambodia seemed to be annihilated. All the efforts put forth for a century seemed reduced to nothing" (1990:57).

Then external events changed the political and religious situation within Cambodia. In 1846, King Ang Doung ascended to the throne of Cambodia after the Siamese and Vietnamese both withdrew from Cambodia. The aggressors were in a stalemate and weary of fighting each other; the Vietnamese were also worried about the French (Tully 2007:75). In 1859, the French assaulted Saigon and overcame the Vietnamese. The French subjugation of the Vietnamese quickly led to Cambodia becoming a "protectorate," effectively ending independence. Part of the conditions of the protectorate was freedom guaranteed to the Catholic Church to preach, teach, and build churches. Peace enabled these activities to continue for nearly one hundred years but the stamp of "Christianity as a foreign religion" was further imprinted on the Khmer sub-consciousness.

1863–1939: Peace and the first Khmer New Testament

The French protectorate was a period of relative peace for Cambodia. France kept Siam at bay and even managed to regain some of the lost provinces but the price was heavy. There was civil oppression and taxes as the French sought to extract finances from the nation (Chandler 2008:178–179). The colonial authorities viewed the Khmer as lazy (168) and allowed many Vietnamese to enter Cambodia as workers and tradesmen as they were perceived as more industrious. About seven percent of the Vietnamese migrants were already Catholic and their large numbers dominated the church. The believers were settled in communities separate from Cambodians on uninhabited land; often awarded by the local French officials with no reference to the Cambodian authorities (Ponchaud 1990:73). This only bred more hatred for Christians, as they were mainly Vietnamese protected by the French.

By the turn of the twentieth century there were about 36,000 Catholics out of an estimated population of three million; but 32,500 were ethnic Vietnamese and there were only 3,000 ethnic Khmer Catholics (1990:87). The long period of peace did enable the establishment of Catholic communities, orphanages, hospitals, schools, a seminary, and linguistic works such as dictionaries and grammars. But the ethnic imbalance and intensity of feelings were so strong that ethnic Vietnamese and Khmer could not be trained in the same seminary (1990:90).

In 1923 Arthur Hammond, the first recorded evangelical missionary, arrived in Cambodia from America. His team had four members, and they committed themselves to translating the Bible into Khmer and establishing a Bible school (Jones 1963:12–13). However, the new converts and the Bible school were viewed as subversive and a royal edict by King Sisowath Monivong forbade proselytizing in 1932 (Ellison 1991); but the work continued and the Khmer New Testament was completed in 1934, and nearly all the Old Testament by 1940. This was a significant achievement considering the team never had more than six members at a time. Despite many trials the Christian and Missionary Alliance (CMA) team managed to evangelize and disciple while translating; having the scriptures in Khmer added a new dimension to church work. The CMA strategy was very different from that of the Catholic Church, focusing on literature in Khmer and outreach to the rural population.

1939–1953: World War II to independence

WW II caused another period of instability in Cambodia. The Vichy French administration let the Japanese enter Cambodia and in return they allowed the administration to continue but important provinces were ceded to Thailand (formerly Siam), which was under Japanese occupation. But after 1945 the French reasserted their authority and claimed the land back from Thailand and a new wave of insecurity began as the Vietminh, Marxist communists, began to infiltrate Cambodia. They saw Catholics as the enemy and many of their settlements were attacked. Priests tried to move Catholics to military posts but this was not successful. In addition, *Issarak,* Khmer nationalists, backed by Thailand, waged guerilla warfare against the French and the nationalists gained control over the countryside (Jones 1963:33). Christian leaders of all descriptions were hampered in their movements and again war destroyed the growth that had been made. But a significant milestone had been reached, the Bible had been translated into Khmer.

1953–1975: Independence to genocide to invasion

In 1953 Cambodia finally gained independence from France. The worsening state of Vietnam and the communist insurgency ironically helped Cambodia gain independence without a fully-fledged war. King Sihanouk abdicated his throne in order to become fully active in politics and set about transforming his nation into a modern state, but global politics ultimately doomed his grand vision for the nation.

However, the first ten years were a golden time for the nation, there was peace, freedom of religion was declared, and the King was even presented with a special copy of the Bible printed in England (Cormack 1997:80); but aside from CMA no other evangelical missions were allowed to enter the country. In the fledgling Khmer Evangelical Church trouble came in the form of CMA's commitment to indigenization. In 1955 finances were withdrawn as plans were made to "indigenize" the church (Ellison 1991), consequently some pastors changed jobs, numbers fell at the Bible school, and there was a general sifting of evangelical Christians (Jones 1963:25). Further trouble came in 1965 when the government, led by Sihanouk, expelled American missionaries (Ellison 1991). This was linked to the entry of American soldiers into Vietnam as Sihanouk desperately tried to keep Cambodia out of the conflict and remain "neutral." However, Catholic missionaries, mainly from France, remained.

The Catholic Church finally declared Cambodia as a separate "Vicariate" from Vietnam and the first Cambodian leaders embarked on contextualization—partly in response to Vatican II. This resulted in celebrating some Christian festivals at the time of Buddhist ones. By 1968 there were about 62,000 Catholics in an estimated total population of six million people (Ponchaud 1990:108). Decades of missionary work had finally achieved the marks of an established Khmer church—local leaders, the Khmer Bible, and widespread Christian ministry in terms of geography and type; but this was all about to be overtaken by events in Vietnam and the Cold War.

1970–1993: From genocide to peace

In 1970 General Lon Nol, backed by the USA, deposed Sihanouk in a coup d'etat. The rallying cry was *Kap Yuon* which means "Kill the Vietnamese." General Lon Nol used the innate Khmer antipathy for Vietnamese to gain support. In the Khmer mind Vietnamese ethnicity was synonymous with Catholicism and Christianity. Racist graffiti at the time spelled the "t" in Vietnamese in the shape of the cross (1990:120), and so Catholics were slaughtered in a surge of nationalist fervor. The country descended into chaos as the new Khmer government tried to drive out the North Vietnamese soldiers from their camps along the Ho Chi Minh trail but they were no match for the Vietcong (Chandler 2008:251). Then the South Vietnamese and Americans invaded Cambodia and attacked the Vietcong, driving them North. Meanwhile the Khmer Rouge, gradually took control of the countryside. By 1972, the armistice was signed between North Vietnam and the USA. Lon Nol controlled only Phnom Penh and a few other urban centers. Relying on the patronage of the USA, the new government allowed American missionaries back into Cambodia. With the capital swelled by refugees to an estimated two million people, different church groups held crusades with international speakers and unexpectedly—revival broke out (Cormack 1997:126).

In 1972 and 1973, Dr. Mooneyham from World Vision spoke and 3,000 made commitments (Ellison 1991). Then Todd Burke's campaign, in 1973, sparked a controversial charismatic outpouring that saw thousands come to Christ with many accompanying signs and wonders (Burke T. and D. Burke 1977). All the while the Khmer Rouge gradually drew the noose around Phnom Penh. Accounts from the time are disconcerting, one of the most poignant images being hundreds of Cambodians being baptized in the Bassac river while Khmer Rouge forces advanced on the opposite side (Cormack 1997:146). As the impending darkness of the Khmer Rouge descended the various Christian groups had meetings about whether to flee or stay. Many Catholic priests, monks, and nuns decided to stay in Phnom Penh knowing they were likely to be martyred. They called two Khmer priests back from France to join them, one was Joseph Chhmar Salas, the first Cambodian Apostolic Vicar (Ponchaud 1990:140). Evangelical Khmer leaders overseas also decided to return, like Chhirc Taing who left his wife and child in Scotland, his impassioned preaching at the well-known Keswick meetings awoke England to Cambodia's plight. All the non-Catholic missionaries left Cambodia before the downfall of the Lon Nol regime.

In April 1975 the Khmer Rouge captured Phnom Penh. So began the nightmare and the whole country was turned into a giant concentration camp (Cormack 1997:179). The population was led out of Phnom Penh into the countryside; the remaining French Catholic priests were separated from their flock and sent to Thailand. Chhirc Taing was last seen handing out tracts to those leaving and the mass killing began. Exactly how many people were killed will never be known. Chandler wrote, "On a national scale it is estimated that over the lifetime of the regime nearly two million people—or one person in four—died as a result of DK (Democratic Kampuchea) policies and actions," (Chandler 2008:259). Many Cambodian Christian leaders and their flocks were killed or died during the genocide. From 1975–78, 50,000 Cambodians fled to Thailand and 150,000 to Vietnam (Ponchaud 1990:166). Catholic and non-Catholic missionaries who had worked in Cambodia ministered in the various refugee camps searching for friends and beloved brothers and sisters in Christ. During these years and into the late 1980s secular and Christian organizations flooded into Thailand where huge border camps were established for the refugees.

In 1979 Vietnam invaded Cambodia, some say prompted by border incursions. It is important to note that Vietnam was under the patronage of the Soviet Union and Cambodia was supported by China. After the defeat of the Khmer Rouge even more Cambodians fled to Thailand where thousands were already being allowed to go to the West. In 1980, amidst all the fighting the Cambodian rice harvest failed. When famine loomed an estimated one million Cambodians fled to Thailand.

During the chaos and trauma many in the camps made professions of faith, more than 25,000 Cambodians were baptized by evangelical missionaries. Ponchaud railed against the "Anglo-Saxon" missionaries who preached in the refugee camps that the genocide was God's judgment (1990:169). There were tensions between various mission groups but despite this the gospel was preached to many thousands who were the seeds of Cambodian churches that would be established in America and France.

Shamefully, Western countries actually supported the Khmer Rouge and the other Cambodian groups in exile as they fought the Vietnamese. Meanwhile the Vietnamese installed a puppet government and Cambodia was renamed, The People's Republic of Kampuchea (PRK), a communist state. The Cold War was in full swing and the West and China turned Vietnam and the PRK into pariah states. Both survived only due to the patronage of the Soviet Union and her allies. The world knew about the genocide but global politics caused the exclusion of the PRK and the West patronized the Khmer Rouge. For a further ten years, from 1979 to 1989, the few Christians left in Cambodia were persecuted by the communist PRK regime; mere possession of a Bible led to imprisonment. The church in Cambodia existed underground, a handful of missions were allowed to operate but only in relief and development work.

In the late 1980s world events again shook Cambodia. *Glasnost* and *Perestroika* broke up the Soviet Union and there were no finances for Vietnam and the PRK. In 1989 Cambodia changed its name again to the State of Cambodia (SOC), Buddhism became the state religion and the persecution of Christians eased as Cambodia turned to the West for help (Chandler 2008:205). However, a dirty guerilla war was still being fought in the countryside and along the Thai border. In 1990 the USA finally stopped supporting the opposition forces, which included the Khmer Rouge; and in 1991 the Paris Peace accords were signed. From 1992–93, Cambodia again became a protectorate, this time under the United Nations. By the end of 1993, and US$ two billion later a new elected government was in power and peace, of a kind, settled on the land. With the peace came a new constitution, a return to monarchy, and the UN established the Kingdom of Cambodia.

1993-today: From the UN to the present

One of the key points for Christians in the new constitution was the freedom of religion. Buddhism was enshrined as the state religion but people were free to choose any religion. Cambodia opened up and looked to the West and Japan for funds; aid poured in and with it many missionaries. In 1989 there were less than thirty missionaries serving in Phnom Penh, by 1995 there were at least 200 non-Catholic missionaries serving in different locations. By 2011 individual missions had hundreds of missionaries. The increase was partly related to a shift in mission strategy initiated in the 1970s.

Before the genocide the mission effort in Cambodia was limited in terms of personnel and finance, partly due to internal resistance but also due to Cambodia being a small nation on the fringe of the global church. However, in 1974 Ralph Winter proposed and expounded the concept of "unreached people groups" at Lausanne (Lewis 2018). With the shift towards unreached people groups, Cambodia became a target nation. In addition, international media focus on the genocide put Cambodia top of the list for Christian sympathy and interest. People, missions, and churches were galvanized into action to help and evangelize Cambodia.

All this effort bore fruit, the Cambodian Baptists even became known as an example of a "church planting movement" by David Garrison (n.d.:28). Bruce Carlton, a missionary who pioneered that movement, stated that from 1993 to 2002 the Baptist convention grew from 6 to 260 congregations (2004:130). Different surveys show how the number of Christians has consistently increased since 1993. The government census of 2008 (NIS 2010) recorded 50,000 Christians. A wide-ranging study by Antioch estimated 240,000 in 2007 (2008) and this study was repeated and estimated 420,000 Christians in 2012 (Hyde 2012:73). More recently a lower estimate of 171,000 Christians was produced by Mission Kampuchea (2018). Despite the wide variance between estimates they all show an increase in the total number of Cambodian Christians and the trend points to continued growth.

"There is no doubt that Christianity has penetrated Cambodia more than ever before, in total numbers, geographical range and across ethnic groups. For some the increase may indicate the time has come for a strategic shift in mission and church strategy."

Regarding geographical coverage another survey carried out in 2009 identified a church in every province and nearly every district; nearly 2,000 villages out of 14,000 had a church (Mission Kampuchea 2010); their most recent survey shows that there are now an estimated 3,204 churches in Cambodia (2018). There is no doubt that Christianity has penetrated Cambodia more than ever before, in total numbers, geographical range and across ethnic groups. For some the increase may indicate the time has come for a strategic shift in mission and church strategy.

Some missions, collectively known as the "closure movement" still use the unreached people group concept as an important criterion for target selection (Higgins 2010:128, Lewis 2018). Higgins explained a scale used by IMB and others which runs from zero to seven; the bottom meaning no evangelical churches and six being more than ten percent evangelical churches. On this scale Cambodia is at least on level three, less than two percent evangelical with widespread church planting in the last two years. In Higgin's mission, Global Teams, this would shift Cambodia from "unreached" to "reached" and so be a target for mobilization versus pioneer efforts. His comments are still relevant today—should missionaries today still be pioneering church planting in Cambodia?

With the rapid expansion of the church have come other issues. For example, the tensions between these: "congregational and mission structures" (Pierson 2009); money—its use and abuse (Johnson 2010); patronage—social (Ledgerwood & Vighen 2002), economic (Slocomb 2010:294–198), spiritual (Thigpen 2015); orphans and orphanages (Knauss 2017); a whole raft of contextualization issues; and nationalism. All are not peculiar to Cambodia but exist in varying degrees throughout the global church. What remains peculiar to Cambodia is the geopolitical context—permanently caught between two powerful neighbors whose influence is countered by the patronage of the global powers of the day.

In contrast to the positive narrative of recent Christian expansion, secular commentators write pessimistically about the recent past. Using phrases such as "Cambodia's curse" (Brinkley 2011) or "Cambodia's metaphorical hunger" (Ear 2013:133) but even Brinkley ends on a positive note about the future and quotes Peang-Meth on the current regime, "If the right spots are pushed at the right time, a seemingly unchangeable situation can be altered. Call me a dreamer if you will, but thoughts give rise to dreams, and dreams to actions," (2011:357). His musings could well be applied to recent Cambodian church history, he sees what Da Cruz never did—hope in Cambodia.

Summary of Historical Barriers and Bridges in Cambodia

The overarching theme of church history in Cambodia is the cycle of advance and then decimation. Periods of closure resulted in rejection of Christianity and violent destruction, openness allowed growth, but with each advance the church expanded further and penetrated deeper. From the sixteenth to the twentieth centuries, this cycle of closure and openness to Christianity repeated several times, and from this pattern certain major barriers and bridges become evident. Major barriers include war and insecurity; the close links between Christianity and patron states; a unique and resistant religious system; and a lack of focus on Cambodia and the Khmer people from the global church.

> "The overarching theme of church history in Cambodia is the cycle of advance and then decimation. Periods of closure resulted in rejection of Christianity and violent destruction, openness allowed growth, but with each advance the church expanded further and penetrated deeper."

The sheer survival of Cambodia as a nation state and Khmer, as a spoken and written language, is a testament to the rugged nationalism and cultural identity of the people. Much of this perseverance of identity has come from the national religion, Buddhism. But Cambodian Buddhism, mixed as it is with Animism and Brahmanism, is distinctly different to other forms of Buddhism (Hansen 2005:5128 and Hyde 2015). This uniqueness, with associated social structures and cultural values has been a formidable barrier to Christianity. The final major barrier was the inattention of the global church to Cambodia, and more specifically the Khmer people. The missionary effort over the centuries was earnest and sincere but constantly suffered from a lack of personnel and resources. However, this was changed by the Khmer Rouge genocide and the strategic shift towards unreached people groups.

Major bridges for the gospel were peace, patronage by Christian nations, missionaries, religious freedom, and the Bible in Khmer. Since the sixteenth century periods of Christian expansion in Cambodia were invariably associated with patronage by Christian nations, the longest period being under the French protectorate. With the patronage of Christian states came freedom for missionaries to operate and freedom for Cambodians to convert. The final major bridge was the translation of the Bible into Khmer, the power of the Bible in a people group's heart language cannot be underestimated.

What are the Lessons from the Past for Today?

Christians cannot ignore the geopolitics of Cambodia even though it may seem the traumas of the past are over. In 2003 Cambodian nationalism rose again as riots against Thailand erupted in Phnom Penh due to the border conflict over temple at *Preah Vihear* (Phnom Post 2003). More recently resentment is stirring in the coastal city of Sihanoukville against Chinese investment in casinos (Prasso 2018). Past and current conflicts represent the tension between the need for assistance provided by patrons and the desire to preserve national identity.

The church in Cambodia needs to make plans in the light of the current geopolitical situation. Most immediately, as the influence of China increases, it is important for Christians to understand the current and potential impact of the Chinese state (Burgos & Ear 2010) and the Chinese church, for example through the "Back to Jerusalem movement" on Cambodia (Hattaway 2003).

None deny the general positive impact of the Christian mission effort but the nature of cross-cultural missions involves the presence of foreigners. Although Hyde notes that seventy-five percent of Cambodian churches have received no assistance from overseas (Hyde 2012:75) one has only to watch Joyce Mayer and Yonggi Cho preaching on national Cambodian television to see the foreign face of Christianity. At one level it can be argued that this is the globalization of mission but with it comes the potential of a nationalistic backlash. Cross-cultural missionaries of all nationalities need to ask, "Are our activities reinforcing the Cambodian notion that Christianity is purely a foreign religion promoted by foreigners, especially considering the growth of the Cambodian church?"

The Cambodian church is maturing. One indication of this is that the Cambodian church is becoming a mission sending church with missionaries in Thailand, Laos, and Vietnam (Hyde 2012:80). Cambodian leaders are recognized internationally by the global church (Himm 2003 and Mam 2012). Cambodian founded and led Christian organizations such as Mission Kampuchea 2021 and the Cambodian national prayer network are active and dynamic, and a new generation of Khmer leaders is emerging some of whom have grown up in Christian homes. The church will continue to face contextualization issues, leadership transitions, and continue to negotiate the global church agenda with the needs of Cambodia but most fundamentally the key question for every Cambodian Christian remains, "How to be Christian and Khmer?"

Conclusion

This chapter has shown that Cambodia has been resistant to the gospel for hundreds of years but was also neglected by the global church. The Pol Pot genocide caused the world to turn its attention to Cambodia and the Khmer people. Hopefully that period on the world's stage and the resulting outpouring of help will mark a turning point in the nation's history away from the destructive cycle of the past to a new future in the new globalized world. Today there are more Cambodian Christians than ever before due to peace, security, the concentration of missionary effort, and the translation of the Bible. However, the history of the church in Cambodia has been marked by sowing, growth, and then eradication and scattering. It remains to be seen whether this dreadful cycle will be repeated again at some point in the future or will there be a "new song" (Isa 42:10)? Only time will tell.

References

Antioch Research. 2008. *Portrait of the Body of Christ in Cambodia: A Detailed Statistical Survey of the Church in Cambodia and its Characteristics.* Phnom Penh, Cambodia: Antioch Research.

Brinkley, Joel. 2011. *Cambodia's Curse. The Modern History of a Troubled Land.* NY: Public Affairs.

Burke, T., and D. Burke. 1977. *Anointed for Burial.* Plainfield, NJ: Logos International.

Burgos, S., and S. Ear. 2010. "China's Strategic Interests in Cambodia: Interests and Resources." *Asian Survey.* 3 (50) 615–39.

Carlton, B. R. 2004. *Amazing Grace: Lessons on Church Planting Movements from Cambodia 2nd ed.* Radical Obedience.

Chandler, D. 2008. *A History of Cambodia* (Fourth Edition). Bangkok: Silkworm Books.

Coe, M. D. 2003. *Angkor and the Khmer Civilization.* London: Thames and Hudson.

Cormack, D. 1997. *Killing Fields, Living Fields: An Unfinished Portrait of the Cambodian Church, The Church that would not Die.* Crowborough, England: OMF International and MARC.

Ear, Sophal. 2013. *Aid Dependence in Cambodia. How Foreign Assistance Undermines Democracy.* NY: Columbia University.

Ellison, P. 1991. "A Short History of the Cambodian Evangelical Church: With Particular Attention Being Given to People Movements and Some Factors related to Church Growth." *Cambodian Christian Services Conference,* San Jose, CA. Unpublished manuscript.

Garrison, D. (n.d.). *Church Planting Movements.* Richmond, VA: International Mission Board of the Southern Baptist Convention.

Hansen, A. 2005. "Khmer Religion." In *Encylopedia of Religion 2nd ed.* 5127–5135. L. Jones, ed. NewYork:Macmillan.

Higgins, K. 2010. "Missiology and the Measurement of Engagement: Personal Reflections on Tokyo." *International Journal of Frontier Missions* 27 (3) 127–32.

Himm, S. S. with Jan Greenough. 2003. *The Tears of My Soul.* London: Monarch Books.

Hyde, S. 2012. *Portrait of the Body of Christ in Cambodia: A Detailed Statistical Study of the Church in Cambodia and Its Characteristics.* Phnom Penh: Antioch Institute.

________. 2015. *A Missiological and Critical Study of Cambodia's Historical, Cultural, and Sociopolitcal Characteristics to Identify the Factors of Rapid Growth and Propose its Future Prognosis.* Bethany International University, Singapore. Unpublished dissertation.

Johnson, J. 2010. "The 'Thinning' Revisited: Dependency and Church Planting in Cambodia." *International Journal of Frontier Missions,* 27 (2) 69–72.

Jones, C. 1963. *Light in Their Dwellings: A History of Forty Years of Missions in Cambodia.* Nyack, NY: Christian and Missionary Alliance.

Knauss, C. 2017. "The Race to Rescue Cambodian Children from Orphanages Exploiting Them for Profit." https://www.theguardian.com/world/2017/aug/19/the-race-to-rescue-cambodian-children-from-orphanages-exploiting-them-for-profit.

Ledgerwood J., and J. Vijghen. 2002. "Decision Making in Rural Khmer Villages." In *Cambodia Emerges from the Past.* J. Ledgerwood, ed. 109–35. DeKalb, IL: Center for Southeast Asian Studies, Northern Illinois University.

Lewis, R. 2018. "Clarifying the Remaining Frontier Mission Task." *International Journal of Frontier Missions.* 35 (4) 155–68.

Mam, B. 2012. *Church Behind the Wire: A Story of Faith in the Killing Fields.* Chicago: Moody Publishers.

Mission Kampuchea. 2010 *Mission Kampuchea 2021.* Phnom Penh. Unpublished presentation.

________. https://cambodiachurches.org/harvest/mapping/CP/map.html?displaylang=EN&lang=sec.

National Institute of Statistics. 2010. National Census 2008. http://celade.cepal.org/khmnis/census/khm2008/.

Phnom Penh Post. 2003. "Mobs Go Berserk in Anti-Thai frenzy Thai Embassy Torched; Businesses gutted." https://www.phnompenhpost.com/national/mobs-go-berserk-anti-thai-frenzy-thai-embassy-torched-businesses-gutted.

Pierson, P. E. 2009. *The Dynamics of Christian Mission: History Through a Missiological Perspective.* Pasadena, CA: William Carey International Press.

Ponchaud, F. 1990. *The Cathedral of the Rice Paddy: 450 Years of History of the Church in Cambodia.* Paris: Le Sarment; Fayard.

Prasso, S. 2018. "Chinese Influx Stirs Resentment in Once-Sleepy Cambodian Resort: How the Belt and Road Initiative has Helped Turn a Quiet Resort Town into a Gambling Hotspot." https://www.bloomberg.com/news/features/2018–06–20/chinese-casinos-stir-resentment-on-cambodia-s-coast-of-dystopia.

Slocomb, Margaret. 2010. *An Economic History of Cambodia in the Twentieth Century.* Singapore: NUS.

Thigpen, L. 2015. "An Emic Understanding of the 'Excluded middle': Spiritual Patronage in Cambodia." http://www.hiebertglobalcenter.org/1103–2/lynn-thigpen-an-emic-understanding-of-the-excluded-middle-spiritual-patronage-in-cambodia/.

Tully, J. 2006. *A Short History of Cambodia: From Empire to Survival.* Chiang Mai, Thailand: Silkworm.

CHAPTER 16

The Definition of the Person as a Family: Lessons Learned from the History of Christianity to Buddhists

Sheryl Takagi Silzer

Historically, in Buddhist countries, Christianity has been viewed as the religion of foreigners (Khai 2010:3). Although there were a number of reasons that Christianity was considered the religion of foreigners, a major reason was that foreigners were not only ethnically different but also had different customs forming different definitions of the person. In China, Westerners' lighter skin color resembled "ghosts," so they were referred to as "ghosts" and "devils" reinforcing their foreignness (Klein 2014:119). Meanwhile, Western missionaries in Thailand regarded both Buddhism and animism as from the devil (Mejudhon 1997:273) and "diabolic manifestations" (Thabping 1974:86, 341). The missionaries' view of other religions such as Buddhism being regarded as the work of Satan reinforced their negative view of the culture (Chaiwan 1984:68–69).

The way early missionaries treated non-believers also caused many local people to view them with hatred and fear (Bigelow 1900:28). Western missionaries often worked alongside colonial powers as well as Western businesses, reinforcing their foreign identification (Khai 2010:3). However, to the collectivist Buddhist, the missionaries and other Westerners were all the same. Therefore, it is understandable that Buddhists equated all Westerners and their religion as foreign (Armstrong 1995:65).

Early Western missionaries viewed Buddhist countries as backward, savage, barbarian, and less advanced compared with the more economically advanced and modern Western societies (Mejudhon 1997:169). This attitude created a "paternalistic" approach towards Buddhists that motivated Western economic, medical, and political efforts to improve the standard of living of the people (Fish 2002:14). As Westerners were accustomed to a higher standard of living, they also had a more isolated "ghetto" lifestyle (Clasper 1959:2–6).

Western foreignness was also reflected by the preference for an individualistic lifestyle as opposed to the collectivistic lifestyle of Buddhist countries (Clasper 1959:2). Buddhists also equate their ethnicity with Buddhism because they were born Buddhist. "To be a Burman is to be a Buddhist" and therefore, anyone who accepted Christianity was also renouncing their Buddhist ethnic identity and their nationality (Khai 2010:88). In Burma Buddhism has shaped their lives and their thinking that it is one and the same with their cultural identity (Fish 2002:5). The missionaries' goal of bringing civilization and the Western way of life focused their efforts on the more common and isolated groups (Chaiwan 1984:68–69) including orphans (Bigelow 1900:29), women and children, and ethnic minority groups such as the Karen, Chin, and Kachins in Myanmar instead of reaching out to the majority such as the Burmese (Khai 2010:274).

Missionaries, in seeking to modernize their converts, provided education and skills to enhance their ability to gain material benefits (Paik 1929:191). This upset the social and economic system, leading to chronic war between the leaders and the missionaries (Bigelow 1900:28–29). Missionaries also competed with other agencies or churches working in the same areas (Cavalcanti 2005:394). The economic system that missionaries brought with them reflected a "competitive" nature due to their own need to compete for their own mission resources. In order to compete, they increased their activities—preaching, teaching, and healing in order to make disciples of Christ (Chaiwan 1984:66). This also included visiting, broadcasting, use of films, literature, evangelistic team ministry, prayer cells evangelism, as well as personal evangelism. The missionaries unconsciously reproduced the economic model that they learned in their home countries (Cavalcanti 2005:383, 392). This economic model views the missionary or missionary work "as primarily the business of full-time specialists" rather the mission of the church to glorify God (Culpepper 1970:34). Culpepper also states that "we have become peddlers of a cheap grace that requires only assent to stated propositions without necessarily the commitment of life" (36).

The missionaries' economic model also shaped a "personalized faith," meaning their faith was closer to their own experience rather than the people they were trying to convert. Although mission agencies provided the structure for mission work, how missionaries engaged with the people was a personal decision. "They bring their brand of religion into a country through the prism of personal interpretive schemas and practices that adapt the faith to its newly found conditions" (Cavalcanti 2005:381–82).

The individual focus of the missionaries also led to less concern for developing family relationships with the new converts. The missionaries did not consider having a community for new converts to join and, as a result, Christianity isolated new converts from their family and social networks (Khai 2010:278–279). This isolation caused the converts to lose their cultural identity and their family relationships (Mejudhon 1996:6). Such a non-contextualized approach can alienate Christians from their own culture, as it did in Korea (Kent 2001:2). For example, missionaries in Burma have been criticized for saying they contextualized biblical stories by the use of local drama, musical instruments, songs, and dress. Instead they needed to explain who God is using local cultural categories and concepts such as *yin yang* thinking of both/and through negation. The use of Western abstract concepts such as "atonement," "sacrifice," "blood offering," and "conversion" did not have religious meanings for Buddhists or other Asians. The classical Christian doctrine of sin interprets evil individualistically rather than in a relational or family context which neglects social sins (Dhin 1976:152–153, 158, 161).

In Thailand a Buddhist referred to Christian dialogue about salvation as "fanatic talk" as he considered that Buddhism, Christianity, and Islam were the same at their core, having the same reality and truth. Buddhists believe that different religions exist because the real truth has not been found. That is why there are many outward religious forms (Chaiwan 1984:68). Buddhists describe Westerners as having an "aggressive-confrontational approach" instead of the Burmese "polite-discreet approach" evident in their evangelistic method (Khai 2010:9) or with meekness in the way they speak, which is characteristic of Thais (Mejudhon 1997:16).The Thai, being "meek, polite, and unassertive," were easily offended by Western missionaries who were more interested in "information and words" than in "relationship and being" (Mejudhon 1997:4, 344).

In response to Western methodology, a number of Westerners have realized the need for a change. In rationalistic thinking, when one strategy does not work, another strategy is considered (Culpepper 1970:29) and "Verbalization is not enough. We must make the gospel incarnate" (37). Judson's missionary success with the Burmese people was his knowledge and understanding of the Myanmar Buddhist world. He used the *zayat* or local meeting place to meet people and share the gospel (Fish 2002:14). De Neui (2003:130) recognized the holistic cultural perspectives of Buddhists and suggested the need for a more holistic approach that uses all the senses in communicating the gospel. He identified the major barriers in Buddhist evangelism to be social rather than religious, including the existence of the spiritual world. Johnson suggests that the barriers that Thai face in converting to Christianity are family pressures, especially offending the mother, as well as the fear of losing friends (2006:140–41).

From an Asian perspective Dhin also suggests a communal versus an individualistic approach which takes the long-term perspective into account (1976:264, 269, 275, 278). He also recommends the incorporation of potential converts, starting with an overall concept such as a God story rather than a Jesus story. Dhin adds that states more comprehensive categories to cover the difference between the Western and Buddhist cultures are needed (163).

Khai says that "the most pressing missiological issue in Myanmar is the problem of the slow progress among Burman Buddhists in converting to Christianity" (2013:3).

The Different Definition of the Person

The lesson that was learned from the history of Christianity missions to Buddhists was that Western culture brought Western methodology based on the Western definition of the person. Therefore, Western methodology did not work well with the Buddhist definition of the person as a family.

"In Western cultures the material world is viewed separately from the immaterial world defining the person as a unique individual, while in Buddhist cultures the immaterial is integrated with the material defining the person as a family."

In Western cultures the material world is viewed separately from the immaterial world defining the person as a unique individual, while in Buddhist cultures the immaterial is integrated with the material defining the person as a family. Chan describes Western culture as "abstract, rationalistic, and dualistic both metaphysically (for example, spiritual-material, God-creation) and epistemologically (subject-object) while the Eastern culture is concrete, holistic, and non-dualistic" (2014:1).

Greek influences on Western thinking is traced back to Descartes, who is credited with dualistic thinking of the body separate from the soul (Russell 1944:18). This separation made it easier to study the natural world and develop the present-day scientific methodology that divides the world into individual units or categories. Dualistic cultures require labels and categories in order to understand reality. Through a process of observation, a hypothesis is made and tested. The results are categorized and truths are established (Gersholz 1991:4). This dualistic process establishes mutually exclusive dichotomies and Mounce says "this dualism of the mind or soul and body has always been central to the Christian faith," referring to the divine and human natures of Christ (2010:4–1, 405).

Scientific methodology also categorizes the natural physical world separate from the supernatural and validates the supernatural world from what can be observed and measured in the natural world (Hultkranz 1983:233). This process also leads to the focus on truth meaning what scientific investigation has proved is truth or right and what is not truth or what is not right.

Asians, rather than focusing on identifiable units or categories, begin with the whole universe or cosmos and view everything in the world as flowing together into a unity rather than into separate parts (Yeo 1994:320). For Asians, what energizes the cosmos or the universe and all of life is "*qi*" or "*chi*," the vital force, breath, air (Cunshan 2008:200) similar to Hebrew "ruach" and Greek "pneuma" which both mean "breath, wind, spirit" (Strong 2009:4151, 7307). Asians view this vital force as affecting change by the interaction of the two opposing forces of *yin* and *yang* (Kim 2001:288). However, *yin* and *yang* are not opposites or exclusive but work together as a unit (Abe 1975:185). They are "mutually complementary" (Yeo 1994:322). In fact, everything, whether animate or inanimate, is interconnected rather than isolated (Cunshan 2008:201). Chai (1957:47) says that the Chinese perception of life and everything that happens is part of a continuous whole making it difficult to fit Asian concepts into Western categories (Pyysiäinen 2003:149).

Not only is the Asian view of life primarily spiritual, it also encompasses the physical body and creation (Kim 1991:11) as well as the unseen realm of cosmic realities (spiritual beings), cosmic forces (fate, karma), local spirit beings (ancestors, ghosts, demons, evil spirits), the use of magic, mediums, and astrology (Hiebert 1999:416–8). Hiebert describes this supernatural or spiritual realm as "the excluded middle" or the area between religion and science which has been largely ignored in the Western world (1982:32–47). Oak says it has been ignored because it was labeled or categorized as "non-religious" (2010:97).

Based on the Western dualistic mentality, Western children are taught to view the world from the perspective of right and wrong in terms of what they like and what they do not like as they believe that humans are only responsible for themselves. They are taught that only individuals themselves can discover the truth about themselves. American children are "socialized by their parents and teaches to have their own points of view, to be independent of the group, and to choose what they personally like or dislike as a way of revealing their distinctive tastes and character" This individualism is reinforced in schools and life in general and the search for the self contributes to a high rate of divorce, use of therapy, and interest in other religions (Lindholm 2007:4–5).

However, Buddhists believe that truth is not easily established as it is not possible for human beings to have all the truth even about themselves and much less about God. Asians believe that it is more important to be sensitive to others and are careful about what they say so that others will not be offended in order to not bring shame on their family or group (Shin and Silzer 2016:127). Younger Asians do not disagree with their elders unlike Westerners who are trained to speak their mind especially when they disagree with others regardless of age (Rösch and Segler 1987:57).

Family-focused identities such as Buddhist cultures are trained to be more aware of others' feelings in contrast to Westerners who hold truth as a higher ideal than harmony of relationships. When missionaries hold to Christianity as the truth, they easily conclude that other religions are wrong. Buddhist family cultures are more tolerant and respectful of other cultures. In Mongolia, Christianity's less tolerant view of other religions created a reputation of bigotry from their persecution of those who did not believe (Young 1989:101).

Asian Culture Reflects the Definition of the Person as a Family

We have also learned how the definition of the person as a family is reinforced by culture. The Chinese character for *person* 人 consists of two strokes—one meaning the person and the other referring to another person, or by implication, more than one (Chan 1967:26). In Japanese the word for *person* is *jibun* 自分 which means the "portion given to self" indicating that a person is only one part of a larger whole (Maynard 1997:38). For Asians there is no clear boundary between a person and others and they tend to de-emphasize their personal distinctions when referring to the family (Hwang 2000:160). The character for person also indicates how the person should behave—that is, one can only become a person by demonstrating love, concern, and care for their family members and by extension to others in society. It is believed that people's actions or behavior with one another is what establishes their humanity by demonstrating how people can become fully human (Hwang 1999:165). A person is made whole "by the exchange of 'hearts' between two bodies" (Sun 1991:2). People who live in isolation are regarded suspiciously because they do not conform to the expectations of the family or society (Shin and Silzer 2016:119–22).

The family-oriented definition of the person considers human nature to be basically spiritual. At birth the spirit takes on a physical body and at death the spirit and the body return to their original place (Liezi, cited in Huang 2016:152). Life and death are viewed as a never-ending cycle where death is not the end but another beginning (Lu 2017: 52). Death is also viewed as the beginning of eternal existence (Lew et al. 2011:175). Animals and inanimate things are also believed to have spirits (Hoshino and Takeda 1987:309–10).

In family-oriented cultures the role of family members is for caring and maintaining order so that the family lines continue in a successful manner. In Asia the concept of filial piety is the cornerstone of the culture, that is, the responsibility of the children to take care of their parents in the same manner as their parents cared for them. When children reciprocate their care to their parents, they develop the virtue of filial piety and Asian children are born with a sense of indebtedness to their parents for the care and provisions they made for their well-being while growing up (Guo et al. 2012:20). Therefore, children reciprocate this debt of care by taking care of their parents when they are older including caring for their own body. In the Book of Filial Piety *Hsiao Ching* it says: "Our body, with hair and skin, is derived from our parents. One should not hurt one's own body in any situation. This is the starting point of filial piety" (Ching 1908:1). This quotation also reflects the family definition of the person.

In Chinese cultures, relationships and resources are shared in order to build and maintain relationships. The receiver of resources incurs a debt and based on their relationship or "*guanxi*" a person can find other resources to secure their need (Hwang 1987:945). The importance of repaying a debt is seen when a person does not reciprocate appropriately; they are considered to be without a conscience, not concerned about face and not desiring to continue the relationship. The reciprocity of a debt is the *yin yang* tension of giving and receiving (Sun 1971:4). Repaying debts is not only sharing resources (*guanxi*) but helps to strengthen relationships and enhance the family face or reputation (Yeung and Tung 1996:55).

The difference between the person or self in individual vs family-oriented cultures is that in individual-oriented cultures people want to know "who" is the person or self is while in Asian cultures the question is "what" is the person or self (Abe 1997:67).

Further Lessons

After considering the depth of Western culture embedded in the definition of the person as a unique individual, it is quite likely that Western missionaries unconsciously continue to use Western methodologies, resulting in the continuance of the belief that Christianity is a foreign religion.

The focus on truth in dualism necessitates dividing the world into categories. This process underlies the consumer perspective which is based on competition for resources. Instead of relationships, various kinds of methodologies are believed to result in success; for example, more converts. When one method does not succeed, it is replaced with another method. Each method focuses on different aspects of the work in order to be able to measure success. If there is not an increased number of converts, missionaries can still report on the number and kinds of activities they engaged in.

The Western separation of the body from the soul makes it difficult to understand the person as a spiritual being with a family or collective identity. When only the physical life is in focus, the spiritual perspective of the human spirit as lasting beyond a physical death is difficult to comprehend. If all the cultural practices of relating to the deceased are ignored, the basis of Buddhist identity is unaddressed. When ancestor veneration is condemned in order to reinforce the truth of Christianity, many Buddhists are immediately offended and are not attracted to learn more about Christianity.

By briefly reviewing some of the history of Christian outreach to Buddhists, we can see that there are substantial differences that are shaped by the different definition of the person. There are likely more implications to be considered including different theological perspectives, but hopefully these considerations will be made more wisely by applying what we have learned about the different definition of the person.

References

Abe, Masao. 1975. "Non-being and Mu the Metaphysical Nature of Negativity in the East and the West." *Religious Studies*. 11 (2) 181–92.

________. 1997. *Zen and Comparative Studies*. Honolulu, HI: University of Hawaii Press.

Armstrong, Ruth M. 1995. "Judson's Successors in the Heyday of Burma Missions." *Missiology: International Review*. 23 (1) 61–70.

Bigelow, Poultney. 1900. "Missions and Missionaries in China." *The North American Review*. 171/524 (July) 26–40.

Cavalcanti, H. B. 2005. "Human Agency in Mission Work: Missionary Styles and Their Political Consequences." *Sociology of Religion*. 66 (4) 381–398.

Chaiwan, Saad. 1984. "A Study of Christian Mission in Thailand." *East Asia Journal of Theology*. 2 (1) 62–74.

Chan, Simon. 2014. *Grassroots Asian Theology: Thinking the Faith from the Ground Up*. Downers Grove, IL: InterVarsity Press.

Chan, Wing-Tsit. 1967. "The Story of Chinese Philosophy." In *The Chinese Mind: Essentials of Chinese Philosophy and Culture*. Charles A. Moore, ed. Honolulu, HI: University of Hawaii Press.

Clasper, Paul D. 1961. "The Buddhist-Christian Encounter in Burma." *Review & Expositor*. 58 (1) 35–49.

Culpepper, Hugh H. 1970. "Reflections on Missionary Strategy." *Southwestern Journal of Theology*. 12 (2) 29–41.

Cunshan, L. I. 2008. "A Differentiation of the Meaning of Qi on Several Levels." F*rontiers of Philosophy in China*. 3 (2) 194–212.

De Neui, Paul H. 2003. "Contextualizing with Thai Folk Buddhists." In *Sharing Jesus in the Buddhist World*. David Lim and Steve Spaulding, eds. Pasadena, CA: William Carey Library.

Dhin, Kin Maung. 1976. "How to Feed His Lambs: The Problem of Burmese Christian Theology Today." *International Review of Mission*. 65: 258 (April) 151–163.

Fish, Lazarus. 2002. Reclaiming the Zayat Ministry: Witness to the Gospel Among Burmese Buddhists in Myanmar. Doctor of Missiology. Wilmore, KY: Asbury Theological Seminary. Unpublished dissertation.

Gersholz, Emily R. 1991. *Cartesian Method and the Problem of Reduction*. UK: Claredon Press.

Guo, Qiyong, Tao Cui, Liu Junping, and Xiong Ying. 2012. "The Values of Confucian Benevolence and the Confucian Way of Extending Love." *Frontiers of Philosophy in China*. 7 (1) 20–54.

Hiebert, Paul A. 1982. "The Flaw of the Excluded Middle." Missiology: An International Review. 10 (1) 35–47.

________. 1999. *Understanding Folk Religion: A Christian Response to Popular Beliefs and Practices*. Grand Rapids, MI: Baker Publishing.

Hoshino, Eiki, and Dosho Takeda. 1987. "Indebtedness and Comfort: The Undercurrents of 'Mizuko Kuyo' in Japan." *Japanese Journal of Religious Studies*. 14 (4) 305–30.

Hsiao Ching. 1908. *The Book of Filial Piety*. Chen, Ivan Chen, trans. London: J. Murray; New York: E. P. Dutton & Co.

Hultkranz, Åke. 1983. The Concept of the Supernatural in Primal Religions." *History of Religions*. 22 (3) 231–53.

Hwang, Kwang-Kuo. 1987. "Face and Favor: The Chinese Power Game." *American Journal of Sociology*. 92 (4) 944–74.

________. 1999. "Filial Piety and Loyalty: Two Types of Social Identification in Confucianism." *Asian Journal of Social Psychology*. 2 (1) 163–83.

________. 2000. "Chinese Relationalism: Theoretical Construction and Methodological Considerations." *The Journal for the Theory of Social Behavior*. 30 (2) 155–178.

Johnson, Alan R. 2006. "Exploring Social Barriers to Conversion Among the Thai." In *Communicating Christ in the Buddhist World*. Paul De Neui and David Lim, eds. Pasadena, CA: William Carey Library.

Kent, Eliza F. 2001. "Collectors' Live: American Colonizers in the Nineteenth and Early Twentieth Century Burma." Essays in conjunction with Art Exhibit, "Collecting Burma" at Denison University Art Gallery, March 2–April 6. Denison University. Granville, Ohio.

Khai, Zam Sian. 2010. Barriers in Conversion (Missional and Indigenous Barriers): Identifying the Potential Barriers Contributing to the Stagnant Progress of Evangelistic Works among the Burman Buddhists. Wilmore, KY: Asbury Theological Seminary. Unpublished dissertation.

Kim, Hun Chul Paul. 2001. "Interpretative Modes of Yin-Yang Dynamics as an Asian Hermeneutics." *Biblical Interpretations.* 93 (1) 287–308.

Kim, Young Ae. 1991. *Han: From Brokenness to Wholeness. A Theoretical Analysis of Korean Women's Han and a Contextualized Healing Methodology.* Claremont, CA: Pomona College, School of Theology. Unpublished dissertation.

Klein, T. 2013. "The Missionary as Devil: Anti-missionary Demonology in China, 1860–1930." In *Europe as the Other: External Perspectives on European Christianity.* Judith Becker and Brian Stanley. ed. 119–148. Goettingen: Vanderhoeck & Ruprecht.

Lew, Seok-Chon, Woo-Yang Choi, and Hye Suk Wang. 2011. "Confucian Ethics and the Spirit of Capitalism in Korea: The Significance of Filial Piety." *Journal of East Asian Studies* 1 (1) 171–96.

Lindholm, Charles. 2007. *Culture and Identity: The History, Theory and Practice of Psychological Anthropology.* Oxford: Oneworld Publications.

Maynard, Senko K. 1997. *Japanese Communication: Language and Thought in Context.* Honolulu: University of Hawaii Press.

Mejudhon, Ubolwan. 1997. *The Way of Meekness: Being Christian and Thai in the Thai Way.* Wilmore, KY: Asbury Theological Seminary. Unpublished dissertation.

Mounce, H. O. 2010. "On Dualism." *New Blackfriars.* 91/1034 (July) 401–7.

Oak, Sund Deuk. 2010. "Healing and Exorcism: Christian Encounters with Shamanism in Early Modern Korea." *Asian Ethnology.* 69 (1) 91–128.

Paik, George. 1929. *The History of Protestant Mission in Korea, 1832–1910.* Pyongyang: Union Christian College Press.

Pyysiäinen, Ilkka. 2003. "Buddhism, Religion, and the Concept of 'God.'" *Numen.* 50 (2) 147–71.

Rösch, Martin, and Kay G. Segler. 1987. "Communication with Japanese." *Management International Review.* 27 (4) 56–67.

Russell, Bertrand. 1944. *The History of Western Philosophy.* NY: Simon and Shuster Inc.

Shin, Benjamin C., and Sheryl Takagi Silzer. 2016. *Tapestry of Grace: Untangling the Cultural Complexities of Asian American Life and Ministry.* Eugene, OR: Wipf and Stock.

Strong, James. 2009. *Strong's Exhaustive Concordance to the Bible.* Peabody, MA: Hendrickson.

Sun, Lung-kee. 1991. "Contemporary Chinese Culture: Structure and Emotionality." *The Australian Journal of Chinese Affairs.* 26 (July) 1–41.

Thabping, J. E. 1974. *The Conversion of Thai Buddhists: Are Christianity and Thai Culture Irreconcilable?* Manila: Ateneo de Manila. Unpublished thesis.

Yeo, Khiok-Khng. 1994. "The Yin and Yang of God (Exodus 3:14) and Humanity (Genesis 1:26–27)." *Zeitschrift for Religions und Geisteschicht.* 46 (4) 319–32.

Yeung, Irene Y. M., and Rosalie Tung. 1996. "Achieving Business Success in Confucian Societies: The Importance of Guanxi (Connections)." *Organizational Dynamics.* 25 (2) 54–65.

Young, Richard Fox. 1989. "Deus Unus or Dei Plures Sunt? The Function of Inclusivism in the Buddhist Defense of Mongol Folk Religion Against William of Rubruck (1254)." *Journal of Ecumenical Studies.*

ACKNOWLEDGMENTS

A volume of this size and scope has its own history. This is truly the work of a global village. I am extremely grateful for the support from each of the members of the international SEANET steering committee. It is a joy to collaborate with you and work through our divergent cultural opinions; I believe we are stronger for it. Thanks to each of the authors of these chapters and for all who contributed comments to sharpen their writings. Thanks go to my colleagues at Serve Globally of the Evangelical Covenant Church and North Park Theological Seminary for allowing me to continue to connect to participate with this network. Special thanks to my enthusiastic and gifted students Ingrid Flechtenmacher and Donna Shegarfi who worked with several of the authors. Many thanks to my office assistant Evy Lennard for her patience and thorough insight for the details along the way. Thanks to my son, Joseph Paul, for the title idea. All of us at SEANET are thankful to Director DG Wynn for reconnecting SEANET with William Carey Publishing. We are glad to be together again, grateful to Ralph Winter's visionary initiative over twenty years ago to make this collaboration possible. Thanks must also go to WCP's copyeditor Melissa Hicks for her eagle eye on the text and helpful suggestions, and for the creative inspiring work of artist Mike Riester designing the cover and interior layout of this volume. Thanks, finally, to all who read this volume, learn lessons from it, and apply them in love to whomever God calls you to serve.

Paul H. de Neui, editor
Chicago, IL, USA

CONTRIBUTORS

Paul Ka-Ming Au was a missionary in Cambodia from 1995–2015 where he was involved in rural development, church planting, and served as adjunct faculty at the Cambodia Presbyterian Theological Institute. He was a missionary with Southeast Asian Outreach and then became an independent church planter in Kompong Speu Province, Cambodia. Au has an MA in intercultural studies from Biola University and is currently pursuing a PhD at Cliff College, on conversion from Khmer Folk Buddhism to Christianity.

Stephen Bailey was involved in relief and development work in Thailand and Laos for seventeen years with CAMA Services. From 2001 to 2011 he was the associate professor of intercultural studies and director of the Alliance Graduate School of Missions at Alliance Theological Seminary in Nyack, New York. He has served as the program officer in Laos for the Institute for Global Engagement promoting religious freedom since 2002. His work on religious freedom and peace building take him to Laos two or three times a year. Dr. Bailey is professor of intercultural studies at Simpson University where he teaches community development and intercultural studies. His academic research has been on SE Asian Buddhism and Christianity.

E. D. Burns is deputy director for collaboration and content for the Lausanne Movement. He serves as director of the MA in global leadership program at Western Seminary, where he also directs the Judson Center. He is the international director of Last Frontier Global, a ministry among Alaska Natives, Christian leaders in Africa, Asia, Central America, and Europe. He, his wife, and their twin sons have been long-term missionaries in the Middle East, East Asia, and most recently in Southeast Asia, where he teaches at Asia Biblical Theological Seminary. He holds a BA from Moody Bible Institute, an MA from Wheaton College, an MDiv from Western Seminary, and a PhD from Southern Baptist Theological Seminary.

Claire T.C. Chong served as a missionary in Cambodia from 1998—2013. She, her husband, and three children are presently based in Singapore. Claire works at Trinity Methodist Church overseeing missions and evangelism. She volunteers with Singapore Centre for Global Missions as a research associate and is studying for her PhD at the Oxford Centre for Mission Studies.

Karl Dahlfred has served as a missionary in Thailand with OMF International since 2006, working in the areas of church planting, theological education, and publishing. From 2012–2016, he taught church history and missions at Bangkok Bible Seminary, assisted in editing and translation of Thai Christian books at OMF Publishers Thailand. He is a founding elder of Grace City Church, Bangkok. In 2017, he began a PhD in World Christianity at the University of Edinburgh. Karl earned an MDiv at Gordon-Conwell Theological Seminary and a ThM at Talbot School of Theology. He is an ordained minister in the Presbyterian Church in America. Karl is married and has three children.

Paul H. de Neui (editor) is an ordained minister with the Evangelical Covenant Church. He and his wife served as missionaries with church planting and community development organizations in northeast Thailand from 1987–2005. He completed his PhD in Intercultural Studies at Fuller Theological Seminary. Paul has been involved in SEANET for many years, dedicated to seeing the writings of emerging non-Western and other practitioners in print for the benefit of the global church. Presently he is the professor of missiology and intercultural studies and the director of the Center for World Christian Studies at North Park Theological Seminary in Chicago, Illinois.

Cristian Dumitrescu is particularly interested in helping people rediscover the beauty of the gospel through their local worldview and value systems. This passion was born during his ministry with the nomadic Roma people in Romania. Cristian earned his BA in theology at the Romanian Adventist Theological Institute, and a license in theology at the Babes-Bolyai University in the same country. After serving as a pastor in post-Communist Romania, he pursued an MA in religious studies at Newbold College in the UK. His PhD is from Andrews University in the US, where he taught for ten years. Cristian currently teaches at the Adventist International Institute of Advanced Studies in the Philippines.

Austin House serves with The Antioch Partners in SE Asia. Since 2004, Austin has served in church planting and discipleship, relief and development and youth ministry work along the Burma/Thailand border. From 2012–2016, Austin served as an associate professor for missions, evangelism and church history at McGilvary College of Divinity, Payap University in Chiang Mai, Thailand. Presently, Austin is forming a business as mission work in a SE Asian country where he and his family will do outreach among an unreached Buddhist people group. Austin received his Doctorate in intercultural studies from Western Seminary. His main academic interests are in seeking out and researching untold historical stories of indigenous Christians engaged in cross-cultural mission work. Austin is married and has three children.

LAWRENCE KO is the national director of the Singapore Centre for Global Missions. He has been a pastor, social entrepreneur, and missions director in Asia for the past twenty-five years. He also serves as commissioner of the Asia Evangelical Alliance's Missions Commission and is a member of the executive committee of the Asia Lausanne Committee for World Evangelization as well as the International Council for Higher Education.

DAVID S. LIM is from the Philippines. He now serves as the president of the Asian School of Development and Cross-cultural Studies, president of China Ministries International-Philippines, board chair of Lausanne Philippines, and coordinator of the Asian House Church Movement. He has served as academic dean at Asian Theological Seminary in the Philippines and the Oxford Centre for Mission Studies in the UK. His PhD in theology (New Testament) was earned from Fuller Theological Seminary. He has authored several books and articles on non-Western missiology, theological contextualization, and transformational development/mission.

RORY MACKENZIE is a retired professor and church planter. He worked with OMF International, assisting in church planting in Bangkok. Since their return to Edinburgh in 1990, he and his wife have been involved in the sizable Thai community there. Rory taught Buddhist studies in a number of locations, including two residencies in Mahachulalongkorn University in Bangkok and at the International Christian College. Rory holds a MTh from the University of Edinburgh, and his PhD was awarded by the University of Sunderland. He was able to publish his doctorate work, *New Buddhist Movements in Thailand: Towards an Understanding of Wat Phra Dhammakāya and Santi Asoke* (Routledge 2007). More recently he has written *God, Self and Salvation in a Buddhist Context* (Wide Margin 2016). sRory currently lives with his wife Rosalyn in Edinburgh, where they are involved in reaching out to international students. They have three adult daughters, two living in London and one in Edinburgh.

JAMES E. MORRISON (pseudonym) is a graduate student at the Cook School of Intercultural Studies, Biola University. He has lived and worked among Tibetans for more than twenty years.

ALEX G. SMITH was born and raised in Australia till age twenty-one. He graduated from Prairie Bible College and later the International Institute of Christian Communication in Kenya, Africa. In the USA he earned his DMiss and MA degrees at Fuller Theological Seminary and an MDiv from George Fox Evangelical Seminary. Veteran missionary to Thailand, he founded the Thailand Church Growth Committee, and co-founded SEANET (South, East, Southeast, and North Asia Network). He served as adjunct faculty at Multnomah University for eighteen years. Presently he is the International Trainer and Advocate in the Buddhist World for OMF International, under which he has worked for over fifty years.

Bouvert Regulas started preaching as a teenager. He received a BTh from Bethel Bible College, Punalur, an MA from Mysore University, an MDiv from Church on the Rock Theological Seminary, Visakhapatnam, a Post-Graduate Diploma in journalism and mass communication from Indira Gandhi National Open University, Delhi, an MTh and PhD in Religion and Philosophy, and in Missions from Acts Academy of Higher Education, Bangalore. Being the author of eight books, he has written more than a hundred articles in Christian magazines and publications. He works as the principal of Mission Theological College, president of Mission of God and the chairman of the Writers Association.

Sheryl Takagi Silzer has served with Wycliffe Bible Translations and SIL International in Latin America, Asia, and the Pacific. She presently serves as a multicultural consultant leading Cultural Self Discovery workshops for multicultural teams in various parts of the world. She is an adjunct professor at Talbot School of Theology and is a guest lecturer for the Asian Doctor of Ministry degree. She received a PhD in intercultural studies from Fuller School of Intercultural Studies. Her main research interest is helping Asians and Asian diaspora to understand how their different definitions of the person create different perspectives on the world. She is married with two married sons and five grandchildren.

G. P. V. Somaratna is from Sri Lanka. He has an MA in missiology, an MA in theology, and a PhD in South Asian history from the University of London. He served as head of the Department of History and Political Science, professor of modern history at the University of Colombo, Sri Lanka, and is now serving as senior research professor at Colombo Theological Seminary. He also served as adjunct professor at Trinity Theological College, as a Post-Doctoral fellow at the Hebrew University of Jerusalem, and in the Global Research Institute of Fuller Theological Seminary. He has published numerous articles and books on the history of Sri Lanka and the impact of Christianity upon Sri Lankan Buddhism. He is widely regarded as one of Sri Lanka's leading scholars on Ceylonese history.

Eiko Takamiza is a Japanese missiologist teaching at Torch Trinity Graduate University in South Korea. She earned her MDiv at ACTS in South Korea, and her PhD in intercultural studies at Trinity International University in the US. She has been the pastor of Hallelujah Community Church, a Japanese congregation. Eiko serves as advisor and representative for the South Korea Japanese Ministries Association. She is also the president of the Asian Society of Missiology.

www.ingramcontent.com/pod-product-compliance
Ingram Content Group UK Ltd.
Pitfield, Milton Keynes, MK11 3LW, UK
UKHW020615180726
13836UKWH00010B/2484